Hegel, Marx, Nietzsche, or, The Realm of Shadows

Hegel, Marx, Nietzsche,

or, The Realm of Shadows

Henri Lefebvre

Translated by David Fernbach

Introduction by Stuart Elden

VERSO
London • New York

This work was published with the help of the French
Ministry of Culture – Centre national du livre
Ouvrage publié avec le concours du Ministère français
chargé de la culture – Centre national du livre

This English-language edition published by Verso 2020
Originally published in French as *Hegel, Marx, Nietzsche: ou, le Royaume des ombres*
© Editions Casterman, 1975
Translation © David Fernbach 2020
Introduction © Stuart Elden 2020

1 3 5 7 9 10 8 6 4 2

Verso
UK: 6 Meard Street, London W1F 0EG
US: 20 Jay Street, Suite 1010, Brooklyn, NY 11201
versobooks.com

Verso is the imprint of New Left Books

ISBN-13: 978-1-78873-373-1
ISBN-13: 978-1-78873-694-7 (HB)
ISBN-13: 978-1-78873-374-8 (UK EBK)
ISBN-13: 978-1-78873-375-5 (US EBK)

British Library Cataloguing in Publication Data
A catalogue record for this book is available from the British Library

Library of Congress Cataloging-in-Publication Data
Names: Lefebvre, Henri, 1901-1991, author.
Title: Hegel, Marx, Nietzsche, or, The Realm of Shadows / Henri Lefebvre ;
  translated by David Fernbach ; introduction by Stuart Elden.
Other titles: Hegel, Marx, Nietzsche. English
Description: English-language edition. | Brooklyn : Verso Books, 2020. |
  Includes index.
Identifiers: LCCN 2019001975| ISBN 9781788733731 (alk. paper) | ISBN
  9781788736947 (hardback : alk. paper)
Subjects: LCSH: Hegel, Georg Wilhelm Friedrich, 1770-1831. | Marx, Karl,
  1818-1883. | Nietzsche, Friedrich Wilhelm, 1844-1900.
Classification: LCC B2948 .L3513 2020 | DDC 193--dc23
LC record available at https://lccn.loc.gov/2019001975

Typeset in Minion Pro by Hewer Text UK Ltd, Edinburgh
Printed and bound by CPI Group (UK) Ltd, Croydon CR0 4YY

Contents

The system of logic is the kingdom of shadows . . . to dwell and work in this shadowy realm is the absolute cultivation and discipline of consciousness.

– Hegel

The spirit of theory, once it has won its inner freedom, tends to become practical energy: it leaves the realm of shadows and acts as will on outward material reality.

– Marx

I will complete my statue: for a shadow came unto me – the stillest and lightest of all things once came unto me! The beauty of the Superhuman came unto me as a shadow.

– Zarathustra

Three Stars, One Constellation:
Introduction to *Hegel, Marx, Nietzsche*
Stuart Elden

Hegel, Marx, Nietzsche, or, The Realm of Shadows was first published in 1975, between *The Production of Space* (1974) and Lefebvre's four-volume study *De l'État* (1976–8).[1] The same year saw him publish a new autobiography, a re-edition of some of his essays on structuralism, and an edited collection on Fourier.[2] Lefebvre was in his seventies at the time, and showed no signs of slowing down – several other significant studies followed, including the third volume of his *Critique of Everyday Life*, the posthumous *Elements of Rhythmanalysis* and the untranslated *Une pensée devenue monde: Faut-il abandonner Marx?*, *La Présence et l'absence* and *Qu'est-ce que penser?*[3]

---

1 *Hegel, Marx, Nietzsche, ou le royaume des ombres*, Paris: Casterman, 1975. *La Production de l'espace*, translated by Donald Nicholson-Smith as *The Production of Space*, Oxford: Blackwell, 1991; *De l'État*, Paris: UGE, four volumes, 1976–8. The last of these is not translated in full, but parts are available in *State, Space, World: Selected Essays*, edited by Neil Brenner and Stuart Elden, translated by Gerald Moore, Neil Brenner and Stuart Elden, Minneapolis: University of Minnesota Press, 2009. Before the present translation, the only part of *Hegel, Marx, Nietzsche* in English was in *Key Writings*, edited by Stuart Elden, Elizabeth Lebas and Eleonore Kofman, London: Continuum, 2003, pp. 42–9.

2 *Le Temps de méprises*, Paris: Stock, 1975; *L'Idéologie structuraliste*, Paris: Anthropos, 1975; *Actualité de Fourier: Colloque d'Arcs et Senans*, Paris: Anthropos, 1975. The book on structuralism reprints some of the essays from the more substantial *Au-delà du structuralisme*, Paris: Anthropos, 1971.

3 *Critique de la vie quotidienne: De la modernité au modernisme (Pour une métaphilosophie du quotidien)*, Paris: L'Arche, 1981; translated by Gregory Elliott in *Critique of Everyday Life: The One-Volume Edition*, translated by John Moore and

Hegel, Marx, Nietzsche is a summation of Lefebvre's considerable debt to these three thinkers, and its organization is clear. It is structured as three main chapters, 'files' or 'dossiers' on each thinker, framed by a long introductory chapter on 'triads' and a conclusion. Lefebvre suggests that the modern world is Hegelian, Marxist and Nietzschean, and while each of those claims separately is not paradoxical, put together they suggest an irreconcilable tension. How these aspects might be understood, and their relations teased out, is the focus of the study. Each thinker grasped something of the modern world, and shaped Lefebvre's own reflections accordingly.

Lefebvre makes the claim that Hegelian thought can be summarized by the word and concept of the state, Marxism through the social and society, and Nietzsche through civilisation and its values. The state and its relation to civil society is of course the focus of Hegel's *Elements of the Philosophy of Right*, and there is much else in his work, but Lefebvre stresses the political here. To take the state as the focus would be a Hegelian view of the world, but there is also a Marxist view, where the state's relations to civil society, classes and industrial change are paramount. Yet this too neglects things that Lefebvre thinks are important, and he finds these in Nietzsche. This would include the assertion of life against impersonal political and economic processes, a stress on the importance of the arts of poetry, music and theatre, coupled with the hope of the extraordinary, the surreal and the supernatural.

The term *royaume des ombres*, the 'realm' or 'kingdom of shadows', or the underworld, is from Hegel's *Greater Logic*, although it is also used in Marx, and in *Thus Spoke Zarathustra,* Nietzsche declares that the overman appears like a shadow. These three passages form the epigraphs to the present work.[4] This poetic aspect is found throughout this book,

Gregory Elliott, London: Verso, 2014; *Éléments de rythmanalyse: Introduction à la connaissance de rythmes*, Paris: Editions Syllepse, 1992; translated by Stuart Elden and Gerald Moore as 'Elements of Rhythmanalysis: Introduction to the Understanding of Rhythms', in *Rhythmanalysis: Space, Time and Everyday Life*, London: Continuum, 2004, pp. 1–69; *Une pensée devenue monde: Faut-il abandonner Marx?* Paris: Fayard, 1980; *La Présence et L'absence: Contribution à la théorie des representations*, Paris: Casterman, 1980; *Qu'est-ce que penser?* Paris: Publisad, 1985.

4 Lefebvre is not the only person to pick up this theme. See, for example, Alenka Zupančič, *The Shortest Shadow: Nietzsche's Philosophy of the Two*, Cambridge, MA: MIT Press, 2003; William Clare Roberts, *Marx's Inferno: The Political Theory of Capital*, Princeton: Princeton University Press, 2017; Robert B. Pippin, *Hegel's Realm of Shadows:*

Lefebvre likening the three thinkers to three stars in the sky – three stars in a single constellation:

> Three stars gravitate, eliminating lesser or invisible planets, above this world in which shadows dance: ourselves. Stars in a sky in which the sun of intelligibility is no more than a symbol and no longer offers anything in the way of a firmament. Perhaps these stars vanish behind clouds hardly less obscure than the night . . .
>
> In myth, from the poetry of Homer to the *Divine Comedy*, the realm of shadows possessed an entrance and exit, a guided trajectory and mediating powers. It had gates, those of an underground city, overshadowed by the earthly city and the city of God. Today, where are the gates of the realm of shadows? Where is the way out? (p. 49)

The links and tensions between Hegel and Marx are well known, and Lefebvre explores some of them here. Lefebvre argues that there is also much common ground between Marx and Nietzsche – their atheism and materialism; their critique of Hegel's political theology, and of language, *logos* and the Judeo-Christian tradition; the stress on production and creation, and the body – though there is equally obviously much to contrast. Lefebvre suggests that Nietzsche's proclamation that 'God is dead' has tragic repercussions more than simple atheism and naturalism; that for Nietzsche rationality is not just limited but also illusory; and that production and society are the focus for Marx, creation and civilisation for Nietzsche (pp. 192–93). Equally, while Marx renders Hegel's dialectic materialist, Nietzsche makes it tragic. Civilisation, while it is discussed here and there in Marx, is distinct from the mode of production, and is most developed in Nietzsche. In Nietzsche, poetry and art take the place of knowledge, and the *oeuvre* is more important than the product. Nietzsche is obviously more interested in the individual, Marx the collective. While for Hegel and Marx it is the notion of *Aufhebung* – lift up, abolish or supersede – which characterizes the transitions of history, for Nietzsche it is the notion of *Überwindung* – overcoming (pp. 26, 31).[5] In this and other later works Lefebvre tends to use the French term

---

Logic as Metaphysics in 'The Science of Logic', Chicago: University of Chicago Press, 2018.

5 See, for example, *La fin de l'histoire: Epilégomènes*, Paris: Éditions de Minuit, 1970, pp. 214–15; *La Présence et l'absence*, p. 95.

dépassement to grasp both processes together, though earlier in his career he had complained that the word was 'contaminated by mysticism and the irrational' because it also translates the Nietzschean term.[6]

We might further explore or challenge aspects of each of those readings, but Lefebvre works through each thinker in detail in turn in this study, and the strengths or limits of his readings can now be evaluated by his Anglophone readers. Instead, in this Introduction, I want to step back and discuss how Lefebvre reached the point where he could make these claims.

Marx

Lefebvre is best known as a Marxist, and one of his continual claims was that Marxism provides the essential framework to his ideas. He was a member of the French Communist Party between 1928 and 1958, but while he distanced himself from its organizational forms, he never moved away from this framework of thought. Lefebvre would often claim that he was interested in showing how Marxist ideas could be brought to bear on problems or issues that Marx himself had only treated in minor ways, if at all.

His lifelong project on the notion of everyday life, for example, draws on ideas of alienation, and explores how this can be found in many more aspects of the human condition. In the three volumes of the *Critique of Everyday Life* he published in 1947, 1961 and 1981, Lefebvre explored many dimensions, relentlessly examining new aspects and developing his theorization.[7] To these three key moments we should add 1958, in which he re-edited the first volume with a long new preface; 1968, when he published *Everyday Life in the Modern World*; and 1992, when the book he was working on at his death, *Elements of Rhythmanalysis*, appeared.[8]

Equally, in *The Sociology of Marx* he suggested that while Marx was not a sociologist there is a sociology in Marx, and he explored how this

---

6 *Marx 1818–1883*, Genève-Paris: Trois Collines, 1947, p. 152.

7 *Critique of Everyday Life: The One-Volume Edition*, translated by John Moore and Gregory Elliott, London: Verso, 2014.

8 *La Vie quotidienne dans le monde moderne*, Paris: Gallimard, 1968; translated by Sacha Rabinovitch as *Everyday Life in the Modern World*, Harmondsworth: Allen Lane, 1971. The new preface to the first volume is in *Critique of Everyday Life*, pp. 25–121.

might be the case.[9] His work on rural and urban sociology draws on some of the claims made by Marx and Engels in *The German Ideology* and Engels's work on the working class in England, but goes far beyond these works.[10] This is both through detailed empirical work and through making substantial theoretical pronouncements. His doctoral thesis, for example, was a study of peasant communities in the Pyrenees, and he spent several years at *Le Centre national de la recherche scientifique* as a rural researcher.[11] Seeing the transitions in and around his home town led him to his work on the urban condition. The now well-known works on the right to the city and the urban revolution developed from this.[12] *The Production of Space* is the theoretical culmination of his studies of both rural and urban politics, as well as his detailed grounding in the philosophical tradition. Politically, Lefebvre would also make many important contributions, particularly evident in 1973's *The Survival of Capitalism* and his books on the state.[13]

As well as these Marxist contributions, Lefebvre made several significant contributions to scholarship on Marx and Marxism. Right at the start of his career Lefebvre had worked with Norbert Guterman on

9 *Sociologie de Marx*, Paris: PUF, third edition, 1974 [1966], p. 21; translated by Norbert Guterman as *The Sociology of Marx*, London: Penguin, 1966, p. 22.

10 Karl Marx and Friedrich Engels, *The German Ideology*, London: Lawrence and Wishart, 1965; Friedrich Engels, *The Condition of the Working Class in England in 1844*, translated by Florence Kelley Wischnewetzky, Cambridge: Cambridge University Press, 2010 [1885]; *The Housing Question*, Moscow: Progress Publishers, 1954 [1887].

11 See *La Vallée de Campan: Étude de sociologie rurale*, Paris: PUF, 1963; *Du Rural à l'urban*, Paris: Anthropos, 1970. A collection of his writings on the rural, edited by Stuart Elden and Adam David Morton, is forthcoming from University of Minnesota Press. For the recently published thesis, see *Les Communautés paysannes Pyrénéennes: Thèse soutenue en Sorbonne 1954*, Navarrenx: Cercle Historique de l'Arribère, 2014.

12 *La Droit a la ville*, Paris: Anthropos, 1968; translated and edited by Eleonore Kofman and Elizabeth Lebas as 'The Right to the City', in *Writings on Cities*, Oxford: Blackwell, 1996, pp. 63–181; *La Révolution urbaine*, Paris: Gallimard, 1970; translated by Robert Bonanno as *The Urban Revolution*, Minneapolis: University of Minnesota Press, 2003.

13 *La Survie du capitalisme: La re-production des rapports de production*, Paris: Anthropos, third edition, 2002 [1973]; abridged version translated by Frank Bryant as *The Survival of Capitalism*, London: Allison & Busby, 1976. The French edition reprints some material which originally appeared in *L'Irruption de Nanterre au sommet*, Paris: Editions Syllepse, second edition, 1998 [1968]; which is translated by Alfred Ehrenfeld as *The Explosion: Marxism and the French Upheaval*, New York: Modern Reader, 1969. Between *The Survival of Capitalism* and *The Explosion* the English reader can reconstruct the whole of *La survie du capitalisme*.

xiv   Three Stars, One Constellation

Marx. Together, in 1928, they were two of the founders of the journal *La revue marxiste*, one of the first Marxist journals in France. Guterman was a Jewish émigré from Eastern Europe, and a multi-linguist. He and Lefebvre collaborated on many projects – Guterman taking the lead on translations; Lefebvre on introductions – until Guterman had to leave Europe just before the war broke out. Guterman settled in New York where he worked as a translator, and forged links with many of the members of the Frankfurt School. In the late 1920s and early 1930s, Lefebvre and Guterman published the first excerpts from Marx's *Economic and Philosophical Manuscripts*,[14] and in 1934 produced the collection *Morceaux choisis de Karl Marx*.[15] Later criticized by Louis Althusser for not respecting chronology and mixing up material from different periods, without historical information,[16] this collection actually showed Lefebvre's long-standing insistence that we should read Marx as a whole. Nonetheless, its short excerpts and thematic organization means that it provides only a sampling of the richness of Marx's work. Lefebvre wrote several books on Marx over his career, including *Marx 1818–1883*, *Pour connaître la pensée de Karl Marx*, *The Sociology of Marx* and *Marx*.

Marxist Thought and the City is one of the most successful of his books on Marx, developing a systematic reading of this theme in both Marx and Engels.[17] Lefebvre also wrote books on Marxism, including

---

14 Karl Marx, 'Travail et propriete privee', *La Revue marxiste* 1, February 1929, pp. 7–28; 'Notes sur les besoins, la production et la division du travail', *La revue marxiste*, June 1929, pp. 513–38; 'Critique de la dialectique hegelienne', *Avant-Poste* 1, June 1933, pp. 33–9 and 2, August 1933, pp. 110–16.

15 *Morceaux choisis de Karl Marx*, Paris: Gallimard, 1934. The best study of Lefebvre's work in this period is Bud Burkhard, *French Marxism Between the Wars: Henri Lefebvre and the 'Philosophies'*, Atlantic Highlands: Humanity Books, 2000. The work of Michel Trebitsch, in a sequence of articles and his prefaces to the Verso translations of the *Critique of Everyday Life*, is invaluable.

16 Louis Althusser, *The Spectre of Hegel: Early Writings*, edited by Francois Matheron, translated by G. M. Goshgarian, London: Verso, 2014 [1997], p. 260. In the same passage, though, Althusser indicates that Lefebvre's *Pour connaître la pensée de Karl Marx*, Paris: Bordas, 1947 'may also be consulted with profit', though notes that it is better than his *Le Matérialisme dialectique*, Paris: PUF, 1939; translated by John Sturrock as *Dialectical Materialism*, London: Jonathan Cape, 1968.

17 *La Pensée marxiste et la ville*, Paris: Casterman, 1972; *Marxist Thought and the City*, translated by Robert Bonnano, Minneapolis: University of Minnesota Press, 2016.

the bestseller *Le marxisme*, for the popular *Que sais-je?* series.[18] His 1947 book *Logique formelle, logique dialectique* was the planned first volume of a sequence of eight on dialectical materialism written in direct opposition to the Stalinist position.[19] The second volume, *Méthodologie des sciences*, was written and printed, but publication was blocked by French Communist Party censors. It was finally published eleven years after Lefebvre's death.[20] In English, the most substantial statement comes in his early book *Dialectical Materialism*, as well as *The Sociology of Marx*. *Dialectical Materialism* and *Le marxisme* are two important works in stressing the importance of the theory of alienation to Marx's work, showing that this term is not just central to Marx's early writings, but crucial in his later discussion of reification, fetishism and mystification. In 1963 and 1966, Lefebvre and Guterman again collaborated on a two-volume selection of Marx's texts for Gallimard.[21] Unlike *Morceaux choisis*, this presents material chronologically, showing the development of Marxist thought. Relatively little of his extensive work on Marx and Marxism is available in English, so the chapter on Marx in the present volume is a valuable contribution in its own right.

Hegel

Throughout his long career, Lefebvre saw Marx's work as important, indeed essential, to an understanding of our times, but not something that could stand alone. In a 1971 discussion with Leszek Kołakowski he declared that, to understand the present moment, Marx was the 'unavoidable, necessary, but insufficient starting point', even if the work was to be an 'analysis of the deception or of the errors or the illusions that originated with the thought of Marx'.[22] In *Hegel, Marx, Nietzsche* he

18 As well as works already referenced, see *Marx*, Paris: Gallimard, 1964; and *Le marxisme*, Paris: PUF, 1948.

19 *Logique formelle, logique dialectique*, Paris: Anthropos, second edition, 1969 [1947].

20 *Méthodologie des sciences: Un inédit*, Paris: Anthropos, 2002.

21 *Karl Marx, Oeuvres choisis*, Paris: Gallimard, two volumes, 1963–6.

22 Henri Lefebvre and Leszek Kołakowski, 'Evolution or Revolution', in Fons Elders (ed.), *Reflexive Water: The Basic Concerns of Mankind*, London: Souvenir Press, 1974, pp. 201–67, p. 205.

suggests that Marx's thought today is not dissimilar to Newton's work in the light of the modern theory of relativity – a stage to start from, true at a certain scale, a date, a moment (p. 10). As such, Lefebvre continually pushes Marxism beyond simply a reliance on the writings on Marx, Engels and Lenin, and brings other thinkers into the dialogue. Hegel and Nietzsche were the only two other thinkers that he held up as significant to the same degree.

Hegel was a crucial thinker for Lefebvre from his earliest writings, produced as part of the group around the *Philosophies* journal in the 1920s, along with Guterman, Georges Politzer, Georges Friedmann and Pierre Morhange. It was through this work that Lefebvre and his colleagues first discovered Marx, and not unsurprisingly, Lefebvre always insisted on the importance of Hegel to understanding Marx. This was a concern throughout his career, and it is with the benefit of hindsight that we can see this as a fundamental challenge to the Althusserian project.[23] Lefebvre also worked explicitly on Hegel. He plays an important role in the early work *La Conscience mystifiée*, written with Guterman, as well as in his short study of *Dialectical Materialism*.[24] *La Conscience mystifiée* is important in terms of an attempt to work out why large parts of the working classes came to embrace fascism in the early 1930s. Lefebvre and Guterman also produced a selected works of Hegel for Gallimard in 1938, and translated Lenin's notebooks on Hegel's dialectic.[25]

Other figures in the post-war French reception of Hegel were undoubtedly more important. Foremost here were Alexandre Kojève's famous lectures on Hegel, attended by an extraordinary audience including Louis Althusser, Raymond Aron, Georges Bataille, Maurice Blanchot, André Breton, Alexandre Koyré, Jacques Lacan, Emmanuel

---

23 Louis Althusser, *Pour Marx*, Paris: 1965; translated by Ben Brewster as *For Marx*, London: Verso, 1965; and Louis Althusser, Étienne Balibar, Roger Establet, Pierre Macherey and Jacques Rancière, *Lire le Capital*, Paris: PUF, 1965; translated by Ben Brewster and David Fernbach as *Reading Capital: The Complete Edition*, London: Verso, 2016.

24 Norbert Guterman and Henri Lefebvre, *La Conscience mystifiée*, Paris: Editions Syllepse, third edition, 1999 [1936].

25 G.W.F. Hegel, *Morceaux choisis*, Paris: Gallimard, 1938; *Cahiers de Lénine sur la dialectique de Hegel*, Paris: Gallimard, 1938. See Kevin Anderson, *Lenin, Hegel and Western Marxism: A Critical Study*, Urbana: University of Illinois Press, 1995.

Levinas, Maurice Merleau-Ponty, Jean-Paul Sartre and many others.[26] Jean Hyppolite did not attend, since he was developing his own reading of Hegel and was wary of being influenced. Hyppolite's translation of Hegel's *Phenomenology of Spirit*, and his detailed study *Genesis and Structure of Hegel's Phenomenology of Spirit*, together with his readings of the work on the philosophy of history and the *Logic*, were enormously influential.[27] Hyppolite supervised several student theses on Hegel, including the recently rediscovered one by Michel Foucault.[28]

The story of the French reception of Hegel is widely discussed, but Lefebvre has an important minor role in it.[29] His reading was one that was largely independent of Kojève's influence. In his reading of Hegel and Marx together, he is perhaps more significant in terms of debates about Marxism.[30] The presentation of Hegel's work in the *Morceaux*

---

26 Alexandre Kojève, *Introduction à la lecture de Hegel: Leçons sur la Phénoménologie de l'Esprit professées de 1933 à 1939 à l'École des Hautes Études*, edited by Raymond Queneau, Paris: Gallimard, 1980 [1947]; abridged as *Introduction to the Reading of Hegel: Lectures on the Phenomenology of Spirit*, edited by Allan Bloom, translated by James H. Nichols, Jr, Ithaca: Cornell University Press, 1980 [1969]. On Kojève and the seminar, see Michael S. Roth, *Knowing and History: Appropriations of Hegel in Twentieth Century France*, Ithaca: Cornell University Press, 1988; and Ethan Kleinberg, *Generation Existential: Heidegger's Philosophy in France 1927–1961*, Ithaca: Cornell University Press, 2005, Chapter 2.

27 G.W.F. Hegel, *La Phénoménologie de l'esprit*, translated by Jean Hyppolite, Paris: Aubier, two volumes, 1939–41; Jean Hyppolite, *Genèse et structure de la Phénoménologie de l'esprit de Hegel*, Paris: Aubier, two volumes, 1946; translated by Samuel Cherniak and John Heckman as *Genesis and Structure of Hegel's Phenomenology of Spirit*, Evanston: Northwestern University Press, 2000; *Introduction à la philosophie de l'histoire de Hegel*, Paris: M. Rivière et Cie, 1948; *Logique et existence: Essai sur la logique de Hegel*, Paris: PUF, 1953; *Logic and Existence*, translated by Leonard Lawlor and Amit Sen, Albany: SUNY Press, 1997.

28 Foucault's thesis is unpublished, but can be found at Bibliothèque nationale de France, NAF28803 (1) 'Archives des années 1940 et 1950', Folder 1, *La Constitution d'un transcendental dans La Phénoménologie de l'esprit de Hegel* (1949).

29 See, for example, Judith Butler, *Subjects of Desire: Hegelian Reflections in Twentieth-Century France*, New York: Columbia University Press, 1987, though this omits mention of Lefebvre; and Bruce Baugh, *French Hegel: From Surrealism to Postmodernism*, London: Routledge, 2003.

30 This was one of the key ways Lefebvre was first read in English. See, for example, Mark Poster, *Existential Marxism in Post-War France: From Sartre to Althusser*, Princeton: Princeton University Press, 1975; Michael Kelly, *Modern French Marxism*, Oxford: Basil Blackwell, 1982; and Martin Jay, *Marxism and Totality: The Adventures of a Concept from Lukács to Habermas*, Berkeley: University of California Press, 1984.

choisis comprises short, almost aphoristic selections, from a few pages to a few lines. Hegel looks, superficially at least, a lot like Nietzsche. The Introduction stresses the importance of Hegel to Marxism, and the way he might be read in the contemporary context of fascism – the Introduction was written in 1938. Lenin's notebooks similarly stress the importance of Hegel to Marx. The chapter on Hegel here is a helpful indication of key aspects of his reading.

Nietzsche

Lefebvre was also a pioneer in the French reading of Nietzsche. Many of Nietzsche's books had been translated into French in the first half of the twentieth century, though like the English translations from the same period they were not always reliable. In the first part of the century Nietzsche was influential in a range of fields, and politically was read by both left and right.[31] Things changed with the Nazi use of his works, and in the Anglophone world the German émigré Walter Kaufmann did valuable work after the war in rehabilitating his reputation as a philosopher, though at the expense of making him largely apolitical.[32] In Germany, the pre-war work of Karl Jaspers and Karl Löwith was important in this regard too.[33]

In France, Lefebvre led the way with his own anti-fascist study *Nietzsche* in 1939.[34] It can be seen as the third part of an informal trilogy of works condemning the rise of nationalism and fascism in Europe,

31 On the early period, see Geneviève Bianquis, *Nietzsche en France: L'influence de Nietzsche sur la pensée française*, Paris: Félix Alcan, 1929; Christopher E. Forth, *Zarathustra in Paris: The Nietzsche Vogue in France 1891–1918*, DeKalb: Northern Illinois University Press, 2001.

32 Walter Kaufmann, *Nietzsche: Philosopher, Psychologist, Antichrist*, Princeton: Princeton University Press, 1950.

33 Karl Jaspers, *Nietzsche: Einführung in das Verständnis seines Philosophierens*, Berlin: de Gruyter, fourth edition, 2010 [1936]; *Nietzsche: An Introduction to the Understanding of His Philosophical Activity*, translated by Charles F. Wallraff and Frederick J. Schmitz, Tuscon: University of Arizona Press, 1965; Karl Löwith, *Nietzsches Philosophie der ewigen Wiederkehr des Gleichen*, Hamburg: Felix Meiner, 1978 [1935]; *Nietzsche's Philosophy of the Eternal Recurrence of the Same*, translated by J. Harvey Lomax, Berkeley: University of California Press, 1997.

34 Henri Lefebvre, *Nietzsche*, Paris: Editions Sociales Internationales, 1939; re-edition Paris: Éditions Syllepse, 2003.

along with *La Nationalisme contre les nations* in 1937 and *Hitler au pouvoir, les enseignements de cinq années de fascisme en Allemagne* in 1938.[35] All these books shared the fate of being condemned by the occupying German forces following the invasion.[36] Lefebvre holds Nietzsche no more responsible for Nazism than Marx is for state socialism (p. 39). Georges Bataille's own significant book *On Nietzsche*, originally published in 1945, makes some similar moves in defending Nietzsche from the fascist appropriation, and makes brief reference to Lefebvre's book.[37] What set Lefebvre's 1939 book apart was that, as well as his discussion of Nietzsche, it included translations of key passages, probably prepared with the aid of Guterman.

Nietzsche's ideas of moments, time and history, his understanding of life, and his reflections on poetry, music and theatre were crucial inspirations for Lefebvre. Later work on space would also owe something to his influence. The later French interest in Nietzsche is quite widely discussed in the literature, given his importance to Foucault, Derrida and Deleuze, among others, but Lefebvre tends to have only a minor role in these studies.[38] The chapter on Nietzsche here, the longest part of the study, is a very good indication of the importance Lefebvre put on his work.

---

35 *Le Nationalisme contre les nations*, Paris: Méridiens Klincksieck, second edition, 1988 [1937]; *Hitler au pouvoir, les enseignements de cinq années de fascisme*, Paris: Bureau d'Éditions, 1938.

36 *La Somme et le reste*, Paris: Méridiens Klincksieck, third edition, 1989 [1959], p. 492.

37 Georges Bataille, *Sur Nietzsche*, reprinted in *Oeuvres complètes Vol VI: La somme athéologique tome 2*, Paris: Gallimard, 1973, p. 187; *On Nietzsche*, translated by Bruce Boone, New York: Paragon House, 1992, p. 171.

38 See, for example, Alan Schrift, *Nietzsche's French Legacy: A Genealogy of Poststructuralism*, London: Routledge, 1995; Douglas Smith, *Transvaluations: Nietzsche in France 1872–1972*, Oxford: Clarendon Press, 1996; Jacques le Rider, *Nietzsche en France: De la fin du XIXe siecle au temps present*, Paris: PUF, 1999, 189–91. More substantial discussions of Lefebvre are found in Pierre Boudot, *Nietzsche et l'au-delà de la liberté: Nietzsche et les écrivains français de 1930 à 1960*, Paris: Aubier-Montagne, 1970, Chapter 8; and Louis Pinto, *Les neveux de Zarathoustra: La reception de Nietzsche en France*, Paris: Seuil, 1995, especially pp. 93–4, 99–102.

Hegel, Marx, Nietzsche

As well as the three discrete chapters on each thinker individually, in the long opening discussion of 'Triads' and the brief 'Conclusion and Afterword', Lefebvre explores the links between them in a more systematic way. Yet *Hegel, Marx, Nietzsche* is not the only work in which Lefebvre explores the relation between these three key thinkers and his own ideas. Many of his books could be discussed here, but foremost among them would be *Metaphilosophy*.[39] It equally can be found in some of his substantive works on other themes, notably in *The Production of Space*, written around the same time as this study, and in *La Fin de l'histoire* from 1970, which shows that Lefebvre was a significant theorist of time and history as well as space.

For too long, Lefebvre has been seen in English-language debates simply as an innovative thinker in two registers – his cultural studies work on everyday life; and his urban and spatial writings.[40] Both are important aspects, certainly, but only two facets of his writings. The translation of *Metaphilosophy* has, one hopes, helped to indicate the broader reach of his theoretical endeavour. His theoretically catholic approach is especially well exemplified in this book. It provides an excellent orientation to how Lefebvre read, appropriated and utilized Marx. It demonstrates the crucial importance of his reading of Hegel, who was central in understanding his relation to Marx, the state, logic and dialectics. And it sheds a great deal of light on his relation to Nietzsche. In this book, written almost half a lifetime after his first engagement with Hegel, Marx and Nietzsche in the 1930s, he returns to these three figures with the benefit of many years of thinking about them and using their

---

39 *Métaphilosophie*, Paris: Éditions de Minuit, 1965; second edition, Éditions Syllepse 2001; translated by David Fernbach as *Metaphilosophy*, edited by Stuart Elden, London: Verso, 2016.

40 The Anglophone literature on Lefebvre is growing. See, among other studies, Rob Shields, *Lefebvre, Love and Struggle: Spatial Dialectics*, London: Routledge, 1999; Stuart Elden, *Understanding Henri Lefebvre: Theory and the Possible*, London: Continuum, 2004; Andy Merrifield, *Henri Lefebvre: A Critical Introduction*, London: Routledge, 2006; Łukasz Stanek, *Henri Lefebvre on Space: Architecture, Urban Research, and the Production of Theory*, Minneapolis: University of Minnesota Press, 2011; and Chris Butler, *Henri Lefebvre: Spatial Politics, Everyday Life and the Right to the City*, London: Routledge-Cavendish, 2014. For a biography, see Rémi Hess, *Henri Lefebvre et l'aventure du siècle*, Paris: A.M. Metailie, 1988.

ideas. It was to be one of his last major philosophical writings but, over forty years since its publication, its themes remain surprisingly relevant today, especially since Lefebvre's abiding interest is in how these thinkers enable us to think the *world*.

Acknowledgements

I am grateful to David Fernbach and Adam David Morton for comments on an earlier draft.

1

Triads

1) Beginning without recourse to any cognitions[1] other than elementary, any findings other than basic, we can put forward the following propositions:

a) *The modern world is Hegelian.* In fact, Hegel elaborated and drove to its ultimate conclusions the political theory of the nation-state. He asserted the supreme reality and value of the state. Hegelianism posits, in principle, the linkage of knowledge and power; it legitimizes it. Now, the number of nation-states has steadily risen (around one hundred and fifty today). They cover the surface of the globe. Even if it is true that nations and nation-states are no longer anything but façades and covers, hiding wider capitalist realities (world market, multinational corporations), these façades and covers are nonetheless a reality: not the most subtle, but effective instruments and frameworks. Whatever the ideology that inspires it, the state asserts itself everywhere, indissolubly using

---

1 [Lefebvre's interpretation of Nietzsche draws on the contrast between the nouns *savoir* and *connaissance*. Although both are commonly translated into English as 'knowledge', *savoir* refers to an objective and socially established body of knowledge, so that *Le Gai Savoir* is an appropriate French title for Nietzsche's *Die fröhliche Wissenschaft* (in English, *The Gay Science*). *Connaissance*, on the other hand, implies knowledge acquired through personal experience. Of the options available in English, Lefebvre's meaning seems best preserved by keeping 'knowledge' for *savoir*, and in most cases rendering *connaissance* as 'cognition'. – Translator.]

both knowledge and constraint, its reality and its value. The definite and definitive character of the state, conservative and even counter-revolutionary (whatever the official ideology, even 'revolutionary'), is confirmed in the political consciousness it imposes. In this perspective, the state encompasses and subordinates to itself the reality that Hegel called 'civil society', that is, social relations. It claims to contain and define civilization.

b) *The modern world is Marxist.* For the last few decades, in fact, the fundamental concerns of so-called public authorities have been: economic growth, viewed as the basis of national existence and independence, and therefore industrialization, production, which leads to problems around the relation of the working class (productive workers) to the nation-state, as well as a new relationship between knowledge and production, hence between this knowledge and the powers that control production. It is neither obvious nor certain that knowledge should be subordinate to political power, or that the state has eternity on its side. Rational economic planning is on today's agenda, achieved in different ways (direct or indirect, complete or partial). In the course of a century, industry and its consequences have changed the world, in other words, society, more (if not better) than ideas, political projects, dreams and utopias. As Marx had basically proclaimed and predicted.

c) *The modern world is Nietzschean.* If anyone wanted to 'change life', though these words are attributed to Rimbaud, it was certainly Nietzsche. If anyone wanted 'everything right now', it was him. Protests and challenges against the state of things are converging from all sides. Individual life and lived experience [*le vécu*] are reasserting themselves against political pressures, against productivism and economism. When it does not just oppose one policy to another, protest finds support in poetry, in music, in theatre, as well as in the expectation and hope for something extraordinary: the surreal, the supernatural, the superhuman. Civilization worries many people, more than the state or society. Despite the efforts of political forces to assert themselves above lived experience, to subordinate society to themselves and capture art, this contains the reserve of contestation, the resource of protest. Despite what is pushing it into decline. This corresponds to the raging wind of Nietzschean revolt: the stubborn defence of civilization against the pressures of society, state and morality.

2) None of the above propositions, taken separately in isolation, has the look of a paradox. It is possible to show that the modern world is Hegelian – or to refute it by classic procedures. If someone wants to prove it, they would have to reconstruct Hegel's philosophico-political system as far as possible, on the basis of his texts. Then they would study the influence of this doctrine and its penetration by various paths into political life (the university, the interpretation of events, the blind activity of politicians, subsequently elucidated, etc.). The same holds for Marx – and for Nietzsche.

But, stated together, there is something intolerably paradoxical about them. How can this modern world be at the same time one thing and another? How can it pertain to doctrines that are diverse, opposed on more than one point, even incompatible?

Neither can it be a matter of influence, or simply reference. If the modern world 'is' at the same time this and that (Hegelian and Nietzschean . . .), it also cannot be a matter of ideologies that float above social and political practice like bright and dark patches, clouds and rays of light. An assertion of this kind forces us to grasp and define new relations between these theories (doctrines), as well as between the theories and practice. If this triplicity has a meaning, it is that each of them (Hegel, Marx, Nietzsche) grasped 'something' of the modern world, something in the process of happening. And that each doctrine, in so far as it achieved a coherence (Hegelianism, Marxism, Nietzscheanism), declared what it grasped, and by this declaration contributed to what was being formed in the late nineteenth century, to reach the twentieth century and across it, with the result that confrontation between these outstanding works involves a mediation, the modernity that they illuminate and that illuminates them. In an earlier book,[2] these doctrines were confronted with historicism and historicity. Here, this critical analysis is expanded, while seeking to remain concrete.

If it is true that Hegelian thought is focused in one word and one concept, the *state*; that Marxist thought strongly emphasizes the social

---

2 Henri Lefebvre, *La Fin de l'histoire*, Paris: Éditions de Minuit, 1971.

and *society*; and that Nietzsche meditated on *civilization* and values, then through the paradox we glimpse a meaning that remains to be discovered: a triple determination of the modern world, implying conflicts that are multiple and perhaps without end, within so-called human 'reality'. This is a hypothesis whose scope permits us to say that it has a strategic import.

3) To study Hegel, Marx or Nietzsche in isolation, in the texts, would not take us very far; all textual connections have been explored, all deconstructions and reconstructions, without the authenticity of one or other interpretation prevailing. As for situating them in the history of philosophy, in general history or the history of ideas, the interest of such a contextual study seems as exhausted as does textual analysis.

What remains to be grasped, then, is their relationship with the modern world, taking this as the referent, as the central object of analysis, as the common measure (mediation) between the various doctrines and ideologies that insert themselves in it. The 'contextual' thus acquires an amplitude and scope, a richness of unknown and known, that is omitted when reduced to a certain particular or general history. In what way did Hegel, Marx and Nietzsche each respectively anticipate the tendencies of modernity in its nascent state? How did they grasp what was in the course of 'taking'? How did they fix one aspect and define one moment among the contradictory aspects and moments?

Three stars, but one constellation. Sometimes the light from each is superimposed, sometimes one hides or eclipses the other. They interfere. The brightness of each either grows or pales. They rise or descend to the horizon, draw away from one another or converge. Sometimes one seems dominant, sometimes another.

The above statements have only a metaphorical significance and a symbolic value. They indicate the direction and the horizon. They declare (what remains to be shown) that the greatness of these works and these men is no longer like that of the classical philosophers, Plato and Aristotle, Descartes and Kant, who constructed a great architecture of concepts. This 'greatness' consists in a certain relationship to the 'real', to practice. So, it is not of a philological order, representable on the basis of language. New, *metaphilosophical*, it has to be defined on the basis of deciphering the enigma of modernity.

4) Let us look again at Hegelianism (nothing says that this will be the last look!). Enormous, pivotal, Hegel holds pride of place at the end of classical philosophy, on the verge of modernity. A solitary figure, yet he gathered together a historico-philosophical totality and subordinated it to the state. What makes for his 'modernity'?

a) First of all, he gave systematic form to Western logos, whose genesis began with the Greeks, ancient philosophy and the ancient city. Like Aristotle, but after two thousand years, and taking into account what had been learned in the course of history, Hegel identified the terms (categories) of *effective* discourse and showed how they were connected in a coherent ensemble: a knowledge, source and meaning (finality) of all consciousness. Though impersonal, logos does not rest suspended in mid-air. Reason presupposes a 'subject' that is just a particular individual, an accidental person or consciousness. This rationality is embodied in the statesman, and realized in the state itself – with the result that the state is situated at the highest philosophical level, above the eminent determinations of knowledge and consciousness, concept and subject. It envelops these developmental conquests. It even encompasses *logically*, in a supreme cohesion, the results of struggles and wars, in other words, of historical (dialectical) *contradictions*. The state, as absolute philosophical 'subject' in which rationality is embodied, itself embodies the Idea, i.e. divinity. Hence those thundering declarations, which we shall have to return to, as it is impossible to let them settle into the false serenity and lying legitimacy of established philosophy, institutional and recognized as such. Since the state is 'the actuality of the Idea', objective spirit,[3] the individual 'has no objective, truth or ethical existence except as member of the state'. The state conceives itself through the thoughts of individuals who say 'I', and it realizes itself through individuals and groups who say 'we'.[4] The historical origin of the state (of each state) does not affect the idea of the state. Knowledge, will, freedom, subjectivity, are

3 [The divergence in meaning between 'mind' and 'spirit' in modern English causes an insoluble problem as to the best rendering of Hegel's *Geist*. My own preference is for 'spirit', but the particular nuance this has should be always borne in mind. – Translator.]

4 G.W.F. Hegel, *Philosophy of History*, New York: Dover, 1956; Introduction, pp. 22ff.

only 'moments' (elements, phases or stages) of the Idea as it is realized in the state, both *in itself* and *for itself*.[5]

Hegel thus legitimizes the fusion of knowledge and power in the state, the former subordinated to the latter. Organizational effectiveness and constraining violence, including war, link up and compete in the state, the former justifying the latter in a perfect reciprocity, and assembling in the political order things that seemed spontaneous (family, work and trades, etc.). The repressive capacity of the state is thus revealed to be basically rational, hence legitimate, which by the same token legitimizes and justifies both wars in particular and war in general. For Hegel as for Machiavelli, violence is a component of political life and the state. On top of which it has a content and a meaning; it opens the path of reason. Law (constraining) and right (normative) are necessary and sufficient for society and its complex mechanisms to function under the control of the state, and they denote the same political reality.

Thus the rationality inherent to all moments of history and to everyday practice is focused in the state. This legitimately and sovereignly *totalizes* morality and right (law), the social institutions and their particular functions (family, nations and corporations, cities and regions of the national territory), the system of needs and the division of labour (which corresponds precisely to needs). Just as consciousness has a triple origin (sensation, practical activity, abstraction), which raises it to the higher level of political consciousness, so the state has a triadic origin: productive work, history and its conflicts, and socio-political practice that brings it to perfection. These associated and interacting triplicities produce a living totality both organic and rational: the state. Viewed genetically, this is nothing other than reasoning humanity, obeying the call of the Idea, which produces itself in the course of history. In short, the state cements and crowns the social body, which without this would fragment into pieces, would atomize – if such a hypothesis makes any sense.

The Hegelian fetishism of the state may frighten the citizen or the reader of a philosophical work, and the summary that will be submitted (once more) to such a reader may perhaps appear monstrous, without any relationship to political reality. But this impression will fade as soon

5 Cf. *Philosophy of Right*, para. 257ff.

as the exposition goes into the detail of the Hegelian analysis and synthesis, which are striking and astonish by their character, both concrete and actual (modern).

b) According to Hegel, the rational, thus constitutional, state, has a social basis: the middle class. It is in this class that culture is located, which connects with the consciousness of the state. There is no modern state without a middle class, its foundation for both intelligence and legality.[6] Neither the peasants nor the workers, the working and productive classes, can constitute pillars of the state. It is from this middle class that civil servants are recruited, either by co-optation or by competition.[7] A competent bureaucracy, selected by tough examinations, is the true social basis and substance of the state.

For Hegel, there are thus social classes and even struggles (contradictions) between these classes: the *natural* class, the peasants, rooted in the soil; the active *reflective* class, artisans and workers, who produce the accumulation of wealth, these individuals being characterized by their (subjective) skill; and finally the *thinking* class, mediator between the two productive classes, and itself mediated by its knowledge, which maintains and manages the social whole within the context of the state. These three classes constitute civil society, with its intermediary (mediation) towards politics, in other words, the bureaucracy, emerging from the thinking class (*middle*: intermediary, mediating and mediated). Conflicts between these classes, the elements (moments) of civil society, press this outside and above itself, towards the establishment of a *political class*, directly (immediately, that is, without mediation) bound up with the state and thus constituting its apparatus. It is the upper fringe of the bureaucracy that *constitutes* (institutes in the constitution) the lower part of the personnel in power, around princes, monarchs and heads of state.

Thus, it is the contradictions (the internal dialectic) of civil society that engender the state and the political class. This latter, representing and effecting state action, can turn back on its own conditions; it has the capacity of recognizing (social) relations between the moments (elements, members, phases/stages) of civil society, of detecting their

---

6 *Philosophy of Right*, para. 297, Zusatz.

7 Cf. *Philosophy of Mind* [Part Three of *Encyclopaedia of the Philosophical Sciences*], para. 528.

conflicts and resolving them, in such a way that the state is preserved as a *coherent* totality encompassing *contradictory* moments. With this aim, the ruling stratum (political class) is entitled to free itself from all other tasks and obligations, and consequently to receive prizes and rewards (honours, money) for exercising its responsibility. The result is that this fundamentally *honest* class, the summit of the pyramid, does not only represent the social substance: it *is* this substance, in other words 'the life of the whole', the *constant production* (reproduction) of society, state, constitution, the political act itself, which consists in governing.[8]

Philosophy, for its part, is the duplicate and shadow of the completed political system: the perfect philosophical system consecrates, legitimates, founds it. Philosophy as such is perfected in Hegelianism, which sums up and condenses its history; it finds full realization in the state to which the system brings theory. Philosophy accompanies the state as a public service. In the same way that the state rationally totalizes its historical, practical, social, cultural and other 'moments', so the philosophico-political system unites the rational and the real, the abstract and the concrete, the ideal and the actual, the possible and the accomplished. Knowledge (theoretical) and practice (socio-political) likewise coincide in administrative *savoir faire*.

The consequence, or rather the logical implication of this, is that history has reached an end. In terms of production, it has generated everything that it could generate. When? With the French Revolution and Napoleon.[9] Why? Because the Revolution and Napoleon produced what supersedes and consecrates them: the nation-state. Marked by struggle and emergence – the figures of the individual and social consciousness, the phases of cognition – historicity re-produces its initial condition and its final content: the Idea. It contains three moments: productive work, self-generated conceptual knowledge and the creative struggle through which the higher moment is born from the lower, dominating this by subjecting (and thereby preserving) it. Origin (hidden) and end (manifest) of all things, of every act and every event, the Idea recognizes itself in the plenitude of the state. Accident and contingency are either non-existent, or no more than apparent. With the modern state time comes to an end, and the result of time is displayed

---

8 Cf. *Philosophy of Mind*, 542.
9 Cf. *Philosophy of History*, 'The Éclaircissement and Revolution'.

(actualized in total presence) in space. This is the twilight of creation, the setting sun, the West! The trinity or speculative triad (work, action, thought) is completed in its triumph, and enters into its starry night. Into mortal wisdom.[10]

Who would not feel a frisson of terror at comparing the monstrous (monstrously rational) character of Hegel's theory of the state with the concrete character of the detailed analyses that support and actualize this? The rise of the middle class above the working classes; the growing socio-economic importance of this middle class, combined with its illusory political importance; the subordination of this socio-economic 'base' to a bureaucracy; a technocracy; an upper class that emerges from the middle class; the formation of a political class – all these aspects of 'modernity' were grasped, foreseen, announced by Hegel at the start of the nineteenth century. Along with this was the revelation of another aspect that is overlooked, ignored or dissimulated in the modern world: the true portrait of the monster, seen from its cruelly thinking head to its active members – the superhuman and too human giant of the state.

We shall have to return to this paradox: Hegel's tripod monster and his rational vision, the philosopher's approval and the good conduct certificate given by philosophy, the juncture of knowledge and power, of Western logos and *raison d'état*, this intolerable ensemble of 'truth'. Starting from this central conception: the Hegelian state produced its moments, its elements, its materials, in historical time. In the resulting space, it re-produces them in an immobile movement. Since 'each member dissolves as soon as it sets itself apart', the movement, the revolving sphere, the round, in a word, the system, are also 'transparent and serene rest', in the words of the *Phenomenology of Spirit*. Thus, the Hegelian state offers the model of a self-generated and self-maintained system that regulates itself, in other words, the perfect automatism.[11] Architectonic colossus, necessary and sufficient, it is so. *Es ist so.* (These were supposedly the last words of the dying Hegel.)

10 Cf. the end of Hegel's *Phenomenology of Spirit*, already cited and commented on in Henri Lefebvre, *La Fin de l'histoire*, Paris: Éditions de Minuit, 1970, and the final pages of Hegel's *Philosophy of History*.

11 A conception taken up recently by authors unaware of one another and seemingly ignorant of their common source: Michel Clousard, *L'Être et le code*, Paris: Mouton, 1973; Yves Barel, *La Reproduction*, Paris: Éditions Anthropos, 1973; Jean Baudrillard, *Le Miroir de la production*, Paris: Casterman, 1973, etc.

5) Let us now reconsider what is currently known as 'Marxism'. (Do I need to repeat that this is not the first time and will not be the last either?)

Preliminary remark: Hegelianism can be defined as a system. True, specialists in the history of philosophy are familiar with the difficulties arising from the diversity of Hegel's texts and their dates. Agreement between Hegel's *phenomenology* (description and linkage of figures and moments of consciousness, both for the individual and for humanity in its progress) and his *logic* (which includes the relation of formal logic, theory of coherence, with dialectic, theory of contradictions), as well as with *history* (sequence of struggles, violence, wars and revolutions), has nothing like Cartesian self-evidence. Yet we can be confident that Hegelian thought, in the course of the philosopher's life, focused in a definable direction, that of the philosophical and political system.

What then of Marxism? This is only a word, a political label, a polemical amalgam. Only an outdated dogmatism still tries to find in Marx's works a homogeneous body of doctrine: a system. Between the works of his youth, those of his maturity and those of his latter years, there is more than diversity, and anything but a quiet plant-like development. There are fissures, gaps, contradictions, incoherencies. Take dialectics, for example, which is first of all exalted and turned against Hegel like a weapon seized from the enemy, then denied and rejected, then taken up in a renewed form that Marx never clearly explained.

In so far as it is possible to draw a body of doctrine from a monumental work such as *Capital*, it refers to competitive capitalism, whose disappearance Marx foresaw and proclaimed. But why stubbornly stick to constructing an ensemble of this kind, given that the work was not completed? Why conceive it as a totality adequate to the mode of production that it analyses and explains, capitalism? It may well be that the final chapters, no less rich than the opening ones, contain discoveries that appear only by confronting them with what emerged from competitive capitalism in the twentieth century. Marx's thought may today play a similar role as does Newton's physics in relation to modern physics, the physics of relativity, nuclear energy, atoms and molecules: a staging post for going further, a truth at a certain level, a date – in a word, a *moment* – which prohibits, on the one hand, dogmatism, 'Marxist' rhetoric, and on the other, presumptuous discourse on the death of Marx and Marxism. Let us make this attitude clear right away; the reasons for it will appear later. It is not a question of reconsidering Marx's thought, following the usual schema of 'revisionism', as a function of what has been new in the world over the last century. On the contrary: the correct and legitimate procedure consists in the determination of what is new in the world *on the basis of* Marx's work. This is how changes in the productive forces, the relations of production, social structures and superstructures (ideological and institutional) manifest themselves.

Today there are multiple Marxisms, and it is a vain effort to try and reduce them to a single 'model'. The thought of Marx and Engels was grafted on to concepts and values that were already widespread in the countries where it penetrated. Hence the birth of a Chinese Marxism and a Soviet (Russian) Marxism, of Marxist schools in Germany, Italy, France and the English-speaking countries. Hence the diversity and unevenness of theoretical development. The graft took either well or less well. In France, the Cartesian spirit, fundamentally anti-dialectical, offered neither a terrain nor a favourable 'mentor'; the graft only bore fruit belatedly, which did not mean these were of poor quality.

What relationship did Marx's thought have with that of Hegel? This question, which as everyone knows has led to a flood of ink being spilled, requires just one answer: Marx's dialectical thought had a relationship with Hegel's dialectical thought that was itself dialectical, which means unity and conflict. Marx took from Hegel the essentials of his 'essentialist' thought: the importance of work and production, the self-production of the human species (of 'man'), the rationality immanent to practice, consciousness and knowledge, as also to political struggles, hence the meaning of history.

It is possible to find in Hegel (as also in Saint-Simon) almost everything that Marx said, including the role of work, production, classes, etc.,[12] with the result that it is impossible to deny the continuity between the two thinkers. Yet the order and linkage, orientation and perspective, content and form, differ radically, so that the impression of a brusque discontinuity is no less striking than that of an uninterrupted continuity.

Throughout his life, Marx struggled against Hegel, to wrest from him his ill-gotten gains and transform these by appropriating them. What

---

12   In Norbert Guterman and Henri Lefebvre, *Morceaux choisis de Hegel*, Paris: Gallimard, 1995 [1939], fragments 218 to 224 are chosen and arranged with this intention.

was Hegel for Marx? At the same time the father, possessor of the inheritance, and the boss and owner of the means of production, acquired knowledge.

In their struggle, there was a generational quarrel but also a class struggle. This combat went through phases with varying fortunes: highs and lows, victories and defeats, by one or other combatant. The stakes changed: either knowledge as totality or dialectic as method, or the theory of the state, etc. Contrary to Hegel, Marx used whatever he could lay hands on. He passed Hegelianism through the sieve of anthropology (Feuerbach), political economy (Smith, Ricardo), historiography (the historians of the French Restoration, especially Adolphe Thierry and the history of the Third Estate), philosophy (French materialism of the eighteenth century) and nascent sociology (Saint-Simon and Fourier). From this sieving and filtering, this critical negation, emerged a different thought and above all a different project, 'Marxism', built from the materials of a reprised and metamorphosed Hegelianism. This struggle ran from radical critique of Hegel's theses on law and the state, on philosophy (the so-called Young Marx, 1842–5), to refutation of the Hegelian political strategy accepted by Ferdinand Lassalle (*Critique of the Gotha Programme*, 1875). No one today is unaware of how Marx understood and approved the Paris Commune, as destructive of the state. He opposed this revolutionary practice to the state socialism that was unfortunately coming to dominate the German workers' movement, and would do so for a very long period, as it still persists today. In the course of this theoretical struggle, Marx never lost sight for a moment of the practical objective of the real stake, which is not the constitution of a system opposed to Hegelianism, but analysis of social practice and the modern world, in order to act and transform these on the basis of their immanent tendencies.

Continuity and discontinuity. There is therefore a 'break [*coupure*]', a point of rupture. Where should we situate this? Drawing on both texts and contexts, we can maintain that this break was neither *philosophical* (transition from idealism to materialism) nor *epistemological* (transition from ideology to science). These two aspects are encompassed in a more complex break, richer in both content and meaning: a *political* break. It was not true, for Marx, that philosophy (reason and truth, fullness and happiness as conceived by the philosophers) was realized in the state and ended in a constraining system. The working class would *realize philosophy* by a total revolution. But this was no longer classical philosophy (abstract, speculative, systematic); the realization of philosophy is accomplished in practice, in a way of living. By superseding traditional philosophy, by superseding itself, the proletariat opens up limitless possibilities. Time (so-called 'historical' time) continues. Hegelian superseding (*Aufhebung*)[13] takes on a quite different meaning: the state itself has to be dispensed with through the ordeal of supersession. The revolution breaks it and leads to its withering away; it is absorbed or reabsorbed in society. Thus, the political *break* presupposes the philosophical break (rupture with classic philosophy) and the epistemological break (rupture with ideologies, those of the dominant class) as its moments. As for reason, it has no definitive form or formula. It develops through superseding: by resolving its own contradictions (between the rational and the irrational, the conceived and lived experience, theory and practice, etc.).

Thus, the state does not possess any higher rationality, still less a definitive one. Hegel takes it as the *structure* of society, while for Marx it is only a *superstructure*. It is constructed, or rather people – politicians, statesmen – construct it on a *base*, the social relations of production and ownership, the productive forces. The base then changes. So, the state has no other reality than that of a historical *moment*. It changes along with the base; it is modified, crumbles, is rebuilt differently, then perishes and disappears. As the productive forces advance from the use of natural riches to the technical mastery of nature (automatism), and from divided labour (alienated-alienating) to non-labour, the state cannot but be transformed. It has already changed profoundly from the feudal-military period to the monarchical period, and from this to the democratic period introduced by industrialization. Capitalism and the hegemony of the bourgeois class accommodate themselves to a democracy simultaneously liberal and authoritarian. This democracy and its state (parliamentary) are only for a time.

History, which according to Hegel had been completed, continues for Marx. Uncompleted time does not freeze (reify) in space, the space of commercial relations, industrial production or state domination. The

---

13 [In *Metaphilosophy* (London: Verso, 2016, pp. 22–3), Lefebvre cites Hegel's *Science of Logic* on the twofold meaning of *Aufheben*, both 'to preserve' and 'to put an end to', which he notes is inadequately rendered by the French term *dépasser*. The same holds for 'supersede' in English.]

production of things (products) encompasses the production of social relations; this double production, too, cannot be frozen (reified) into a simple re-production of the same things and the same relations. Thus, there is no re-production of the past or the present without the production of something new. This is the original form that the Hegelian dialectic acquires with Marx. The revolutionary creation of new relations cannot be avoided, even by the use of political instruments, constraint and persuasion (ideological). Rationality? This turns out to be inherent to social practice, and culminates, though without conclusion, in industrial practice. The everyday? Transformed along with social relations, it will bring happiness to men, Marxist optimism intrepidly maintains.

As for the state, a double movement runs through it. On the one hand, it manages the whole society in terms of the hegemony of the dominant and ruling class: in terms of its present interests and its strategic projects. It accordingly generates an educational system, practical knowledge [*connaissance*] and ideologies, social 'services' such as medicine and teaching, according to the interests of the hegemonic (dominant) class. At the same time, it raises itself above the whole of society, with the result that those individuals who possess the state (whether fraction of the hegemonic class or *déclassés*) may end up dominating and even exploiting for a time the economically dominant class, taking away its hegemony. This happens with Bonapartism, fascism, a state resulting from a military coup, etc. This contradiction *internal* to the state is added to the *external* contradictions that arise from its conflictual relations with its *base*, itself pervaded by contradictions. Hence the impossibility of a stabilization of the state. A provisional form of society, with its more or less integrated moments (moments, in other words, more or less dominated and appropriated: knowledge and logic, technology and strategy, law and moral ideology, etc.), the state does not rest on the middle class. Its base does not coincide with this class, but encompasses all social relations. Today, accordingly, it is the state of the bourgeoisie. It needs a bureaucracy, which effectively means a middle class, which tends to become parasitic as well as 'competent', by raising itself above the whole society along with the state (not without conflicts with the owners of the means of production, that is, with the other fractions of the ruling class).

Marx places at the centre of his analysis of the real, and likewise of his project, the social force able to overturn the state and the social relations on which it is based and which transform it, in other words, to destroy it first of all so as to bring it to an end. If the working class asserts itself by becoming a 'collective subject', then the state as 'subject' of history will die. If the state escapes this fate, if it does not collapse, if it does not fracture and wither away, this means that the working class has been unable to become an *autonomous* collective subject. By becoming autonomous, the working class replaces the dictatorship of the bourgeoisie with its own hegemony (its dictatorship). What prevents the self-determination and assertion of the proletariat as 'subject', as ability to manage the means of production and the whole society? Violence. Violence is inherent to the 'subject' when it breaks obstacles; this is its only meaning and scope. In the case of the working class, violence puts an end to the state, and to politicians raising themselves above the social. Proletarian (revolutionary) violence self-destructs instead of destroying the world. By itself it produces nothing, is in no way creative. We may say of violence that it is a permanent quality or 'property' of a self-asserting social being. According to Marx, this class cannot realize itself without superseding itself. By this act, it realizes philosophy by superseding it. For Marx, the *social* can and must reabsorb the two other levels of so-called 'human' reality, on the one hand politics and the state (which lose their dominant character and wither away), and on the other hand economics, the productive forces (which organize themselves within society, by a rational management according to the interests of the producers, the workers, themselves). The social, and consequently social needs, those of society as a whole, define the new society that is born from the old by revolution; socialism and communism are characterized on the one hand by the end of the state and its primacy, and on the other hand by the end of economics and its priority. In the 'economic-social-political' triad, it is the social and society that Marx emphasizes, and the concept of which he developed. Some would say that he banked on the social against the economic and the political, which had priority before the reversal of this world in which they had primacy. Others would say that Marx established a strategy on the basis of analysing tendencies in the real (the existing), with the social asserting itself as such.

Marxist thought is inspired by an immense optimism (an optimism that many people today label with a word that has lost its favourable connotations and is seen as denoting an uncertain naïvety: humanism). Happiness would arise from the conflictual play of forces, and especially from the conflict between nature (the spontaneous creation of wealth, reserves and resources) and anti-nature (work, technology, machines). The triad of nature, work and knowledge is the bearer of fortune.

A certain paradox continues to surprise, always new despite being very well known: the lasting influence of this optimism, despite its repeated setbacks. Marxism has failed, particularly and especially in the large number of countries that claim to adhere to it. In these so-called socialist countries, specifically social relations (association, cooperation, self-management [*auto-gestion*], etc.) are crushed between economics and politics, to the point of having no acknowledged existence; they are reduced, as in capitalist countries, to 'private' relations, personal communication in everyday discourse, the family, relations of formal socializing and business, at best to friendship or complicity. This crushing of the 'social' under the banner of socialism adds a further mystification to an already long list (rationalism against reason, nationalism against the nation,[14] individualism against the individual, etc.). In this strange list, certain labels gradually fall into disuse (rationalism, for example, and its relationship with the irrational and the rational), but others take their place; 'socialism against the social' is a good replacement for any other opposition that is now obsolescent.

And yet, here or there, a ray of sunlight breaks through. It emerges from the economic against the political,[15] which shows the complexity of the situation. Failures of Marxist thought? Yes. Death? No.

---

14 [A reference to Lefebvre's *Le Nationalisme contre les nations*, published in 1936.]

15 One example: the Lip affair in France, summer 1973. [A strike at the Besançon plant of the Lip clock manufacturer led to a prolonged occupation with self-managed production by the workers, attracting wide support across the country. – Translator.] The 1968 events may be interpreted in the same sense, as a breakthrough of the 'social' above economics and against politics. These circumstances show the dominant feature of the class struggle today in an 'advanced' industrial country with a revolutionary tradition. Self-management is no longer an 'ideal', a remote possibility. The struggle is waged on the ground of self-management, the site and the stake of action. And today, self-management defines the social between (against) the economic and the political, according to Marx's thought. [Lefebvre discussed these themes in *The Explosion: Marxism and the French Upheaval* (1969), *The Survival of Capitalism* (1976) and the essays collected in *State, Space, World*.] We should also note the tenacious confusion among Marxists between the *relations of production* (including the *technical* division of labour in the productive process) and the *social relations of production* (including the association controlling hierarchies and decisions, with its tendency to self-management). This allowed the reduction of the latter to the former.

This situation is eminently paradoxical, and also one we shall have to return to.

6) We turn now to Nietzsche and Nietzschean thought (in as much as this is still a 'thought'). This does not mean that the following reflections exhaust the situation of which this thought is part. We should not approach it without circumspection. 'The Cartesian mind is seized by terror as soon as it enters the world of Nietzsche.'[16]

History? For Nietzsche as for Marx, contrary to Hegel, it continues – under a double form: on the one hand, absurd wars, endless violence, barbarities, genocides; and on the other, an immense, cumulative knowledge, ever more crushing, made up of scholarship, quotations, an amalgam of actions and representations, memories and techniques, speculations that are of little interest but supremely 'interested'. What continues, therefore, is not history (historicity) as conceived by Hegel, a genesis of ever more complex realities, productive capacities that finally culminate in the edifice of the state. Nor is it history according to Marx, leading towards neither divinity nor the state, but towards 'humanity', the fullness of the human species, perfection of its essence, domination over matter and appropriation of nature. The Hegelian hypothesis (which Nietzsche was familiar with, and attacked violently in his *Untimely Meditations*),[17] and the Marxist hypothesis (which Nietzsche rejected, via Hegel, without knowing it), were for him no more than theological. They presupposed that thought or practical action had a meaning, without demonstrating this. They postulated a direction: an immanent rationality, a divinity in humanity, or in the world. But God is dead! The atheism of Feuerbach, Stirner or Marx misunderstood the import of this assertion. Philosophers and their accomplices continued to reason – to philosophize – as if God were not dead. But along with God died history, man and humanity, reason and rationality, finality and meaning. Whether proclaimed by theologians as a higher entity, or secularized, placed in nature or in history, God was the support of philosophical architectures, systems, dogmas and doctrines.

---

16 P. Boudot, *Nietzsche et l'au-delà de la liberté*, p. 151.

17 [Lefebvre particularly has in mind here the first of these essays, 'On the Use and Abuse of History for Life', which dates from 1874.]

What then is history? A chaos of chances, desires, determinisms. In this Nietzschean triad, taken over from the Greeks, *chance* holds the first place. The revelation and acceptance of chance, even the apologia for it, give a new dimension to freedom, declares Zarathustra, by breaking the slavery of finality. There is no event without a conjunction or conjuncture of forces initially external to one another, which meet up at a point in space and time where something happens in the wake of this encounter. Chance offers opportunities, favourable conjunctures (the *kairos* of the Greeks). 'Chances end up being organized according to our most personal needs', wrote Nietzsche. Why? Because what emerges in the face of analysis as well as in life is the *will*: not the pallid 'faculty' of classical psychology, the will of the subject who says 'I want', but the *will to power* [*puissance*], the active energy that seeks not a particular advantage from power [*pouvoir*], but power for itself: to dominate. As Hegel saw, following Heraclitus, there is struggle, combat, war; but for Nietzsche, the struggle of wills to power replaces Hegel's rational historicity and dialectical overthrow (which Marx followed, modifying the Hegelian terms), an overthrow through which the slave conquers the conqueror (the master), so advancing in the direction of history. The third term of the triad: determinism, necessity. According to Nietzsche, there is not and cannot be a unique necessity, an exclusive determinism (physical, biological, historical, economic, political, etc.). There are multiple determinisms, which are born and die, grow and disappear after having undergone a certain path, played a certain role in nature or society. A role more often disastrous than beneficial . . .

So, history is not strictly speaking a chaos; it can be analysed and understood; but the understanding of history shows it to be irreducible to an immanent rationality, a progress determinable in advance. In any historical sequence, elements and symptoms of decadence can be discerned, even within something still strengthening. The shocks of violence shatter anything that seeks to establish itself in a fixed mould. Partial determinisms (biological, physical, social, intellectual) allow *genealogies*, such as that of a particular family, a discovery, an idea or a concept, far more than they do *geneses*, explanations by a producing activity.

Hegel, and Marx after him, refused to disconnect the rational from the real. They took the point of view of a logico-dialectical identity of the two terms (unity in contradiction and struggle, victory of a third term born from this struggle). According to Nietzsche, however, this is the root of a fundamental error. It rationally associates fact with value or meaning; but facts have no more meaning than a pebble on a mountain or an isolated noise. As for nature, it has no meaning, rather offering the possibility of countless meanings, in a mixture of cruelty and generosity, joy and suffering, pleasure and pain – a mixture with no name. 'Man', by a choice, confers a meaning on nature, on natural life, on the things of nature. 'Man' is not a 'being' that endlessly questions the world and himself, but a being that creates meanings and value – which he does as soon as he names things, evaluating them by speaking of them. Very likely, there are only facts and things for and by such evaluation. Does knowledge contribute a value, does it give meaning to objects and things? No, says Nietzsche against Hegel. In fact, as 'pure' and abstract knowl- edge, it strips the world of meaning. As for work, Nietzsche agrees with Marx that it has and gives meaning and value, but not the labour that manufactures products, only work that is creative. 'Who evaluates? Who names? Who lives according to a value? Who chooses a value?' This is how the question of the *subject* is posited, to which a response is neces- sary in order for the quest for a new meaning to retain a meaning – a question that it is hard to answer, since the answer presupposes a return to the original, by giving the 'subject' and its relationship with meaning a genesis. Hence Nietzsche's uncertainties (significant in themselves). Sometimes he says that *peoples* invent meanings, create values. The philosopher and the poet keep aloof from the crowds, yet they emerge from the peoples, even and especially when opposed to their people.[18] It is peoples that invent, and not states or nations or classes, which give no more meaning and value to anything than does knowledge or politics. This thesis posits in principle a complete relativism, a 'perspectivism' that is nonetheless convergent with Marxist positions, as it attributes to peoples, and consequently to the 'masses', the creative capacity of gener- ating a perspective on the basis of an evaluation. Sometimes Nietzsche replies on the contrary that only the individual (of genius) has this capacity – an 'elitist' position: 'We, who indissolubly perceive and think,

---

18 Cf. *Thus Spoke Zarathustra*, Chapter 15, 'The Thousand and One Goals': 'Much that passed for good with one people was regarded with scorn and contempt by another . . . A table of excellences hangs over every people. Lo! It is the table of their triumphs; lo! It is the voice of their Will to Power.'

we ceaselessly bring to birth that which is not yet', he proudly declares in
Die fröhliche Wissenschaft. Nietzsche's thought, in other words, in as
much as it is a thought, does not flinch from contradictions and incoherencies. But is it necessary to choose between these propositions? Are we
faced with a system, a knowledge, or rather the transition from one
knowledge to another, from sad science to *Gay Science*?

What then is this 'gay science', opposed both to the absolute science of
Hegel and the critical science of Marx? Without awaiting a deeper recon-
sideration of this central point, it is useful to give right away here the
genealogy of the *fröhliche Wissenschaft*. It has its origin in what is deepest in the West: a subterranean current combatted and buried by Judeo-
Christian morality and Greco-Roman logos, against which Nietzsche
waged a combat that was all the more terrible in that this was the matrix
from which he himself emerged, which gives this struggle an exemplary
and paradoxical character.

At the origin of Christian thought we have a work both illustrious and
misunderstood, Augustinianism, relegated into the shadows by official
doctrine. Augustine contemplated with all the resources of Greek,
Platonic and Judeo-Alexandrian philosophy, in other words, with all the
still-fresh memories of the Roman tradition, on the specific characteristic of Christianity, the doctrine of the fall, of sin and redemption. He
interpreted the image of the *mundus*, of Greco-Italian origin, as a function of ordeal and purification by pain: the hole and the gap, the abyss
deepening in the earthly depths, the shadowy corridor opening to the
light by a path hard to find, the trajectory of souls who return to the
maternal womb of the earth to be later reborn. The *mundus*: a ditch in
which newborn infants were abandoned when their father refused to
raise them, along with the condemned to death, refuse, corpses that
were not returned to the celestial fire by burning them. Nothing was
more sacred, that is, more accursed, more pure and more impure. The
'world': an ordeal in darkness to gain redemption, light. '*Mundus est
immundus*', Augustine proclaimed, at the dawn of the Christian world –
the moment when the pagan world collapsed. He had found a motto for
Christianity, its slogan.

Augustine, the first Westerner, did not posit in principle a 'something'
pertaining to knowledge, whether an *object* (like the majority of the pre-
Socratics: water, fire, atoms, etc.) or a *subject* (such as the *noûs* for
Anaxagoras, or the active intelligence for Aristotle), or again an absolute

knowledge (the Platonic Idea, forerunner of the Hegelian). For Augustine, being was defined (if we may put it this way) by will and desire, not by knowledge. Being (divine) is desire and infinite: desire not inherently finished, thus inexhaustible, and desire for the infinite, for another being equally infinite. This makes possible a presentment – like the sun through the clouds – of the mystery of the divine triad, the Trinity. Man in the image of God, the analogue of the divine, initially *is* infinite desire. The fall and sin broke this subjective infinity by separating it from its infinite 'object'. If the 'world' is no more than a heap of filth, reason is revealed in the rupture and finitude of desire. Fallen into the dereliction of the finite, desire seizes on finite objects but encounters there only anxiety and frustration, in place of the infinite joy that it still and always senses. Rampant in the darkness of the *mundus*, this broken desire, divided from itself and yet reduced to pursuing only itself (in 'self-love'), this infinite desire fallen into the finite is nothing other than *libido*, yet not unique but triple. According to the Augustinians there are three *libidines*, at the same time inseparable in fallen being and yet clearly distinct: *libido sciendi* (curiosity, knowledge and the need for knowledge, a need always disappointed and always reborn, attracted towards each thing instead of probing its own corruption and its own failure); *libido sentiendi* (the concupiscence of the flesh, the need for enjoyment, the endless and always disappointed pursuit of physical pleasure, a parody of infinite love), and finally *libido dominandi* (ambition, the need to command and dominate: the will to power). The triple libido of the Augustinians re-produces derisorily, in the dereliction of the finite, the divine triplicity of the Father (true power), the Son (the word, true knowledge and wisdom) and the Spirit (true love). Each libido is only the shadow of infinite desire, only desiring itself (self-love) through finite objects.

What relationship does this have to Nietzsche, other than purely abstract? In what way does Augustinianism (crushed by a theory of absolute knowledge, Thomism with its Aristotelian origin, which would pass through the sieve of Cartesian critique without suffering too great damage, and continue as an ingredient of Western logos) form part of the genealogy of Nietzschean thought? By way of seventeenth-century France. The underground current of Augustinianism inspired constant protest against the official theology of the Catholic Church; it also sustained protest against the establishment of the centralized state, the

absolute royal power supported by *raison d'état* and knowledge:
Jansenism against Louis XIV. Jansenism, however, was not confined to
the thought of Cornelius Jansen, Saint-Cyran, Pascal and Port-Royal. It
passed into literature: in Racine, and above all in La Rochefoucauld.
Augustinian libido was referred to as 'self-love' in this author's *Maxims*,
which cruelly analyse all forms of self-love to denounce its detours and
masks: ambition, the search for pleasure, curiosity.[19] La Rochefoucauld,
a sophisticated duke, was well acquainted with worldly society and knew
what should be known about it. He was a Jansenist by both heart and
spirit. This 'moralist' destroyed the social world [*le Monde*]: the court,
courtiers, royal power. To official knowledge, the Cartesian (state) logos,
he opposed the asceticism of a non-knowledge full of bitter clarity.
Nietzsche both read and reflected on La Rochefoucauld's *Maxims*. Not
only did he know them but he imitated them. The aphorisms of *Human,
All Too Human* (first volume 1877–8; second volume 1879) extend to the
modern age the harsh analysis, intrepid penetration and sad knowledge
of the French 'moralist' (who might be more properly called an 'immor-
alist'). They have the same frame of mind, the same pointedness and
alacrity. If Nietzsche revealed the *libido dominandi*, self-love as ambition
and struggle for power, it was to denounce it down to its roots. The
Protestantism of this son of a pastor drew nourishment and strength
from a Jansenism diverted from its aim and its meaning, and soon
turned in protest against those who destroy the 'world' but do not know
what to do with the debris.

So much for the 'sad science'. As for *The Gay Science* (1881–2), it has a
close origin and a (dialectically) opposite meaning.[20] Outside of Greco-
Roman logos (logic and law) and Judeo-Christian morality (the hatred
of pleasure, enjoyment viewed as sin and defilement), what did the West
invent? A madness that gives meaning to actions and things: individual

19 On this last point, see Henri Lefebvre, *Pascal*, two volumes, Paris: Éditions Nagel,
1950. Nietzsche dedicated his *Human, All Too Human* to the memory of Voltaire, but he
quotes La Rochefoucauld in many places, and the imitation is perfectly visible in both
content and form. 'Like a herald who goes forward without knowing whether his knights
are following him', he wrote to Wagner about this book in 1878.

20 Cf. also the above-cited *Pascal*. Other authors have risen to the challenge and
shown both the originality and the contributions of southern French *civilization* against
the state power and social pressure from the north of the country. The enemy here (in
the language of the romance of the Round Table) is Denis de Rougemont, author of a
foolish book *L'Amour et l'Occident*.

love, mad love, absolute love. But the West misunderstood, ignored and crushed the best that it had. Southern French civilization – that of the Midi and King Sun – which assimilated images, metaphors and concepts from the Arabs of Andalusia as well as from Celtic legends,[21] brought courtship into love, which did not just mean respect for the beloved 'being' (the individual, the person), escaping the ancient status of beautiful object, but the sharing of pleasure. The 'gay science' was not simply a rhetoric of love, or a way of assembling words. It was the art of living in and through love: the art of joy and amorous pleasure. The lover, in the act of love, honours his lady. He serves her instead of using her for his sexual need. Respect for the beloved being – the beautiful woman – not only meant refusing to consider her as an object, not only submitting to her will and even her caprices, but also giving her control of physical pleasure. Courtly and absolute love proclaimed itself above ambition and power, beyond the will to power. The 'libido sentiendi' was redeemed, purified by passion. Desire was once again infinite, as it no longer had a finite object before it but a divine being, 'deus in terris': beautiful, active, sentient and conscious. The 'gay science' supersedes sin and redemption. It rediscovers the innocence of the body and great health. It contains a deeper understanding [connaissance] than the bitterness of critical analysis, and 'truer' than the 'pure' knowledge of the learned. Better than work, and more than knowledge, it gives meaning and value to events, actions, things. It is a constant festival.

Nietzsche brought together 'gay science' and 'bitter science', superseding the one with the other, subordinating lucidity to joy[22] without losing it, and likewise knowing [connaître] to living. From their conflictual unity he sought a third term that he believed would arise: a poetic life of the flesh to transcend both the 'sad science' and the 'gay science'.

Living and lived experience forcefully reassert themselves, with violence if need be. Against whom and against what? Against the coldest

---

21 The various episodes of the Round Table: the magician Merlin and his love for Niviane; Lancelot and his love for Guinevere; the quest for the Grail and the epic of Percival. (The Celts invaded the lands that would become France, down to the north of Spain, where they formed a people known in antiquity under the name of 'Celtiberes'.)

22 It is not hard to find in La Rochefoucauld's Maxims an indication of this project. The tradition of absolute love marks a large number of literary works in France, especially The Princess of Cleves, a novel that La Rochefoucauld may have had a hand in. On the myth of the Grail and the quest for the absolute, cf. Nietzsche's curious letter to Seydlitz, 4 January 1878.

of cold monsters, the state. Against sad (conceptual) knowledge, against oppressive and repressive violence. Against the everyday, against unacceptable 'reality'. Against labour and the division of labour and the production of things. Against social morality and constraints, those of a society without civilization that seeks to perpetuate itself by any means. Around 1885, shortly after Marx had died, Nietzsche the poet, Nietzsche the megalomaniac, cried out his anguish and his joy. He wanted to save the world and Europe from the barbarism they were falling into. Western society, that of logos (Greco-Roman: logic and law) and morality (Judeo-Christian: Puritanism), had become monstrous beyond belief, beyond all measure. Production for destruction, making children for wars, accumulating knowledge to dominate peoples, Nietzsche saw these absurdities in Germany under the sign of reason. He sensed, denounced and stigmatized the fundamental error, philosophically consecrated and legitimized by Hegel: the conjunction and fusion of knowledge and authority, abstract cognition and power, in the state and the state model of modern society. Today, he would see the destruction of nature (both outside and within 'man') as a manifestation of the will to power in all its horror, rather than its negation. And the same with the potential self-destruction of the human species (nuclear danger, etc.).

The West had tried out its values, in an immense assertion: logic, law, state (Hegel), work and production (Marx). The result tended to prove the failure of the human race. The reverse and counterpart of this colossal assertion was a hidden nihilism and a malevolence pertaining to pathology. European nihilism was not the product of critical thought, but of its ineffectiveness. It did not come from the rejection of history, nation, homeland, but from the defeats of history. Its secret, its enigma? They lie in the assertion itself, that of logos, an assertion that appears full yet reveals its emptiness.

Did Nietzsche ignore work, industry, the working class, capitalism and the bourgeoisie? He speaks little of these directly. He speaks of them only through the critique of culture and knowledge. If he dismisses them from his field, it is because in his view none of these terms, none of these 'realities', contributes a perspective other than nihilistic. Where Hegelianism had seen the triumph of reason, where Marx saw the conditions of a different society, Nietzsche perceived only a 'reality' that he did not strive to recognize at such, except to refute and reject it. For it would tumble into mud and blood.

Should Nietzsche be defined as *anarchistic*? Yes and no. Yes, as he rejects en bloc the 'real' and knowledge of the real considered as higher reality. Yes, as with him subversion is distinguished from revolution. No, as he has nothing in common with Stirner or Bakunin, who define themselves by a consciousness, a knowledge (not political in the case of the former, basically political with the latter). Anarchists remain on the ground of the 'real': of what and whom they combat. They want to see and possess a 'property', albeit unique, or expropriate those who possess 'reality'.

Nietzsche wanted to supersede the real – transcend it – by poetry, appealing to carnal depths. Did he struggle for the oppressed? No. According to him, the oppressed have often, if not always, lived better, in other words, more intensely, more ardently, than their oppressors: they sang, they danced, they cried out their pain and their fury, even when subject to the 'values' of their conquerors. In their own way, they invented. What? Not what would bring down their masters and over-turn the situation, but something else, closer to Dionysus, god and myth of the earth, of the vanquished, of the oppressed (women, slaves, peas-ants, etc.).

For Nietzsche there is thus an inaugural act: redemption, supersession. Renouncing the will to power after having experienced it, thus renouncing the political acts by which oppression and exploitation are maintained – this is how the initial act is placed in perspective. Will to live? This remains deri-sory if one (the 'subject') sticks to an intuition, an intention – which dismisses voluntarist and vitalist philosophy: Schopenhauer, Stirner and many others. Classical tragedy marked the place of redemption; it repeated the sacrifice of the hero to show how his fate is accomplished and what leads him to his loss; it redeemed the spectator-actor from the obscure wish expressed in wanting power. As a popular festival, it opened up new possi-bilities: in Greece, urban life and rational law supplanted custom. Music offers the example of an ever prodigious metamorphosis, transforming anguish and desire into joy, in the course of a purification deeper than Aristotelian 'catharsis'. It creates meaning. The 'subject'? This preoccupation of the philosophers proves derisory. There is no other subject than the body; but the body has its depth, and music is born from it and returns to it, with its sounds more luminous than light that speaks only to the gaze.

On the basis of this exaltation of art, myths and religions are to be interpreted instead of falling into derision (superstition). Myths and religions sought redemption, but missed the real aim as they served as masks for the will to power, generating practices (rites) and institutions (churches). If religions are understood and interpreted, the causes of decadence are found in them, particularly in the West where Judeo-Christianity generated capitalism and the bourgeoisie, phenomena that were derivative but that aggravated their causes.

Nietzschean overcoming (Überwinden) differs radically from Hegelian and Marxian *Aufheben*. It does not preserve anything, it does not carry its antecedents and preconditions to a higher level. It casts them into nothingness. Subversive rather than revolutionary, Überwinden overcomes by destroying, or rather by leading to its self-destruction that which it replaces. This is how Nietzsche sought to overcome both the European assertion of logos and its opposite obverse side, nihilism. Is it necessary to add that this heroic struggle against Judeo-Christian nihilism on behalf of and through carnal life has nothing in common with hedonism? There is a triad (three terms), but in the course of the struggle what is born casts the other terms into nothingness (sends them *zu Grunde*, as Heidegger would say), with the result that they then appear as 'foundations', depths. Dialectical? Yes, but radically different from either the Hegelian or the Marxist dialectic. By the role, the import, the meaning of the *negative*. By the intensity of the tragic.

The superhuman? This is born therefore from the destruction and self-destruction of all that exists under the name of 'human'. It is the possible-impossible *par excellence*, as already implied by the initial and initiating redemption: rejection of the will to power, the gay science and joyous pessimism. As for what should be (*Sollen*), this is an imperative of living rather than morality. A distant possibility? No! So close to everyone that nothing is able to grasp it, the superhuman resides in the body (cf. what Zarathustra says of 'those who have contempt for the body'). This body, rich in unknown virtualities, unfurls some of its powers in art: the eye and the gaze in painting, touch in sculpture, the ear in music, speech in language and poetry. The total body, in a conjuncture that favours it, is unfurled in theatre and architecture, music and dance. If this total body deploys all its possibilities, then the superhuman penetrates into the 'real' by metamorphosing it. As in poetry and music. Not without certain ordeals, such as the terrifying idea of eternal recurrence: the reproduction of the past, absolute repetition or the absolute of repetition, chance and necessity dizzily united . . .

7) Do we now, in the second half of the twentieth century, possess all the elements of a vast confrontation, all the pieces of a great trial (in which all that remains is to denote accusers and accused, witnesses, judges, lawyers)? No. The files are incomplete, by a long way.

If we examine the great 'visions' or 'conceptions' of the world (under-standing by this, in a rather imprecise way, theologies and theogonies, theosophies, theodicies, metaphysics and philosophies, representations and ideologies), we perceive that they put to work a small number of 'principles': one, two or three. Rarely more.[23] The sacred numbers include seven, ten, twelve and thirteen. Philosophico-metaphysical principles are limited to the One, the Double, and the Triad.

Do the most vigorously and rigorously unitary conceptions have their birthplace in the East? Very likely. Hegel already thought this in his *Philosophy of History*.[24] Are their preconditions revealed by an 'Asiatic mode of production', incompletely defined by Marx, which according to him differed from the Western modes of production in terms of the role of the state, cities and the sovereign, as well as in its social base (stable agricultural communities)? With the result that the entire mental and social space, agricultural and urban, was organized according to a single law. Whatever the case, immanent (in nature, the palpable) or transcendent (being or spirit), the One asserts itself as absolute principle in several conceptions of the world. Many others accept two principles, generally in struggle: the male and female prin-ciples, or goodness and evil, good people and bad, light and darkness. These dualist (binary) conceptions received their most elaborate expression in Manichaeism. Almost everywhere they draw on the magical and ritual content of popular religion. The Mediterranean basin and the Middle East seem to have been the birthplaces of this dualism, or at least its places of predilection. Is its 'precondition' the conflictual relationship between sea and land, plain and mountain, the

---

23 Schopenhauer extricated the 'quadruple root' of the principle of sufficient reason. A few poems of Hölderlin, and a few texts of Heidegger, speak rather enigmatically of the four (elements?). The number five held a privileged position in ancient China (four directions in space, plus the centre and the vertical, the site of imperial thought).

24 *Philosophy of History*, Part I, The Oriental World, pp. 111ff.; on the Asiatic mode of production there have been numerous publications, starting with the book by Wittfogel. [Karl Wittfogel, *Oriental Despotism: A Comparative Study of Total Power*, New Haven: Yale University Press, 1957.]

settled and the nomadic? Perhaps, but it does not matter. Here we shall emphasize the differences between conceptions of the world, leaving aside their history.

The European West seems committed to triadic or trinitarian thought. And from a very early date, if we believe the research of pre-historians and anthropologists. As early as the establishment of a stable agriculture and settled villages, with the great migrations that unfurled across Europe for many centuries. The Greeks already thought in triads: chance, will, determinism. It was in the West that the Christian doctrine of the Trinity took shape, shedding unitary and dualist doctrines (respectively monophysitism and Manichaeism, the latter still being influential in the Middle Ages, as with the Cathars). Why? In what conditions? Perhaps because of the triadic structure of agrarian communities (houses and gardens, arable land in private ownership, pasture and forest in collective possession). Or perhaps due to the process of their origin: the formation of towns on an already developed agricultural basis, so that the town appeared as a higher unity, combining villages and hamlets, familiar places with those distant and thereby foreign. Or again, did this threefold model have its origin in Euclidian geometry and the theory of three-dimensional space (though it seems to pre-exist this, and to develop outside of science). Why not look for the reasons and causes of the dominant representations in social or mental space? We only raise this question here in passing.[25]

An underground current runs through Christianity, deeper and more hidden than Augustinianism, because it's more heretical. It could be compared with a water table that irrigates the roots of trees, surfaces in springs and fills wells. Joachim di Fiore's 'eternal gospel' very probably owes its form to Abelard as much as to its attributed author. Removed from their mysterious and mystical substantiality, their eternity, they form part of 'reality' and historicity. The Father? This is nature and its wonders; the infinite and terrible fertile power in which are dimly discerned creation and the created, consciousness and unconsciousness, suffering and pleasure, life and death. Hardship is not added to natural existence, it is inherent to it. The Son, the word, is not

---

25 [Lefebvre's *La Production de l'espace* had been published in 1974, a year before the present book.]

eternally coextensive with the paternal substance but emerges from it, is born from it in time: language, consciousness, cognition, coincide with the birth and growth of the Son. In the course of his rise, knowledge cannot fail to acquire self-confidence; this faith goes hand in hand with consciousness and its troubled certainty, conquered over doubt. The word believed it would save the world. It failed. Knowledge is not enough for redemption – neither is the suffering of the unhappy consciousness. Not only did Christ (the word) die in vain, but his death enabled the worst of powers to establish itself, the Church that celebrates the death of the word by killing it each day: killing thought. In order for redemption to be accomplished, the Spirit, the third term of the triad, a triad eternal and temporal, immanent and transcendent, has to be embodied and turn the world upside down. The Spirit is subversive or is nothing. It is embodied in heretics, rebels, the pure who struggle against impurity. It brings with it revolt and joy. Only the spirit is life and light.

Joachim's eternal gospel divides time into three periods: the law, faith and joy. The law belongs to the Father and comes from him: the harsh law of nature and the power that extends this. Faith belongs to the word, the Son, with its corollaries of hope and charity. The Spirit brings joy, presence and communication, absolute love and perfect light. But also struggle, adventure, subversion, thus a violence against violence . . .

Misunderstood by the customary history of philosophy, as by that of society, this triadic schema had an inestimable import. We should note that it has, as a schema of reality and model of thought, far greater flexibility than a binary or unitary one. It contains rhythms; it corresponds to processes. It cuts across Cartesian thought, in which the divine infinite embraces the two modes of existence of the finite, extension and thought. It triumphs in Hegel. What is Hegelianism? An interweaving of triads, emitted and recaptured by the third higher term, the Idea (the Spirit).

First triad: nature, history, concept. Second triad, implicit and explanatory: thesis or assertion; negation or antithesis; synthesis or positive (affirmative) supersession. Third triad: need, work, enjoyment, or rather, satisfaction. Fourth: the master, the slave, the victory of the slave over the master, a victory that transforms him into the master's superior, superseding him. Fifth: prehistory, history, post-history. And so on. As for Marx, his triadic schema modifies but preserves the Hegelian schema, taking it (according to Marx and Engels) to a higher level – affirmation, negation, negation of the negation – which accentuates the role of the negative.[26] The developed communism of the future restores primitive communism but with 'the full wealth of development'. Private property of the means of production supplanted the collective possession of these means (the land), but will give way to a social possession and management, hence collectives and automatic machines. Even Marx presents a bourgeois Holy Trinity: capital, land, labour (profit, rent, wages). And so on.

Oddly enough, the positivism that opposed any philosophical speculation adopted the triadic schema. According to Auguste Comte and his famous law of three stages, the metaphysical age followed on from the theological age, and the scientific age will replace it.

As for Nietzsche, if we accept that he identifies himself with his spokesman Zarathustra, he also adopts the triadic schema: 'Three metamorphoses of the spirit do I designate to you: how the spirit becomes a camel, the camel a lion, and the lion at last a child.' The camel demands the heaviest task, the most onerous law. The lion seeks to win its freedom and assert itself, by finding itself, by becoming capable of creating; it has faith in itself and in its future. The child is innocent and forgotten, a beginning, a game, a self-rolling wheel: joy. Zarathustra said this while staying in a town called The Pied Cow. Did Nietzsche have in mind the quest for the Grail (the absolute), and Percival (Parsifal) whose story tells of his youth, purity and even simplicity of spirit? After Merlin (divine/diabolical) and Lancelot (man and superhuman) comes the Spirit-child.

Why not apply to our own triad Hegel-Marx-Nietzsche the same triadic model? Hegel would be the Father, the law; Marx, the Son and faith; Nietzsche, the Spirit and joy! Such an application does not hide its parodic intention . . .

Why this reflection or retrospection on triads? Because nothing guarantees the eternity of this model. Will it not also suffer obsolescence, exhaust itself? Should we today, after detailed examination of the

---

26 In his writings on contradiction, Mao Zedong rejected the triadic schema or rhythm of European thought. Among other things, this enabled him to ignore a fundamental problem raised by this thought, that of the relation between logic and dialectics.

triads, not reject this schema and supersede it, either by *Aufheben* or by Überwinden? Or else leave it only a share, perhaps the sacred/accursed share, of 'our' reality or our understanding?

Does this appreciation (also for the moment at the stage of a tactical hypothesis) lead to a return, recourse to the substantialist (absolute unity) or binary model (formal oppositions, non-dialectical contrasts and dualities)? This is neither obvious nor probable. More likely we shall have to adopt a different route: an approach that takes account of a greater number of moments and elements, levels and dimensions, in brief, a multidimensional thought. Will this maintain, in contrast, that thought, by taking account of greater numbers, loses itself in too great a number of parameters, variables, dimensions and flows? Not necessarily!

8) The ensemble of categorical assertions posited by Western logos is surrounded by a network of problems. Among these, that of cognition emerges and deepens, abyss and mountain. Philosophy raised it in the late eighteenth century, and from then on it formed part of the theoretical situation in Europe. Previously, in Cartesian thought, in the critical project associated with the *Encyclopédie* that arose in France, and in the empiricism and positive science that emerged in England, no doubt appeared as far as knowledge was concerned. The critique of religion and the political regime was pursued in the name of cognition. Logos was questioned but was not itself put in question.

The scene changed with Kant's critical philosophy. 'What is it to know [*Qu'est-ce que connaître*]'? This simple question ravaged questioning thought. From this time, it would pursue its path no longer by seeking the absolute (the mythic Grail), but instead the answer to the question of understanding. The horizon changed. This ravaged thought would hesitate between rationalism and 'classical' humanism, a humanism that received its formulation from Goethe, and romanticism, itself dual: either reactive or revolutionary.

Unfortunately, philosophy and professional philosophers restricted the problematic of understanding to make it more precise, so that it would belong to their 'discipline' which was tending to become a speciality. They saw science as an incontestable process, an activity both sufficient and necessary. A reduction that reduced philosophy to epistemology, a meticulous   sorting   between   acquired   knowledge   and   uncertain

representations. From Kant on, philosophy put the problem of understanding as follows: 'Where are the limits of knowledge, either provisional
or definitive? How can these markers be crossed? How can we know
(*connaître*) more and better: more knowledge and more certain
knowledge . . .'

Philosophy like this sidestepped the wider problem, the real question
of understanding: 'Knowledge is necessary, but is it sufficient?' What is
cognition worth, not in terms of results – conceptions, methods, theories – but as activity? Various responses were immediately proposed: the
sufficiency of knowledge was countered by the notion of a necessary and
insufficient knowledge, and that of a necessary non-knowledge: cognition was referred beyond or below itself, to intuition, 'learned ignorance',
or pure and simple faith.

Who formulated the problematic of understanding in its full scope?
Goethe. Not in *Werther* or *Wilhelm Meister*,[27] but in *Faust*, in other
words, a tragic play rather than a novel.

This play (hardly stageable, particularly the second part) opposes
living to cognition. Faust, who knows all that could be known in his
day, belatedly perceives that he has failed to live. For his happiness and
unhappiness, he is visited by the demonic principle: the absolute Other,
the accursed of God, who knows what Faust does not know, who
possesses the secret of living: passion, delirium, madness, crime, in a
word, evil (sin). Mephistopheles (with the authorization of his hierar-
chical superior, the eternal Father) allows Faust to pass through the
ordeals of living after having undergone those of knowing. He leads
him to Gretchen, the woman still passive, beauty (the beautiful object),
but able to suffer and complain, and then to Helen, the active woman,
still more lovely, but more ungraspable. The old triptych God–man–
devil is joined by a fourth character: woman. She differs equally from
the eternal virgin and the eternal mother. She is duplicated: victim and
servant of sensual pleasure (Gretchen); queen of beauty, joy and delight
(Helen). The eternal feminine is revealed only by way of initiation and
ordeal.

---

27 Georg Lukács constructed his Marxist humanism on the basis of the great classic
humanism of Goethe: the novels, and especially *Wilhelm Meister's Apprenticeship*, a
model story of education and training. Overestimating the novel as a genre and its critical teaching, Lukács neglected or misinterpreted poetry and theatre. He misunderstood
Faust, which led him to misunderstand Nietzsche – not to mention various other errors.

To the great question that opens like an abyss on the path of 'modern man', Goethe gives only a poetic response: all that happens is only symbol, hieroglyph, and only the eternal feminine calls and shows the way of redemption. This is how the great Western idea pursues its course, that of absolute love as a counterpoint to logos. This great image runs right through the West, from the medieval romances down to *Le Grand Meaulnes*, where it dissolves in the pallid moonlight of the beautiful soul. Unless it rebounds . . .

Still in Goethe's lifetime, Hegel divinized knowledge. For him, the negative places itself in the service of positivity: absolute knowledge. And we could interpret the demonic in Goethe (Mephistopheles) as an accentuation of the negative, given that its role remains ambiguous. For Hegel, then, God is the concept, the concept is identified with divinity. The concept of history and the history of the concept coincide. From nature emerges logos, the word: then nature and word (science and consciousness, language and logic) unite in the recovered spirit, absolute spirit. God-knowledge and history converge in the state. Absolute spirit, logos as principle and end, is ultimately defined as a philosophical trinity: concept (father), becoming (son), state (spirit). And Kierkegaard was not wrong to rail sarcastically at the speculative Good Friday by which the god in three persons incarnated in history climbed the Golgotha of dialectical ordeals to reach the glory of the last judgement (as pronounced by the philosopher).

With Hegel dead, Hegelianism disintegrated. What a strange situation European thought found itself in after Hegel and Goethe, after Kant and Schopenhauer! At first with the Young Hegelians, then after them, Marx hesitated between knowing and acting. He retained the project of constructing an imprescriptible knowledge, resistant to all refutation and reaching the essence of society (bourgeois, capitalist), but he took up the Promethean-Faustian formula: 'In the beginning was the deed.' He maintained the Hegelian ideas of a rationality underlying history, a philosophico-scientific certitude inherent to the analysis of practice, a finality subordinating causality and necessity. At the same time, he hesitated before the rationality that in this schema was immanent to existing society and reality. How long would the bourgeoisie survive? Would it exhaust its inherent rationality? Did this reason itself have to be broken, along with the state and property relations? Would the bourgeoisie continue its historic mission for a long time, the growth of the productive forces until the inevitable qualitative leap? Where were the internal limits of capitalism? If there is a rationality everywhere, it is also to be found in this society, which is easily qualified as absurd on the grounds of its injustice and inhumanity.

Marx posited a meaning of becoming, of history, without demonstrating it; he accepted Hegelian (Western) logos without subjecting it to a fundamental critique. Hegel's still-theological hypothesis passed through the sieve (the 'break') in Marx's thought. No more than Hegel did Marx question the origin of Western rationality, its genesis or genealogy: Judeo-Christianity, Greco-Latin thought, industry and technology. Marx was content with an attenuation of Hegelian theology (theodicy) and the epic of the Idea. Sometimes Marx and Engels came up against some conceptions that were irreducible to their schematization; for example, logic and law. Why had logic (born in Greece) continued across the Western societies and their modes of production? What relationship was there between ideologies and the dialectic? As for law, elaborated in Rome, this lasted until its renascence in the bourgeois-democratic revolution, with the Napoleonic *code civil*. Accordingly, the social transition to communism would not be able to do without law and laws, with the result that the triadic schema – from unconscious customs under primitive communism, through law in the course of history, to conscious custom within 'developed communism' – remains abstract. Equally, Marx was unable to say much about the future communist society, other than that the long transition would be punctuated by *ends*: end of capitalism by revolution; end of labour by automation; end of law by custom; end of state, nation, homeland, working class, bourgeoisie, a separate economy and a dominant polity, etc. Nietzsche would add to this list: the death of God and man.

One question arises when thought reflects on this path signposted by ends and deaths, as a set of reefs are signalled by crosses and shipwrecks: 'Will not logos itself come to an end, exhausted, passed into writing and writings – even writing itself, born as it was from living speech and word?'

If Hegel maintained with incomparable vigour and intolerable rigour the primacy of knowledge as code of the 'real', hence the primacy of theory, system, concept (thus doing away with rifts, separations, splits and conflicts), Marx already hesitated between cognition, partially transferred to *production*, and creative action, *practical* living and experience, the key preoccupation of the famous *1844 Manuscripts*. With Marx, the productive activity intended to assure doctrinal unity divides in two: a) production (manufacture) of material things, exchangeable goods, commodities, machines, in other words, means of production; b) production of social relations, creation of artworks, ideas, institutions, cognitions (*connaissances*), language, aesthetic objects, innovative acts. While Hegel had successfully attempted a unitary concept in the narrow context of knowledge, Marx failed in the wider framework of action. Production and creation fell apart, despite his efforts to combine them, each threatening to go its own way.

9) This is how avant-garde European thought led towards what we can retrospectively call the 'Nietzschean crisis'. The problem of understanding had received no solution. The revolution failed in 1848 and again in 1871. What was the outcome of the rationality that Hegel had seen as immanent in the state, and Marx in social (industrial) practice? Wars. At the same moment as Nietzsche, and for quite similar reasons, Rimbaud declared that it was life that had to be changed, and love reinvented. But the proud edifice of Hegelianism bridled, outdoing in arrogance and power the Bonapartist state that had issued from the great French Revolution. Bismarck, a political strategist with great vision, understood that certain objectives of the democratic revolution could be realized 'from above', by consolidating the state instead of transforming it – national unity, for example. He also envisaged integrating into the national state the new class that was in the course of formation, the proletariat. From this point, Germany, which had brought the modern world philosophy, committed itself to the most pedantic historiographic erudition, to philistinism. It threatened to conquer Europe, initially through a 'culture' that denied civilization. The recourse to myth (Wagner) showed this decadence of Western logos, with its two aspects that were seemingly incompatible but actually mutually supporting: knowledge and power. A descent into hell began, starting with descent into the abyss of consciousness, psychism, the unconscious, will and desire – with Schopenhauer. A vain fascination, as Nietzsche said and showed . . .

Shameless and unheeding logos, proud of its accumulated knowledge and methods, conveyed some myths of its own. The first among these, in the name of which it exerted its worst blackmail, was irrationality: any criticism of reason would lead to unreason and an apology for violence. Whereas it is logos itself that has cruelty as its obverse side, its counterpart and counterpoint. Whereas the appeal from conceptual knowledge to a higher form of understanding has a meaning and must be heard.

Yet Nietzsche did not exhaust the list of myths, manipulations and blackmails bound up with the exercise of logos, power and cognition. He could not have known them all in his day, and some of them might have turned against him. The myth of the Titan – the modern Prometheus – who breaks the great social and political machine, a myth that exalted the modern working class, Nietzsche took up in his own way when he sought to 'philosophize with a hammer'. Similarly, with the opposite and corollary myth of the clever little imp who somewhere disrupts a little cog in the same machine, so that it comes to a halt and stops functioning,[28] the forces of negation (protest, contestation) are themselves dislocated. But this remark leads on to a different story . . .

10) To continue the confrontation between the members of the Hegel-Marx-Nietzsche triad, in other words, between the three dominant thoughts on the modernity that they each sought to grasp, we have to do away with political encumbrances and hypotheses. This point deserves close attention.[29]

a) Hegel and Hegelianism may be charged with reaction pure and simple. A *rightist* politics that saw itself not just as *Realpolitik* but as theoretically true, would be justified in Hegel by analysis of the 'real', of the nation and the *pays réel*, the necessary institutions. This would also legitimate both state and state apparatuses, along with political apparatuses in general and the predominance of the statesman over all other 'moments' of knowledge, culture, etc.

---

28 These two myths, that of the Titan and that of the evil demon [presumably a reference to Descartes], have continued to exert their influence. Thus, Freud and his successors (including Wilhelm Reich) have sometimes been seen as Titans, and sometimes as clever little imps. Among the myths referred to elsewhere, I draw attention to that of the Foundation (Asimov), and that of the typewriting monkey (myth of the productive combinatory, of chance and necessity, which is not without connection to 'eternal recurrence').

29 Cf. Henri Lefebvre, *La Fin de l'histoire*, though already in my *Nietzsche* (Paris: Éditions sociales internationales, 1939) I rebutted the political accusations made against Nietzsche, particularly by Georg Lukács.

Now, there is this in Hegel: theorization and rationalization of the political act. There is in him the justification, along with the state, of a 'state of things' in which the totality of the real comes to a halt, stagnates and is blocked.

If there was only this in Hegel, would he merit the present confrontation? Would there be ground and cause for a hearing? No. First of all, Hegelianism contains, together with this theorization, the confession and denunciation of this 'state of things'. It makes possible an analysis. Second, Hegel, who sought to be and believed himself a defender of freedom, also rejected and rebutted this extreme case: stagnation, the display of the accomplished. He conceived a compromise that would bring harmony between authority and freedom. Only the liberal state left room for its 'moments' and for the flexibility of its members. It alone was able to regenerate itself, re-produce itself with an inherent dynamism, a vitality both immanent and rational. For Hegel, obsolescent recourse to fait accompli, to unrestrained violence, indicated that the final equilibrium had not been achieved; it was either incomplete or had failed. If, in the last century and a half, the state has revealed its 'worst side', which Hegel had theorized, we cannot make Hegel's doctrine responsible. A symptom more than a cause or a reason, Hegelianism cannot be got rid of as easily as something like the legal historicism of Savigny, for example. It can be used (and certainly has been) to justify sticking to the past, in terms of historicism, nationalism, even chauvinism. These interpretations and alterations are part of the file, but they do not prevent us compiling this.

b) The same is true of Stalinism for Marx. If there is a 'revisionist' ideology in relation to Marx's thought, it is certainly this dark cloud. True, the Stalinist mystifiers launched the 'revisionist' epithet to cover up their own ideological operations (based, it goes without saying, on the economic, social and political 'reality' of the USSR after Lenin). The Stalinists cleverly muddied their tracks, for example by describing Hegel as a 'philosopher of feudal reaction', whereas they themselves were Hegelians and even super-Hegelians. If the class struggle after a proletarian revolution leads to a strengthening and increased centralization of the state, this may be a 'historical necessity', but it has nothing in common with the thinking of Marx. Still more: if this thesis is *true* in the theoretical sense of the term, then so-called Marxist thought collapses.

It crumbles into pieces, even if well-intentioned people gather up the pieces and try to reconstruct something with the debris.

Against this pseudo-theory we can cite so many texts by Marx, Engels and Lenin that they would fill volumes. Moreover, the violent controversies aroused by Stalinism and the anti-Stalinist opposition have revealed a contradiction internal to the revolutionary movement and the workers' movement itself. This already appeared with Saint-Simon and Fourier. The latter was happy to dispense with the state, whereas Saint-Simon no less happily contradicted himself, at one point demanding a state that would be effective because run by the '*industriels*' (producers and scientists), elsewhere the replacement of state constraint by the direct administration of things. This contradiction erupted in Europe around the year 1870. When political historians and publicists tenderly examine the workers' movement, with a view to eliminating or at least attenuating its contradictions, they overlook the double process that led in France to the Commune and in Germany to the Social Democratic Party. The French movement resolutely attacked the state and demolished it in 1870, when the workers of Paris set out to 'storm the heavens'. German socialism, in contrast, influenced by the Hegelian Lassalle, accepted and integrated the state. An integration which, as we know, was envisaged by the great political strategist Bismarck. Do we need to recall once again the content of Marx's *Critique of the Gotha Programme*, in which, despite a cautious formulation that hardly mentions the Paris Commune, Marx's full approval of this is clear enough, in what was his political testament? The contradiction is manifest even in the thought and work of Marx.

Hence the terrible bitterness of the last line of this text: '*Dixi et salvavi animam meam*.' ('I have spoken and saved my soul.')

If state socialism has triumphed in the workers' movement, and in the world, this means that the workers' movement has abandoned both Marxism and Leninism; that it has succumbed to Lassalleanism; that Marxism has become an ideology, a philosophy serving the state, a *public service* in the Hegelian sense. Marx holds no responsibility for this situation, other than having left in obscurity a conflict of decisive importance.

c) The same holds, finally, for Nietzsche and Hitlerian fascism. A forced falsification twisted Nietzsche's texts, pulling them towards fascist ideology. True, ambiguous fragments are not lacking. In his analysis of the will to power, Nietzsche expresses admiration for questionable heroes: adventurers, condottieri, conquistadores. Marx might equally be classified as an anti-Semite on the basis of his text on the Jewish question! Developing a radical critique, a fundamental refutation, a refusal and rejection of the *libido dominandi*, Nietzsche envisaged all its aspects, all its masks, both political and otherwise: imperial and imperialist action, Machiavellianism, warlike ambition and activity, as well as goodness, charitable action, 'good works', even renunciation and humility.

As for Nietzsche's success, in other words, the reception of his theoretical analysis as ideology, this underwent a change of sign: anarchists and immoralists at the turn of the twentieth century, then fascist politicians, and today philosophers, so-called 'Nietzscheans', have all contributed to his misunderstanding. These errors of interpretation have to figure in the file. They are not directly imputable to the author.

This rejection of political appreciation implies a devaluing of politics as such, something we should emphasize. The political criterion, which during the Stalinist and fascist period was presented as *absolute*, is in no way definitive. It changes and falls. For a short space of time, it took on a 'total' appearance because imposed by the double means of ideological persuasion and violence. It then induced errors whose derisory character was later apparent.

11) 'Is it out of a mania for triads, or a caricature of the supposedly triadic model, that you focus here on just three bodies of work, three thinkers? What leads you to place Hegel, Marx and Nietzsche at the gateway to modernity and as its guiding lights? Why not others?'

It is free for anyone to claim that shadows and the realm of shadows came to an end with Freud, Heidegger, Lenin or Mao Zedong, or even Wilhelm Reich, Georges Bataille, etc.

Let us look at Freud and his work. Why not include him here, and place him in the dominant constellation?

Freud's thought and his psychoanalysis acquired much of their strength from being connected with clinical observation, with a therapeutic practice. Often effective, but sometimes in vain or even worse, this medical practice has a 'real' existence. It is a real gain that it brought sexuality, so long a blinkered zone, into language and conceptual thought. As for practice, the connection of Marxist thought and revolutionary practice (attempts, defeats) gives it a good position to reply to 'practicists'. Only Nietzschean thought suffers from the comparison, being linked only to a practice of *speech*. Unless it is placed in relationship with the mediocre practice of writing. Psychoanalysis, for its part, led to a trade, a profession with its place in the social division of labour, and tending from the start towards institutionalization. In such a situation, partial (clinical) practice gave birth to an ideology that seeks to justify it by overstepping it. By tackling every problem, it seeks to be total.

Hence the weakness of psychoanalysis: a formless mixture of a linguistic technique with fragmentary cognitions (*connaissances*), and with representations proclaimed beyond their sphere of validity (by reduction and extrapolation). This ideology conveys its own myth, the unconscious, a box of tricks that contains everything put into it: body, memory, individual and social history, language, culture and its results or residues, etc. Finally, and above all, Freud only grasped, described and analysed the *libido sentiendi*. Psychoanalysis after Freud only indirectly tackled the *libido dominandi*, so profoundly explored by Nietzsche. It completely neglected the *libido sciendi*, the domain of cognition, the *social* status of knowledge. Why? Because Freud, though influenced by Schopenhauer's deep-going studies, never abandoned the Hegelian schema of knowledge. He thus failed to recognize the great underground tradition, the clandestine legacy that made for the greatness of European thought and through which the dead or rotten branches of logos were given new life. Psychoanalysis does not go as far in its analysis as had Augustine, Jansen, La Rochefoucauld, Pascal and Nietzsche. When Freud had to face the terrible discovery that sex and sexuality led only to failure, drama and pathos, thus the pathological, he took up the very old theme of *concordia discors* or *discordis concors* – adding very little to this besides the clinical effort to cure neuroses. Do psychoanalysts succeed in this? Do they control the terrible *negative* power of language – by means of language? That is a different matter.

If understanding perceives desire at the lowest depth of 'being', it puts in question understanding itself. For Nietzsche, who pursued this line of questioning to its end, the great desire whose potential energy was hidden in the total body (and not in sex alone), this great desire that becomes 'supreme grandeur', born from the body and in the body, reveals itself as dance, song, then desire for eternity, eternal itself. It has nothing in common with the poor sexual libido, nor even with Platonic eros.

'*Meine weise Sehnsucht*', says Zarathustra: 'my wise yearning': wisdom embraced, desire across the mountains, desire on trembling wings, this ardent reason shouts and laughs.

In the investigation pursued here, it would be interesting to study the movements that shake religions and religious institutions, in particular the Catholic Church, rather than psychoanalysis, a 'modernist' ideology that is somewhat arrogant.

Would not Nietzsche himself have seen the success of psychoanalysis as a further symptom of decadence? An aggravated sickness? A form of European nihilism? Certainly. There is something morbid about this new avatar of Judeo-Christianity, which seeks to recycle itself by making up for the curse cast on sex, but preserves in its language and concepts all the 'signs of non-body'. Psychoanalysis, as theory and ideology, practice and technique (of discourse), has succeeded neither in restoring the total body nor in preventing the phallic from assuming an 'object' existence.[30] Besides, the ideological breakthrough of psychoanalysis continues to obscure Nietzschean thought by relegating it to a blind zone that replaces another blind zone, that of sex, a zone that is nothing other than the *libido dominandi*. As a result, psychoanalysis as ideology serves the established order in a number of ways: by hindering the critique of the state and power, by displacing thought and substituting another centre, etc.

'Why not Heidegger?', a questioning voice demands, rather malevolently. For several reasons, this philosopher does not figure in the constellation here. He followed the triadic model in the most naïve manner: Being, its eclipse, its resurrection or resurgence. This history of Being (the creative power, the word, the spirit) was seen as original by people unaware of Joachim de Fiore's 'eternal gospel'. It obscured the more concrete history offered by Hegel and Marx, without attaining the force of Nietzsche's critique of history. Heidegger's philosophy, a dissimulated theodicy, hardly secularized, tends to rescue the philosophical tradition without passing it through the sieve of radical criticism. Heidegger eludes the notion of *metaphilosophy* despite touching on it. He substitutes for it an ontology said to be fundamental, a variant of metaphysics whether we like it or not. True, he makes a contribution to the critical analysis of modernity, being one of the first to have perceived

---

30 Cf. the remarks of Gustave R. Hocke in *Labyrinthe de l'art fantastique*, Paris: Denoel, 1977, p. 189.

and foreseen the ravages of technology and understood that *domination* over nature (by means of knowledge and technique) becomes domination *over people*, and does not coincide with *appropriation* of this nature which it tends to destroy. Heidegger speaks (writes) an admirable language, almost too fine, as for him the dwelling of Being – what saves it from endless wandering – is language (the word) and constructions (architecture: temples, palaces, monuments and buildings). From this 'admirable' idea (we use the word ironically) the philosopher draws a disturbing apology for the German language. This prevents him from a radical critique of Western (European) logos, despite bordering on this. What he says of Nietzsche and against Nietzsche does not convince – that Nietzsche went too far and too deep, that he followed the mirroring surfaces of consciousness, veridical and deceptive – any better than his predecessor.

As for other contemporary 'thinkers', what have they done except launch into circulation the small change of Hegel, Marx and Nietzsche – along with some counterfeit coins . . .?[31] This judgement may seem severe. Actually, there is nothing pejorative about it, it simply means that theoretical struggles and ideological tests do not pass without harm.

12) The same voice is raised again: 'You only include German thinkers. Are you not concerned at privileging unduly a particular culture and language? And by what right do you refuse Heidegger what he dares to demand, precisely this privilege?'

Marx gave a peremptory reply to this argument in outlining the course of his own reflection and that of Hegelian thought. Because of Germany's economic and political backwardness in the first half of the nineteenth century, German thought kept a distance that enabled its

---

31 One star of first magnitude is absent from the constellation – Clausewitz. As a political strategist he requires a different study and a radical critique of politics as such. The same for Lenin and Mao. What is Leninism, today also subjected to critical analysis? A turning of Marxism towards non-developed (i.e. primarily agricultural) countries, which has a deep rationale and serious consequences. As for Mao, his prodigious political action does not involve a theoretical advance of the same order, despite his texts on contradiction, practice, etc. Nothing is more vexatious and sterile than the fetishism of an individual or their work.

N.B. The writer of these lines, in autumn 1973, declares himself as pro-Chinese, hence 'Maoist', strategically. (To be continued.)

philosophers to understand what was happening in England (economic growth, capitalism, the bourgeoisie) and France (the political revolution, the formation of the nation-state with Robespierre and Napoleon). The great Germans were able to bring to language and to the concept what was happening and being done elsewhere. In uneven development, the 'bad side' (sometimes) has its productive counterpart.

This privilege of distance came to an end with the economic and political rise of Germany – as Nietzsche saw very well in 1873, with his *Untimely Meditations*. Marx, who continued in a conflictual relationship with the great German tradition, had already left his homeland, which was only able to view him by way of a crucial misunderstanding (Lassalleanism, state socialism, the fetishism of the state). Where is the sharpest critique of Germany to be found? In the works of Marx and Nietzsche. They spoke as connoisseurs, Nietzsche being inspired more than Marx by French thought – not the official Cartesian tradition but the underground currents. Marx, as we know, received his main impulse from the great English writers Smith and Ricardo.

As for France, why not boldly recognize the turn taken by French thought after Saint-Simon and Fourier? Cartesian rationalism was weakening, but it resisted and put up a counter-attack. We know all too well that this dethroned universalism threw off its grafts – dialectic, radical criticism and self-criticism, etc. – in a chauvinistic nationalism. It swung between apologetic affirmation of Western logos – confounded for the needs of the cause with Cartesian rationalism – and indeterminate negation, with recourse to ruthlessness, good or bad, and to barbarism. With this conversion of what was said elsewhere, the repeated affirmation of logos has made possible a recuperation of attempts at emancipation by economism or the national state.

As for subversive negation, indeterminate, anarchistic and destructive of knowledge (without replacing it), this has led to a recuperation by literature, philosophy and ideology, including institutionalized psychoanalysis.[32]

---

32 Only George Bataille escapes this judgement, up to a certain point. The items bearing on the difficulties of modern thought (Hegelian, Marxist, Nietzschean) in France figure in the files, but incompletely, as they would swell them to the point of hypertrophy.

The contention that in France social and political practice anticipates reflection was confirmed in 1973 by the 'Lip affair' – not so much the 'affair' itself as its extraordinary echo.

For nearly a century and a half now, theoretical thought in France has remained *below* its theoretical possibilities, below political practice and events: the revolutions of 1848, 1871 and 1968 (not forgetting the 'liberations' of 1919 and 1944). These political events already go beyond (supersede) both reality and political reflection. Thought in France dwells on illusory brilliance, diversions that lead it only into a siding. Marx had already noted this backwardness, due to 'deep' causes and reasons that he saw as not unique to this country. French thought sometimes hurls itself into the verbal depths of philosophy separated from practice. It then rediscovers the Cartesian logos, attached to the cogito, the thinking 'subject', which suits an isolated knowledge, a subjectively abstract intellectuality. In the age of Descartes, the philosophical thesis of the thinking subject had a subversive edge; it was bound up with an individualism on the offensive and with an understanding of practice (social and political). Three centuries later, it is simply a convenient escape route.

Or else this thought falls into journalism, accepting or presupposing the confusion between information and cognition. A passionate and passive interest is taken in what happens far away: in Russia, Spain, China, Italy, Czechoslovakia, in the Third World, in Chile, etc. These experiences, generally unfortunate, are expected to provide a recipe applicable to France. Little attention is paid to what is happening close at hand, under our own eyes. It is forgotten that for Marx and Engels, France was the 'classic' country of revolutions, and that *political practice* here runs ahead of thought.

When the German philosophers, at the start of the nineteenth century, sought to reflect theoretically on what was happening outside their own country, in the rest of Europe, they made up for German backwardness instead of aggravating it. They gained a theoretical function and exercised this, down to Marx and Nietzsche. Besides, nothing happened at home that had great theoretical significance, and even Bismarck's role was only to adapt to a new situation, the Napoleonic model of the state, as elaborated by Hegel.

The weakness of French thought is striking, even after the Commune of 1871 – until the Dreyfus affair at the turn of the century. Revolutions in France, from the first successful one down to the latest abortive one of 1968, have failed to arouse political reflection and critique (implying the critique of politics). The devious combat between a France openly reactionary in both thought and daily life – a Byzantine France – and the France of boldness (sometimes *fuite en avant*) has never ceased.

13) We now come to the title phrase, 'kingdom of shadows'. What does this mean? It did not proclaim an unconditional apologia for the works discussed here.

Hegel saw and foresaw the omnipresence and omnipotence of the state. He described its rationality, borne by definite social classes and strata: middle class, bureaucracy, technocracy, army, political apparatuses, etc. He even described the deadly boredom that results from this: the shadow on earth of the sun of the Idea and the gloomy edifice of the state. The satisfaction of the Spirit that had completed its task, the satisfaction of all needs by appropriate work and objects, the satisfaction of the conscious 'subject', and the self-satisfaction of everything that had reached its plenitude, could only produce a flat and heavy bourgeois happiness: possession extended to the absolute. Hegel thus declared his science and his own wisdom to have reached its twilight, along with the whole of philosophy. Knowledge, like the owl of Minerva, emerged only as night was falling. The state? It was the old age of the world, the end of history and creative consciousness, an exhaustion proclaimed and provoked by philosophy, by the system, by knowledge and wisdom. As for philosophy, it painted 'grey on grey'. This greyness has what one might call a privileged symbol and symptom: the death of art, an illusion of youth and human folly.[33] After youth and maturity, the *third age* brings the process to a close, in a final equilibrium.

Unlike Hegel, Marx did not take as his principle and starting hypothesis the 'real', the accomplished, but rather the *possible*. He developed the reasons for revolutionary possibility and its entry into the real by overturning it. He thus sought to rationally establish faith in the possible. Like the Gallic cock that he celebrated in his youthful writings, he trumpeted the eternal dawn, the immortal youth of the Revolution. What in fact has been 'realized'? The shadow, the very opposite of the possible proclaimed by Marx, and this with its own signboard, its own vocabulary. Nothing of what proclaimed its end has actually reached this. Not

---

33 On the ageing of consciousness and science that have reached their end-point and exhaustion, cf. the conclusions of Hegel's *Phenomenology*, *Philosophy of History*, *Aesthetics*, etc. Art dies after romanticism, itself an exaltation of death.

even the old philosophy! Nowhere has the working class conquered the status of political 'subject' (collective and revolutionary), carrying society *beyond* politics. Was Hegel right? Yes, but on all sides there are phenomena of disassociation to be seen, of corruption, of the rottenness of the centralized state; everywhere there is opposition, appeal, differences and decentralizations. Everywhere state structures are shaking and then reconstructed. And yet, if we can see in every part of the world a tendency *towards* what Marx proclaimed, nowhere has this tendency indicated anything but a poorly traced path, an uncertain horizon. Hence the immense disappointment already sensed by Marx himself: '*Dixi et salvavi animam meam.*'

Nietzsche? His life and his work have a meaning, a goal: to say the unsayable, to grasp the ungraspable, to think the unthinkable, to fathom the unfathomable, to realize the impossible – to metamorphose the 'real', moribund or already dead, into a new life. The poet sought to achieve redemption by what was closest to him, so close that it was unsayable, unthinkable, unfathomable: the body. 'There is more reason in your body than in your wisdom', said Zarathustra. But what did Nietzsche do, if not dream his body and speak aloud the dream of the body? His Promethean (Titanic) effort to live the agony and death of the modern world by transmuting (metamorphosing) its exhausted values and its reality in the course of full self-destruction – did it lead towards something? Towards the superhuman. Is this not also a figure of consciousness – of its dissatisfaction, its sickness – hence a metamorphosis of the divine, a metaphor of the Idea? Or rather still an adjuration, a conjuration, an invocation? At worst, an opera image for the use of a cultivated elite? Still God, still the Idea, still the unhappiness of consciousness and 'culture' . . . Nietzsche went forward. In his forward flight, his shadow accompanied him.[34] Who is Zarathustra? The sick man and the doctor? The bridge or the other bank? If it is true that the state devours society from above by integrating it into itself, if it uses institutionalized knowledge and cognition, then *civilization* resists. But this resistance is only maintained in an ever more narrow elite, ever more threatened.

Nietzsche's madness is rightly seen as evidence of his authenticity. But what does 'authenticity' mean if meaning and truth are shattered?

---

34 Cf. *The Wanderer and His Shadow*, the continuation and end of *Human, All Too Human*.

Perhaps he became mad deliberately, to join Dionysus, god of metamorphoses. Nietzsche's madness is a (poor) response to Hegel's greyness and
Marx's disappointment. Night is deeper than day! What should we
conclude from this?

14) And now we have the dossiers opened wide, displayed, accessible
to the broadest public if it takes the trouble to consult them. These
preliminaries govern the procedure of the present work, its conception
and composition. *Procedure*: a term that we use instead of 'method',
abused on all sides, used as an alibi and a retreat, the Cartesian echo of
which permits its abuse. As for composition, is this the best or the only
one possible? No, it is what is appropriate here, unless we are mistaken.
Every work, every book, is somehow different, requiring its own procedure, its requirements of construction.

The path here proceeds 'fanwise'. At the start, the centre, what we
have been dealing with here: the 'Hegel-Marx-Nietzsche' conjunction.
Already with this first articulation, differences and challenges appear.
The work will unfurl and open the fan. 'Unfurling' means more than
just 'unfolding', more than making explicit. The implication/explication
will be developed. The unfurling will take the implied differences all the
way; it includes a well-ordered development, a captured process of
increasing complexity, a convergence between the actual and the
conceptual, without either having priority over the other. It avoids
separating the three moments of thought: the categorical (concepts),
the problematic (the questions raised), and the thematic (the statements made, the proposals elaborated).

On the unfurled surface will appear (perhaps) a picture of modernity, paths and perspectives, in other words, the modern world in its
terrible complexity, with all its contradictions.

This procedure presupposes *reprises*. A reprise implies a difference
that is grasped. It does not always avoid repetition. The present work
itself takes up problems treated elsewhere, but it reconsiders these
differently, giving them a different import and a different perspective.

At the end of this unfurling, will there be just a picture? A map of
modernity, showing those who view it certain paths, obstacles, perspectives, blind alleys? Perhaps there will also be a decision to make.

15) To whom is this book addressed? What 'public' does it invite to consult the files, and if possible set themselves up to judge?

This book is addressed to 'us'. Nothing is easier to misuse than this pronoun. And yet Nietzsche, despite advising against it, makes wide use of it: 'We, the new Europeans, the new philosophers who supersede philosophy, the "feeling-and-thinking", the seekers-attempters, those without a homeland . . . How sad it is that we have, vis-à-vis the fine words that "the others" spread around, very ugly second thoughts.'[35]

This was said and happened before the invasion of pragmatism (functionalism). The avowed or unavowed champions of this pragmatism reject the 'we'. Very well. 'We' also need enemies. If the pragmatists and empiricists believe they can emerge from the shadows and enter the light, they make people laugh as soon as they open their mouths.

'We' – what is meant here by this word? Western man questioning himself and his unique property, logos? Modern man with his love of technology? The philosophers of modernity who trap it by one corner or another. The list goes on. All of us! We, those who advance on tiptoe, in a paradoxical world: in a penumbra. If only this world presented itself like architecture, with clear contours, edges and angles! We flatter it by calling it 'complex', which is highly contradictory. Now, contradictions are blunted or seem to be blunted in favour of various logics, but these logics confront one another in a game in which contradictions reappear as surprises, as paradoxes. And the shadows go among the shadows.

Three stars gravitate, eliminating lesser or invisible planets, above this world in which shadows dance: ourselves. Stars in a sky in which the sun of intelligibility is no more than a symbol and no longer offers anything in the way of a firmament. Perhaps these stars vanish behind clouds hardly less obscure than the night . . .

In myth, from the poetry of Homer to the *Divine Comedy*, the realm of shadows possessed an entrance and exit, a guided trajectory and mediating powers. It had gates, those of an underground city, overshadowed by the earthly city and the city of God. Today, where are the gates of the realm of shadows? Where is the way out?

---

35 [Here Lefebvre is somewhat paraphrasing section 343 of *The Gay Science*. – Translator.]

2

The Hegel File

1) What was the *social* status of knowledge in France, and in Europe, before the nineteenth century?

The standard history of philosophy, one of ideas and ideologies, which examines abstract constructions 'from within', has difficulty answering this. As for the *epistemological* question, one of theoretical status, that is a different matter – secondary and derivative if we accept the terms of the question; theoretical status follows and derives from social status.

In the old triad of orders or 'estates' (*Stände* in German), nobility, clergy and 'third estate', knowledge belonged to the clerics. The nobility had action: war, festivals, tournaments and pleasures. For the 'third' estate, productive work: agriculture, handicrafts and commerce. For the clerics, contemplation, knowledge and tranquillity. What knowledge? An unholy mixture of theological metaphors and philosophical concepts; ideology had official status, institutionalized in the Church. In relation to this 'corpus' (doctrinal body), solidly maintained (kept in hand) by very varied means, cognition was born only on the margins. It therefore had a fundamental critical edge: starting with Abelard, then Rabelais and Montaigne, Kepler and Galileo, Descartes and Newton.

The prevailing history of ideas gives a good account of the growth of knowledge, but a very poor one of the conflictual relationship between this marginality (going as far as heresy and apostasy, rebellion against all authorities), and the various statuses (estates). This history reduces the relationship to a 'criticism of authority', whereas the conflict had a wider reach. The uncertain status of cognition shook all forms of assured status in the social and political context. To whom should knowledge be imputed? Who managed it? The Church and its institutions, the clergy and clerics, could not possess critical knowledge as such, neither transmit it nor increase it. They transmuted it into ideology. Now, cognition has a cumulative character and demands management (self-management by those responsible: scholars). Through contradictions, cognition pronounces its logical judgement: 'All or nothing'. With the result that the social status of cognition shook the existing society as much as did its actual content, in the same way as the growth of the productive forces and the rise of the bourgeoisie – causes that *precisely* exercised their action *by way of* knowledge and its management.

The facts are familiar enough, but there is often a failure to interpret, appreciate and connect them. In the seventeenth century, the so-called 'great century' which saw the consolidation of the centralized state in France, a gulf developed between knowledge and power. Cognition was hardly less heretical, in political terms, than religious heresy. Even mathematics seemed subversive, and still more so physics. As Descartes showed, the connection of algebraic signs has nothing in common with scholastic abstractions and the properties of 'substantial forms'. His theory of refraction ruined the old symbolism of the rainbow. Despite a drift of Cartesian reason towards *raison d'état*, Descartes exiled himself to Amsterdam. Scientific heresy linked up with religious heresy in Jansenism and Pascal. Scientific 'societies', functioning partly by correspondence (letters) and almost clandestine, practised the self-management of knowledge: the state combatted this practice by institutionalizing cognition in the form of academies and academicism. We need not recall in detail how in the eighteenth century the growth of knowledge accompanied the rise of the bourgeoisie. Cognition found unforeseen support and invaded social and political practice. On the one hand, it was linked to art and music, which saw an extraordinary upsurge in the wake of discoveries in physics, mathematics and technology. On the other hand, it was linked with production – initially not so much with industry, which was still weak in France, as with agriculture, which demanded improvement and perfection. The connection of science and industry by the mediation of technology would soon strengthen the connection between knowledge and productive activity foreshadowed by the *Encyclopédie*, and operating already in England by the end of the century.

The *Encyclopédie* (and the work of Diderot) marks an epoch, not only because a philosophy, materialism, emerged from it, or because the Church and the monarchy recoiled in the face of this bold intellectual enterprise, but because the social status of science changed. Wrested from the clergy and clerics, entrusted to a new 'stratum', intellectuals, managed by them to a large extent outside of state control, it established itself as a power alongside political authority.

Here again, the break was political more than philosophical or epistemological, the former encompassing the latter. Any new science – political economy, for example – supplants another in the '*corpus scientiarum*'.[1] Cognition, considered from within, was certainly transformed, but also and above all its social status, which was the dominant aspect. As far as knowledge was concerned, its socio-political demand and command changed profoundly during this period. The French Revolution confirmed this change and continued it by accentuating the process already begun: the connection between knowledge, bourgeoisie and nation-state. Not without introducing new contradictions, for example the rights of the individual (designated 'man' and 'citizen'), which almost inevitably conflicted with those of the nation-state. This casts light on the contradictory character of this great revolution, both bourgeois and democratic, the compromise between these conflicting terms being immediately subjected to harsh tests.

It is a historical fact that the bourgeois-democratic revolution revisited the *social* status of knowledge in order to *nationalize* it. Not only did it secularize the entire edifice of cognition, it rationalized (and thus state-ized) it. It also wrested it from self-management, even though the interested parties sought to keep some responsibilities (this was the demand of the '*idéologues*' under Napoleon). The French Revolution created a number of scientific institutions separate from each other, though unofficially it maintained cognition under the sign of encylopaedism. By the same token, it created contradictions that would subsequently follow their own course: between universalism and nationalism, for example.

---

1 Cf. Michel Foucault, *Archaeology of Knowledge*, New York: Vintage, 1982, pp. 222ff. This author misunderstands the social status of knowledge, concerning himself only with its epistemological status in the 'pure' sense.

The cult and festival of Reason, so often ridiculed, had the eminent meaning that knowledge and power tend towards a unity, with knowledge drawing prodigious energy from its struggle, and (revolutionary) power submitting (in appearance) to Reason. Hegel was not mistaken.[2] For him, the French Revolution represented the negative power of the concept, absolute knowledge asserting itself by clearing the ground, as the end of history approached. In French thought and the French Revolution, Hegel distinguished three aspects: a destructive and *negative* aspect, poorly understood and received, but the most important; a *positive* and constructive aspect; and a philosophical and metaphysical, hence transcendent, aspect, that he, Hegel, had extracted after having done justice to the negative aspect. French philosophy and politics, lively and mobile, *were* (ontological assertion) the actual work of the *spirit*. The Revolution, for Hegel, was the concept in action, and even 'the absolute concept that turns against the whole domain of accepted ideas and frozen thoughts'. The Revolution brought the fall of those entities that had falsely governed consciousness and science: good and evil, faith in God and his providence, the power of wealth and the power of divine or natural right, duties and submission to imperatives external to knowledge. With French philosophy and the French Revolution, and still more so with Napoleon, the Absolute Spirit manifested itself by accepting and receiving into itself its movement, negative and positive, destructive and creative, hence its self-generation, its *moments*. As for the serious danger that differences would disappear in the 'objectivized essence' (actualized in the national state), Hegel had a hard time averting it.

Hegel thus rightly appears in history, with a greater claim than other German philosophers (Kant, Fichte), as the thinker of the French Revolution. He perceived and reflected it, along with its continuation in the Napoleonic epic, from the depths of his backward Germany. The German philosopher was not content simply to transcribe political facts into his own language. He placed these in perspective and created for this the language of the concept. A clarity emerged that seemed definitive. This conceptual language corresponded to the languages current in Europe; it took these to a higher level of mutual comprehension.

---

2 Cf. *Philosophy of History*, 'The Eclaircissement and Revolution', pp. 438ff., and *History of Philosophy*, paragraph 295.

Moreover, it extracted and formulated the essential feature of the Revolution by proclaiming its future: the bourgeois rather than the democratic side.

The ascendant movement leading to absolute knowledge did not proceed only through science or the sciences, the adventures and avatars of consciousness, or the slow progress of institutions. Hegelian logos summed up and focused Western logos by way of a production that the whole world would imitate – the nation-state. Hegelianism did not present itself as a second-degree discourse on philosophy, science and its history, but as a first-degree discourse on a political action that no longer had a direct expression.

With the same scope as Clausewitz, though in a different language, Hegel held a strategic discourse and defined a strategy, that of absolute politics and the political absolute.

2) At the centre, then, the vertical pivot or axis: knowledge. In other words, the concept, or, more rigorously, the concept of the concept, its objectively reflected essence (rather than the subjective reflection, 'I think that I think that I think', which gets lost in the bad infinity of illusory subjectivity, whereas in the concept according to Hegel, subjective freedom constitutes itself as substance).

The concept, the power of truth both negative and positive, clears the path by eliminating what does not suit it: errors, illusions, lies, appearances, accidental representations. To this concept, generally seen as impotent abstraction, Hegel attributed every capacity: it lives, it works, it produces, it fights. In 1844, Marx would mock these activities of the Hegelian concept. By the same gesture, this animated concept does away with the crazy, the abnormal, the pathogenic and pathological. The weaknesses of consciousness in the process of becoming, the despairs of the unhappy consciousness and the hopes of the beautiful soul, logically disappear, whereas the least trace of knowledge, from sensation to reason, is preserved.

In a language that is not exactly Hegelian, we could say that conceptual knowledge eliminates ideology and along with it the poetic delirium of speech. The dramatic ordeals of the concept include this struggle and this meaning. They have a cathartic function, in the last instance *epistemological*, so that Hegel did not have to discern in philosophy a core and a periphery. The circle drawn around the centre forms part of knowledge; animated from bottom to top and from start to finish, it contains the absolute.

To be sure, neither Hegel nor any Hegelian suspected the infernal vicious circle, the remarkable tautology: 'knowledge knows the real; the real is knowledge'. Tautology or magic? Logology and/or incantation? Both. The concrete and the abstract coincide, the fact and the idea, thus the end and the means of knowledge. The real, what we know, defines knowledge, and knowledge defines the real by rejecting the unreal: not just the apparent, but also the '*vécu*', lived experience, identified by decree with appearance, with the phenomenon, with accidental representations and the illusions of subjectivity. No Hegelian, down to our own time, is aware of the gulf that opens up between lived experience and the concept, and that this conflict has serious consequences. None of them can admit that the necessary is not therefore sufficient, and that the sufficiency of knowledge as such represents only a postulate (an accidental representation proclaimed as essential). Knowledge accumulates; it alone, for Hegel, has this cumulative character. It has superiority over memory, reminiscence, recognition, the imaginary, the symbolic, all of which have no autonomy, so no novelty. Yet the duplication of self-consciousness, reflectivity (the capacity to *reflect* on things and oneself), already proclaims the cumulative power of cognition. Around the axis, the crystalline column, the moments of knowledge are arranged; they support each other and mount up in two dimensions: horizontally and vertically. Knowledge extends in width around its centre, and grows in height towards the pinnacle of the Idea and the Spirit. Discontinuities and disjunctions in the process compromise neither its cohesion nor its arrangement. If it has *moments*, none of these substantial moments disappear into nothingness along with illusions and appearances. The edifice regularly grows. Its pieces adjust and cement themselves. In contrast to this, for example, discontinuity reigns in art, and in the phenomenology of consciousness, which emphasizes subjectivity. Knowledge in the strict sense escapes these inconveniences, which explains a certain paradox, without suppressing it. Hegel appeals to the Revolution (French, bourgeois-democratic). He theorizes it. And yet, according to him, the Revolution abolished nothing apart from a few illusions. The essential aspect – the 'moments' – persist and subsist: family, corporations and trades, morality and even religion; in short, whatever pertains, or seems to pertain, to reason. Neither Hegel nor the

Hegelians understood a paralogism inherent to their logicism. Sometimes logic, as theory of coherence and cohesion, dissolves into dialectic, the theory of contradictions; sometimes logic absorbs dialectic, and cohesion prevails over contradiction. On many occasions Hegel asserted the priority, anteriority, essentiality of the dialectical process. Becoming, the first concrete thought, the first notion, outclasses the empty abstractions of being and nothingness. Pure being and pure nothingness coincide, truth lying neither in the one nor the other, 'but in the fact that being does not pass, but is passed, into nothingness, and nothingness into being', as Hegel declares early on in the *Science of Logic*.[3] A philosophy that starts from Being as being, or Nothingness as nothingness, deserves to be called a system of *abstract* identity. It ignores movement. The power of the concept and movement, in other words, dialectical movement, coincide: 'The concept's moving principle . . . I call *"dialectic"*', 'This dialectic is not an activity of subjective thinking applied to some matter externally, but it is rather the matter's very soul putting forth its branches and fruits organically.'[4]

What then does Hegel's famous dialectical method consist in – a method that so many people claim to use, yet is defined so rarely and so poorly, given the difficulties that mount up? First of all, that knowledge according to Hegel, in other words, the concept, *progresses* and *produces* its determinations in immanent fashion. Second, that analysis, which Hegel calls the Understanding, discovers determinations in the things analysed, but discerns and thus posits them separately, each outside the other (*partes extra partes*, in the words Spinoza used to characterize the first and lower of the three types of cognition). *Dialectical reason* dissolves these determinations of the Understanding by grasping their unity, with the result that it positively *produces* the universal. Above the senses and the Understanding, the highest level raises itself: intelligent reason and rational understanding. At this level the knowledge that initially posited distinction, 'this is that', 'A is B', denies it. Then, and only then, it is 'dialectical', situating A and B in their relationship and their becoming – in their conflicts. For example: 'the leaf is green . . . the pencil is red' (concept of leaf or pencil) is transformed: 'the leaf is no longer green, it is drying up', etc. Reason re-establishes its starting point,

---

3 *Science of Logic*, para. 137.
4 *Philosophy of Right*, para. 31.

the separate determination 'A', as a particularity grasped concretely in its relations and movement, by the universality of the concept.[5] Third, dialectic consists in the opposition of true and false being no longer in any way fixed: common sense, in other words, the Understanding, accepts or rejects an assertion or a system *en bloc*; it does not conceive the difference of (philosophical) systems as the development of the true; for it, diversity means absurdity, unacceptable contradiction. However: 'The bud disappears when the blossom breaks through, and we might say that the former is refuted by the latter . . . These stages are not merely differentiated; they supplant one another as being incompatible with one another.'[6]

Is this perhaps the place and time – the 'moment' – for confession? Hegel turns the situation upside down, reverses his own movement. He begins by presupposing and positing the dialectic, taking this to the ultimate paradox of rejecting mathematical method as abstract and empty, logico-quantitative.[7] Only the dialectical method gives access to the concrete (the real). Hegel describes the eternal movement in almost Dionysian terms; a Bacchanalia in which 'not a member is sober'.[8] He refers explicitly to Heraclitus, and then suddenly the background, perspective, even essence is changed: logic is in command; it ensures the cohesion of the construction, resolving the contradictions that it raises, except in appearance and in the conflict between the apparent and the real (the concrete). 'To see that thought is in its very nature dialectical, and that, as understanding, it must fall into contradiction – the negative of itself – will form one of the main lessons of logic'. According to this passage from the Introduction to the *Encyclopaedia Logic*, it is at the level of the *understanding* that thought contradicts itself.[9] It follows that dialectical reason puts an end to the contradictions of analysis, which then seem to arise from what the analytical understanding separates by discerning the aspects and moments of things. This is indeed what the

---

5 *Science of Logic*, preface.

6 Lenin commented on the text of Hegel's *Science of Logic* (and just this) in his *Philosophical Notebooks* [which Lefebvre and Guterman translated into French]. When Hegel explains dialectical movement, he refers metaphorically to organic nature, which seems a satisfactory example. The same is not true of Lenin's thought, in which the reference is rather to politics. Cf. *Phenomenology of Spirit*, Preface, para. 2

7 *Phenomenology of Spirit*, para. 42ff.

8 *Phenomenology of Spirit*, para. 47.

9 *Encyclopaedia Logic*, introduction, para. 11.

continuation of this passage states: 'When thought grows hopeless of ever achieving, by its own means, the solution of the contradiction which it has by its own action brought upon itself, it turns back to those solutions of the question with which the mind had learned to pacify itself in some of its other modes and forms.' According to Hegel, at the higher level of the spirit, logic is re-established and carries the day. The spirit makes the separate determinations and the contradictions between them disappear. It resolves conflicts. Solution means resolution, within the very process. No contradiction affects the spirit. Everything happens in the Hegelian system as if contradiction was born with and from alienation. The absolute Idea emerges from itself, alienates itself in nature, then finds itself, recognizes itself or re-produces itself in full consciousness and cognition by way of history and conceptual knowledge. Dis-alienation makes contradiction vanish, and hence dialectic. What is the role of the negative at this level? It has disappeared. It served only as mediator in Absolute Spirit between the finite and the infinite, simultaneously containing and superseding this spirit, the one in the other, the one by the other, and yet the one after the other.[10]

The metaphorical reference to nature that Hegel constantly employs, as in the *Phenomenology* (the flower replaces the blossom, the fruit replaces the flower, the organic ensemble *produces* branch, flower and fruit), confirms this critical analysis. It turns out that the processes to which Hegel refers have a cyclical determination (or character) rather than a dialectical one. The blossom generates the flower, which generates the fruit, which generates seeds and blossoms, and so on. The process is re-produced. But this raises a problem. Organic beings (plants, animals) are relatively stable totalities. Hegel, seeing nature as the first product of the Idea (which emerges from itself to project itself into matter), perceives not so much contradictions as balanced developments – a contrary situation to that of history. Spirit finally re-establishes the organic, at the highest level. Hegel and Hegelianism thus proceed to the self-destruction of the dialectic that they generated. And we understand why Marx, and then Engels, re-established the rights of thought and the dialectical method against the Hegelians and Hegel himself, as a particular and privileged case of 'turning the world upside

---

10 Cf. *Science of Logic*, Chapter 2.

down'.[11] What remains of Hegelianism after such harsh operations? By defending 'his dialectic', do we not risk demolishing it? Dismantling dialectical thought itself, which cannot be defined as a method *indifferent* to its content, indifferent to the 'system'. Is it better then to keep, though modifying, the triadic system that Hegel took to an apogee? And what is the exact relationship between logic and dialectic? Does logic shatter in dialectic? Is it continued, or articulated to something else?

Nothing in the world dies away except by self-destruction, said Nietzsche. Hegel was remarkably embarrassed by the self-destruction of his own dialectic. This produced a paradox, an aporia: *difference*. What is difference, Hegel ponders at length in Book Two of the *Science of Logic*. He finds it hard to reach an answer. Identity repeats itself: A is A. But the second A differs from the first; it re-produces it, but is not the same, simply because it is second. A thus differs from itself, and difference goes back into identity. And yet it stipulates the non-identity of the identical itself. In difference, the One separates from the Same, and the Same from the Other. But then difference becomes oppositions, 'in so far as', in other words, in the various and separate determinations that the understanding posits and that reason supersedes. It seems then that, for Hegel, difference represents simply an attenuated case of dialectical contradiction, without negative power, which leads him to ask whether the statement 'All things are different' has any interest at all. Without diversity, there would not be things. The proposition is reduced to a tautology. On top of which, the difference thus represented is general, abstract and vague, thus indeterminate. When Leibniz invited ladies to look among the leaves of a tree for two that were identical, it was a happy time for philosophy; no other proof was needed than the leaves of a tree.[12]

Hegel is unable to escape his embarrassment by irony. He extricates himself with formulations that are too simplistic: is not difference *indifferent* vis-à-vis both identity and non-identity (contradiction)? This would later generate a number of problems. Is difference resolved or dissolved, either in the identical or in the conflictual? Is it

---

11 As we shall see in an important item in the Marx file.

12 Cf. the adverse interpretation of difference, apropos the tree and the leaf, first of all in the very well-known passage from *The Holy Family* on (against) the Hegelian idea of the tree and the fruit, then in Nietzsche's *On Truth and Lies in a Non-Moral Sense*.

simply a specific (differentiating) activity? Among differences, is there a crucial difference between those that can be reduced, being internal to a system, and the irreducible ones, residues resistant to any reductive operation, which characterize either distinct systems, or non-systems?

3) What form does Absolute Spirit assume in order to definitively establish the cohesion of the construction? The *political* form. The edifice is built up brick by brick, moment by moment; it seems to be that of knowledge (pure and absolute), but it is actually none other than the state. For state and knowledge coincide. More rigorously, they are two aspects, two 'moments' of one and the same actuality as indissoluble as the ideal and the real, theoretical philosophy and practical action. The necessity that governs the whole process has three moments: *condition* (the presupposed moment, which realizes itself in the course of the process); *thing* (produced as content and external existence); and *activity* (movement that proceeds from the conditions to the thing, that produces the thing by making it emerge from the conditions).

Fundamentally rational, all the way from organic nature that is restored at the level of the Spirit (the Idea, and therefore the state, this embodiment of the Idea), necessity does many things. It successively posits the condition, then what the condition makes possible: thing (reality) and activity (productive: work, political action). A triple effectiveness that goes further than causality and finality taken separately. Activity taken in isolation remains subjective; it requires particular conditions to produce it. The thing taken in isolation has no interest or meaning, it is inexplicable; and if nothing generates it, it does not come into existence. Only the organic ensemble of three moments has a meaning and an *intelligible* (spiritual) necessity. The same necessity at work in its three moments is recognized in knowledge, in productive activity, and materially in political action. In other words, the triadic rhythm is found in each term, together ensuring the organic ensemble. In each domain, the activity summoned by the ensemble discovers its specific conditions; from this point, it can simultaneously assert itself (subjectively) and generate things (objectively), which reacts – reciprocal action – on the conditions, initially to reaffirm them, then to supersede them.

In Hegelianism, a rationalization of the historical and revolutionary process that constituted/instituted the nation-state, as already in

Robespierrean ideology, knowledge is the foundation of power; it legiti-mates this by subordinating it (discreetly). 'The revolutions that until now have changed the face of empires have had as their object simply a change of dynasty . . . The French Revolution is the first to have been founded on theory' (Robespierre's last speech to the Convention). 'If you want factions to disappear, and that no one should seek to raise themselves on the debris of public liberty by the platitudes of Machiavelli, then make politics powerless' (Saint-Just, the same day). Hegel seems at first to reject the Napoleonic experience, which re-established harsh reality by erecting the state above society and its 'moments', and indeed to misunderstand it. He sees in Napoleon the immense vigour of a char-acter embodying the world spirit, who governs by imposing respect in place of deference, and then turns his force outward, spreading liberal institutions everywhere. Hegel says nothing of Bonapartism, except that it led to the 'impotence of victory', and that the irony of history worked against it.

At the centre of the state, the pivot and core, Hegel puts the political class; this takes charge of knowledge and possesses competence. A genuine 'estate' within the state, a power elite, a body that recruits itself by rational means (competition), it ensures the functioning of society. And the ideology used, religious or secular, seems of little importance for Hegel. His *Philosophy of Right* offers an apologia for this social stra-tum or class: being both selective and stable, it deserves every praise. Why? Because it knows. It is acquainted with the social ensemble, and can thus make it work. There is no trace of determinism or blind automatism in this functioning, nor again of arbitrary domination. From this centre, in the political class, knowledge holds the state and makes it hold. Immanent rationality is concentrated in this higher stra-tum of the 'thinking class' (middle class), which coincides with the lower stratum of those who govern and who nominally exercise power. It bears and supports them. Hegelianism thus makes the following presupposition: given that the rationality diffused and infused in the *whole* society is concentrated at the apex, the political instances are able to *cognize* (by knowledge) and *resolve* (by decision and action) all contradictions and conflicts that may arise at lower levels, between the 'moments', components and elements of the edifice. If there are such conflicts, they can only be of minor importance. They do not shake the construction of state and nation. Knowledge-power is capable of reducing them or finding a solution that makes them disappear. Contradictions are reducible, apparent rather than real: temporary incoherencies in a coherent whole.

This is how Hegel posits the problem that would dominate both the new, so-called human or social sciences, during the nineteenth and even the twentieth century, and also philosophy when this refused to be tied to metaphysical entities of being and consciousness, thought and life, intuition and reflection in general. This is the problem of the whole or totality in human reality. 'How is it that a multitude of often rival activities are unaware of one another, or compete with one another, yet constitute an ensemble? How is it that after disturbances, revolution or war, this ensemble reconstitutes itself? Why does it not fall into pieces and fragments? What prevents it from atomizing into individuals or groups? What is it that makes a people a people, a nation a nation, a class a class . . .?'

It is not hard to wax ironic at Hegel's response (and we may as well do so here). Hegel answers: 'There is a whole because it is a whole!' An obvious tautology. And very likely, after a detailed critique, we will reach the conclusion that the Hegelian presupposition of a global logic, a system, a coherent ensemble, is summed up in this tautology. But the proposition, which appears ridiculously repetitive, takes another aspect when expressed differently: 'There is a whole because there is a totalizing reason'. And this is how Hegelianism shows its strength. Reason? Knowledge? Concept? They exist, they have a role, a function, an action. Why not presuppose them and place them at the centre, at the core, in the axis around which the whole establishes itself? How can a whole be constructed and maintained, except by cognition of it?

It is true that both before and after Hegel, other philosophers and scholars defined the whole differently. For vitalists and romantics, the properties of the organic whole precede thought. Only the living being, qua living, 'is' a whole, generating and maintaining itself by the force of life until this abandons it. Thought has no need to rise to life, in order to confirm and complete the qualities of life in its own form; it has first of all to accept them in their immediacy; and reflection has something posterior and even foreign about it in relation to the first essence of things. For vitalism, philosophy starts from intuition, the alpha and omega of cognition. The Absolute is not conceived or perceived; it is sensed. At the start of the *Phenomenology* Hegel rejects this mystic naturalism, that of Schelling and romanticism. 'These apocalyptic utter-ances pretend to occupy the very centre and the deepest depths; they look askance at all definiteness and preciseness of meaning; and they deliberately hold back from conceptual thinking and the constraining necessities of thought, as being the sort of reflection which, they say, can only feel at home in the sphere of finitude. But just as there is a breadth which is emptiness, there is a depth which is empty too' (para. 10) – '[This intuitionism] tramples the roots of humanity underfoot' (para. 69). For the nature of humanity is to tend to rational agreement, to communication, to the community of consciousnesses through science. These texts aimed at Schelling would also be applicable to Schopenhauer, and we can say, a century and a half later, that they foreshadow Nietzsche.

It is also true that already before Hegel, the English economists (Adam Smith, etc.), and others as well (Saint-Simon), had conceived the economic-social-political whole in a more 'realist' manner than Hegel, without any mysticism. For Adam Smith, the market, productive work and the division of labour, the exchange of products, was enough to explain the cohesion of the ensemble. For Saint-Simon, rationality lay neither in the concept, nor in knowledge as such, but in productive work: in industry. The French Revolution, the rise of the Third Estate, allowed this underlying rationality, previously denied or concealed, to surge forth.

According to the economists, the market arises from a vast interac-tion of demand and supply. A 'spontaneous' process, as Marx would show in his analysis of exchange-value, it obtains a certain regulation 'blindly', in the manner of processes governed by physical laws (rather than by a mysterious internal unity), hence a rationality that excludes neither accidents nor contradictions nor difficulties (crises).

Productive activity? Industry? Their rationality results from a practi-cal relationship between activity and its object. From the moment that a man fashioned an object with his hands, with his body, with an instru-ment (a flint, a bone, a stick), this rationality was at work. 'Man' who operated rationally once could do so a second and a third time. He knew where to place the tool, where to find the material, how to hold it in his fingers. And what is true of industrial activity is also true of collective activities: workshops, firms. Saint-Simon was aware of and familiar with this emergence of the rational, starting with a conceived primordial practice, already in Hegel's lifetime.

Should we then disavow Hegelianism, ridicule it? No. It is precisely here that it shows its strength. Hegel was familiar with the work of the English economists, he took these into account. Saint-Simon, Hegel's rival in the power and scope of his concepts, was either ignorant of them or misunderstood them. Yet he cannot be accused of 'irrealism'.

The *system of needs*, and the *division of labour as system*, were demonstrated by Hegel with a positivity equal to that of the Saint-Simonians of his time. With him, these two systems fit each other precisely, like pieces in a puzzle; two sub-systems are inserted and integrated. They correspond to one another objectively (whereas the political class constitutes the subjectivity of the state), ensuring law and right a foundation endowed with cohesion and equilibrium.

Here Hegel's line of argument is on firm ground. Is it not necessary for the needs of individuals living together to define themselves? And for them to harmonize with rather than destroy one another? Need has first of all a subjective existence; but it obeys the universal movement (rational and dialectical) by which the subjective seeks to objectify itself, yet manages to do so only by transforming the object into subjectivity. We know that this movement culminates in knowledge (in the concept, higher unity of the objective and the subjective). Need both seeks an object and arises from the object sought. What does it expect from its quest and from the object? Satisfaction. How does it obtain this? By possession of the object, followed by its destruction (consumption). And yet this object was produced by others. It corresponds to other needs, to other wills and other activities. For Hegel, these relationships give rise to the sphere of political economy:

the science which starts from this view of needs and labour but then has the task of explaining mass-relationships and mass-movements in their complexity and their qualitative and quantitative character . . . This is one of the sciences which have arisen out of the conditions of the modern world. Its development affords the interesting spectacle . . . of thought working upon the endless mass of details which confront it at the outset and extracting therefrom the simple principles of the thing, the Understanding effective in the thing and directing it.[13]

---

13 *Philosophy of Right*, para. 189, Zusatz.

According to common sense, the baker, builder, teacher, etc. already exist, and from their activities there results something that maintains and reproduces itself: everyday life, that of the family, the trade, the group, the village or the town – in short, what Hegel calls the life of civil society. This is simple, even if there are petty quarrels among these moments. The economist sees things as rather more complicated, so that the '*concordia discors*' of activities in civil society requires an analysis and a theory. Hegel arrives as a philosopher, and pronounces that he supersedes both common sense – the domain of the Understanding, unaware of itself as such – and the particularized science of political economy, which discovers a rationality whose source it is unaware of. He, the philosopher, will give political economy a foundation by showing the origin and complementarity of the system of needs and the system of labours, despite the accidental conflicts that arise. What happens to need and labour? The two things – each separately, the one as social need and the other as social labour – necessarily become *abstract*. This leads them to pass from nature to the concept (or rather it reveals the conceptual rationality inherent to the immediate and the natural). Natural and subjective singularities fall away, to make room for defined and thus general needs. In what way? That of reciprocal action, which implies communication, exchange, the mutual recognition of needs. If subject A seeks to impose his need on subject B, the latter does nothing for him; each consciousness confronts the other in a struggle to the death. To put an end to this unending confrontation, A recognizes the need of B, and B the need of A. What they exchange is not only things (objects) but also their (subjective) needs. By way of this mutual recognition, B's need becomes A's as well, and vice versa. In the reciprocal act (communication and exchange), needs are socially *divided* and *multiplied*, and so are the modes of their satisfaction. Individual needs form part of the generally recognized need, which is both abstract and definite (particularized) within universality (the ensemble). Thus, individual A may have his particular tastes, his secret tendencies, he may like this or that. By becoming social, however, his need can find satisfaction only in the products of social labour: food, clothing, habitation, etc. Thus, the *social moment* frees the individual from what was singular, unique, incommunicable about him. Communication (through language) and exchange (of objects) each work towards this result, knowledge (at this level, understanding and representation) dominating natural necessity.

In the course of the interaction (between objects and subjects), therefore, an important mediation intervenes: labour. This follows the same process as need; it becomes abstraction, a social abstraction. Individual efforts and natural gestures that are pleasant for the individual – those of play, of childhood – lose their meaning. The disciplined gestures of production, imposed by collective activity, make up according to Hegel a *practical culture*, complementary to the *theoretical culture* arising from objects already in use. Here, it is language that ensures the match. Like needs, social labour divides by multiplying; the division of labour (which Hegel never criticizes) has this dialectical aspect, the multiplication of labours and needs. The result of this is the system of (productive) labours, complementary to the system of needs. It results from the harmony between the two systems that social needs are produced and reproduced with an apparent spontaneity (an automatism). And labours likewise. Abstraction, a 'universal element and objective of labour', extends to the means, tools. Like skill or hands, tools increasingly form part of knowledge and demand cognition. In their own way they also become abstract – a third term along with need and labour. The ensemble thus leaves the sphere of the natural and immediate, to form part of concrete *abstraction*. 'The abstraction of one man's production from another's makes work more and more mechanical, until finally man is able to step aside and install machines in his place.'[14] An eminent truth that the *Encyclopaedia* also repeats. Abstract labour becomes both uniform and easy; it enables an increase in the scale of production, by subordinating fragmented technical activity to the social whole. 'The skill itself becomes in this way mechanical, and gets the capability of letting the machine take the place of human labour.'[15]

In the extreme case, therefore, 'universal fortune' simultaneously allows the general satisfaction (of needs), the mechanization of labour (production), and the self-regulation of the social ensemble (each subjective activity of individuals and groups being necessarily transformed into a contribution to the satisfaction of everyone else).

This rational optimism thus foresees a stabilized and balanced 'state of things', a state in which relations between the partial systems, the

14 *Philosophy of Right*, para. 198.
15 *Philosophy of Mind*, paras 525–6.

moments and elements, the sub-systems themselves, support one another, being produced and reproduced in an assured equilibrium and stability. This is the perfect *automatism* of the ensemble within *abstraction*, in an edifice coherent both horizontally (the complementary elements) and vertically (from the bottom, production, to the top, the political leader). Does this structure not seem stable enough to withstand any test? At the bottom, the two producing classes: peasants and workers. Above these, the middle, thinking, bureaucratic class, from which come the managers, the executives, the expert and competent. If the state cements and crowns the edifice, this is because it is the supreme identity of knowledge and power.

Need we insist on the grandeur of this analysis, this picture?

First of all, there emerges from it the concept of *social labour*, with its implications (exchange, commodities, division of labour) and its consequences (the automatic machine). Hegel refines the discoveries of Adam Smith, and the theoretical elements of the new science of political economy. Marx would take these over completely, without neglecting the critical aspect, which is found in Smith but which Hegel misunderstands (the division of labour mutilates the individual, obscures the process of production and consequently cognition of the socio-political ensemble). With this reservation about alienated and alienating labour, Marx would present the *concrete abstractions*, commodities and labour, in the Hegelian line as modified by political critique.

Second, how can the amazing topicality of Hegel's exposition be denied? The modern state, run by a 'political class' that combines technocrats and professional politicians (they sometimes coincide) has no other aim, end, meaning or perspective than the *automatic reproduction* of its own structure, coinciding with the *production* that it controls. In the political automatism, 'man' – promoted to 'citizen' and defined by citizenship – is supposed to accept without protest or murmur the satisfactions offered to him by the state (physical, cultural, political – an admirable triptych). No joke. By caricaturing a little (hardly), we could say that 'man', who has disappeared as such, changed into citizen-soldier and, in the extreme case, into political-soldier in the Bonapartist mould, figures as a 'piece' of an admirable machine of the military type. Even if ignorant of Hegel, or familiar only second hand, how many leaders, notables, politicians and technocrats would not recognize this picture and themselves!

However it arises, we have here Nietzsche's 'eternal recurrence': the circle of circles (vicious, infernal, perfect), the sphere of spheres. We are in an immediacy rediscovered by way of mediations (history, action, cognition), in an identity recaptured by way of conflicts and contradictions. The political machine – the automatic ensemble – becomes a reality with the replacement of labour by specialized machines. Well-oiled and maintained by techno-mechanics, the great political machine will turn forever – turn on itself, with all its wheels and cogs. If it does not come unstuck, it may even expand. The eternal recurrence of the same and the identical is the state, which generates itself and is self-generated, which is perfected and self-regulated, and remains stable in the consumption of objects and the consumption of subjects. Eternity, the eminent, the supreme, is presented and achieved in this ensemble and its divine plenitude.

At what price? We have a sense of the price paid for this access to absolute and divinized politics.

4) Knowledge founded on power, and power founded on knowledge, determine what escapes them, thus what they dismiss, in full knowledge of the causes and effects. Since reason contains the code of being, and can decipher the existing with no other residue than the unnameable and insignificant, the rational defines the irrational. What does this mean? The dominant logic defines differences in order to reject them, but not differences internal to the system; in fact, it never achieves the homogeneity of a monolithic bloc, even though politicians pursue this design. It contains and includes a diversity – executives, classes, organs, institutions, laws. What state rationality cannot tolerate is what does not conform to its form, external difference. Philosophically speaking, the system defines alienation, understanding by this nonconformity as well as revolt and madness. In relation to the central and axial logos, Hegelian alienation is determined as with the Greeks: hubris, disturbance and even merely suspect ambiguity. Worse, knowledge set up in power rejects or misunderstands subjectivity as such, hence lived experience [*le vécu*]. This can be manipulated; it disappears along with the unhappy (rebel) consciousness or the beautiful soul (which dreams of a more beautiful life, so severely judged by Hegel in the *Phenomenology*). Lived experience may protest and challenge, demand or rebel, but it is in the wrong. Why? Because it does not have reason on its side. We perceive that among

the Hegelian 'moments' there are those that disappear because they pertain to the phenomenon, and moments that are preserved because they form part of knowledge. Alienation from the system is defined by the system, but this definition can never be published officially; which in practice leaves a large part to circumstances, thus to the arbitrariness that the system claims to eliminate.

Severe conceptual knowledge refuses to take into consideration non-knowledge, knowledge halfway to the concept, or even critical thought. It removes them from the luminous centre, casting them into outer darkness. Thus silence about everyday life. Sex? This is completely contained in the concept of the family, the state being defined from this point of view as substance that combines the family principle and the principle of civil society (labour and needs, other groups than the family). As the *Encyclopaedia* declares without ambiguity (para. 536). Love, the natural sentiment, 'no longer exists in the state'.[16] As sentiment, love is simply an enormous contradiction, since the subject ('I') seeks to realize itself in another person. Ethics (morality) resolves this contradiction, making the alienation of love disappear: in the family, and only here, the sexual and emotional relationship gains its significance (a moral one, naturally). As for the destination of woman, this is housework.[17]

Non-knowledge or semi-knowledge, halfway between ignorance and cognition, that concerning physical pleasure and fertility which was formerly transmitted in secret by old and young women, oral knowledge (unwritten and impossible to write down), this fount of social practice is misunderstood, ignored, despised and rejected by Hegel, Hegelianism and the Hegelian state, which seek to crush it. The body is seen as pertaining to natural immediacy: outside of rationality, in alienation and contradiction, in the singularity of the incommunicable.

In an incontestably brilliant manner, Hegel grasps and envisages the threatening possibilities of a liberation of lived experience, hence of the body. Children have the right to education. Why? Because of 'their own feeling of dissatisfaction', because they long to grow up. But if pedagogy should see the infantile element as having any value – play, for example – it ceases to be serious. It represents children as mature in immaturity, and thus falls into contradiction. It makes them satisfied with

---

16 *Philosophy of Right*, para. 158ff.
17 Ibid., para. 166.

themselves, driving them into alienation. Children will not respect it, as it communicates to them a contempt for adults.[18]

Order defines disorder. Hierarchy acquires precision and consolidation, according to Hegel, in his state, at every degree of the political edifice, that of knowledge and of life. Logos means the triumph of logic, theory and practice of coherence, which arrogates to itself the right to exclude incoherence, hence whatever disturbs cohesion. The logic of state brings with it a broad strategy, and coincides with this.

It is embodied to varying degrees in rulers, more or less eminent: big and little leaders, various dignitaries. We already know a good deal about the political class and its knowledge. What Hegel sees as the most important aspect, however, is still to come; these people, the political class, whose only task is to think, to manage the conceived ensemble, and to decide at the highest level, are above the division of labour. Do the great leaders need to know everything? Able to decide, unable to know everything, they have to surround themselves with competent advisers, scientists, diplomats, etc., themselves candidates for the roles of leaders and future leaders. We can examine the state edifice either from outside in, from the internal to the external (the central axis to the peripheries), or from inside out: philosophically, from the discursive and analytical understanding, which remains among the separated things with separate activities, to the necessary and sufficient rationality that cleaves to the centre. Outside, on the periphery, analysis encounters such external necessities as the police, for example, or corporations. Penetrating within, it encounters justice and administration. At the most central position stands the government, close to the Idea and the Spirit, as Hegel declares without the least irony.[19] At the top position there is satisfaction, that of people who carry out their task well (honestly). 'Blessedness is a satisfaction', Hegel says in his *Aesthetics*, which places the satisfaction of political virtue above aesthetic joy, individual happiness and the serenity of knowledge, as their synthesis.

5) In order to properly situate the Hegelian conception, we have to say that *in a sense* it takes to perfection a great idea that inspired the thought of the eighteenth century: the idea of harmony, or harmony as idea.

18 *Philosophy of Right*, para. 173ff.
19 Cf. in particular *Philosophy of Right*, para. 184.

This concept is born from music, or rather from the close contact between (materialist) philosophy and music in the eighteenth century. The history of ideas has little to say on this paradox. Harmony appears as a reality that is palpable (hearing), rational (based on numbers and relationship), and technological (with new instruments: the harpsichord, then the pianoforte). It adds a new dimension to music; or, more exactly, it recognizes a dimension already existing in musical practice, especially in the West; hence the three dimensions of melody, rhythm and harmony. The latter lends itself to great vertical constructions, utilizing chords and textures (harmonics), whereas melody and rhythm follow horizontal lines (the various 'voices'). The elaboration and development of harmony, in the eighteenth century, gave rise to new musical genres: the *symphony*, among others, which superimposes the ascending and descending verticality of chords and textures onto the horizontality of voices (in the fugue). Harmony maintains and retains in a totality its elements and moments: directions, intervals, voices, rhythmic elements, chords, various instruments and their timbres, etc. To each moment taken separately it adds a 'reflexivity': the elements are in relation with themselves in the ensemble, all correspond to one another in the harmonic construction, each reflects the other and they all reflect the unity of the ensemble. This makes for the 'beauty' of a symphony by Mozart or Beethoven.

The idea of harmony can fade into sentimentality (that of the 'beautiful soul' which Hegel so hated), but is exalted in great musical constructions. Hegel himself, in his *Aesthetics*, characterizes his age, that of romanticism, by the domination of music. *In a certain sense*, the great philosophical systems of the late eighteenth and early nineteenth centuries strive to embody the idea of a cosmic or human (social) harmony. Just as does Beethoven's Ninth Symphony! This assertion needs a certain qualification; it is more true for Fourier than for Saint-Simon, for the theories of economic harmony than for the naturalists, more for Hegel than for Kant. And it is also more true of the *Phenomenology*, a real symphony of the spirit, than for the severe *Philosophy of Right*. The unconditioned universal that the *Phenomenology* seeks to achieve (or reveal) still tolerates differences in an overall movement that is not yet reducible to the ensemble of a movement. 'In the figure of the content, the moments of the aspect under which they were initially presented: to be on the one hand a universal milieu of multiple subsisting materials, and on the other, a reflected place in which their independence is dissolved.'[20] This phrase analyses the movement of a symphony in Hegelian terms. It describes a moving (in both senses) dialectical animation.

We have to do justice to Hegel, so as to motivate and strengthen the fundamental criticism: he perceived his vertical construction as a sovereign harmony rather than a broad political thought, an intellectual symphony in which the philosopher is the author and the political leader (monarch) the conductor. He saw and defined himself as a liberal, champion of a constitutional monarchy. If we imagine Hegel faced with the political events of the twentieth century, he would probably say something like this: 'The modern state swings between two extremes: corruption, disintegration, conflicts between the various powers that ensue from the decomposition of Power – and the authoritarian rigidity, military, fascist and reactionary fetishism of the leader. As theorist of the state, philosopher and political thinker, I have defined a position of relative equilibrium and regulated functioning. Around this position the political balance leans to one side or the other. It inevitably returns to the state as supreme consciousness of society, more and better than arbiter or arbitrary, synthesis of moments, site of policed harmony.' To which we can immediately reply: 'Dear philosopher, you prove – as you always wish to and believe you prove – that your state inevitably departs from equilibrium and returns to it only with difficulty. You reveal a social body that has removed itself from nature and the natural body, and risen towards abstraction. This state that you erect as an absolute so dominates the hierarchy over which it presides that a day comes when it exploits the whole society and uses it for its own account. We call this "Bonapartism" or "fascism". Unless it fragments, and we have a political crisis.'

For the philosopher, biological life – the result of an alienation of the Idea, but a moment of dis-alienation – forms part of logic, as an element. In the theory of Hegelian logos, there is a convergence between auto-dynamism, which presupposes life, and rational structure, which implies coherence.[21] The living being remains stable, preserves its energy,

---

20   [Here Lefebvre seems to be paraphrasing paras 115ff. of the *Phenomenology*. – Translator.]

21   Cf. *Philosophy of Nature*, para. 285.

maintains its conditions. It has in it the three moments of activity, objects and conditions. Life produces and re-produces itself. In biological reproduction, there is simply an extension of the act of production and perpetual re-production of itself, which ceases only with death.

The state, as earthly divinity, is thus also the supreme living being. Hegel would adopt, in the modern vocabulary, the concepts of auto-regulation and re-production. He would reject the concept of automatism, and still more the image of the great machine. *Organic* life, at the level of the Absolute, would be irreducible to a mechanical automaton. And yet, should we take the philosopher at his word? He also demands trust (faith). Why grant him this? Does not the identification presupposed between the ardent life of a symphony, the animal life of an organism and the internal life of the state, abuse this metaphor? Even a dragon has an internal life, and monsters lack neither grandeur nor beauty. Let us hear what Hegel declares about the Idea and the state:

> [E]verything turns on grasping and expressing the True, not only as *Substance*, but equally as *Subject* ... the living Substance is being which is in truth *Subject*, or, what is the same, is in truth actual only in so far as it is the movement of positing itself ... Thus the life of God and divine cognition may well be spoken of as a disporting of Love with itself; but this idea sinks into mere edification, and even insipidity, if it lacks the seriousness, the suffering, the patience, and the labour of the negative.[22]

Is there not something ominous and disturbing in this passage from the *Phenomenology*? What exactly is this seriousness, the labour of the negative? As opposed to the second negation in Engels and Marx, which strengthens the first and completes its work, the Hegelian negative seems to deny negation, to reject it into appearance (with contradiction and dialectic). It works in the positive, seeking a certain result. But what should we say of this passage from the *Philosophy of Right*: 'Individuality ... manifests itself here in the state as a relation to other states ... This autonomy embodies mind's actual awareness of itself as a unit and hence it is the most fundamental freedom which a people possesses and its highest dignity.' This is therefore the moral (ethical)

---

22 *Phenomenology*, paras 17–19.

moment of war. 'It is the moment wherein the substance of the state . . .
makes the nullity of these finite things [life, property, and their rights]
an accomplished fact' (paras 322–3).

No, Hegel did not clearly discern what is disturbing in these declarations. A century and a half of political experience casts a different light
on them from what they have in his conception.

6) The state, in major countries (major in terms of their strength, the
smaller ones eagerly following in their wake), has become so complex
that its protagonists – high officials and political leaders – no longer
have cognition of it. Their entourage of advisers (public or private)
suffers a division of labour, which can be inconvenient for knowledge
and domination of the 'all'. This political summit and its surrounds, in
the Hegelian model, are supposed to *cognize* the whole and consequently
understand the conflicts and contradictions of the ensemble in order to
bring a solution to these sooner or later. Can they still do this? If they
rule it, is this not from afar and too high?

It is hard therefore to say whether the modern state conforms to the
Hegelian stereotype or differs from it, so that this model only retains its
interest as an 'ideal type', even just a 'brand image'. What is hard to deny,
however, is that the state, almost everywhere, has monopolized or tried
to monopolize its entire space in order to control it, and likewise knowledge, to use this as a means of both management and controlled integration of the parts and elements of the political ensemble. We know that
capitalism and the state based on this mode of production have absorbed
pre-capitalist formations (agriculture, the life of the towns) and institutions (universities, courts), not forgetting the extensions of capitalism
(leisure, housing), largely by using knowledge (information, the
so-called human sciences).

If legal aspects have been modified, and there is now a right to work,
to trade unions, rights that are more or less codified (those of children,
women, old people, tenants, 'users', etc.), we know that the fundamental
principles, the very ones that enabled this codification, have not changed
in the capitalist countries, and especially not in France: the right to
property, the rules of inheritance and transmission of assets. Besides,
these *rights* have as their counterpart the competence of the state in
sectors and domains that formerly escaped it. By introducing these
possibilities of conflict, the different rights and new institutions have

extended the state's capacity for intervention. Such interventions, whether sporadic or total, have constantly grown, and the improvements to the contractual system, apparent or real, have not diminished the omnipresence and (supposed) omniscience of the state. On the contrary. It turns out that politicians, including those of the bourgeois state in capitalist society, have assimilated the *theory of growth*, glimpsed by Hegel and elaborated by Marx. Hegelians without knowing it, or even sometimes knowing it, have understood to a large extent the *conditions* for growth, in particular the indispensable *objects* (capital, technology, investment) and the necessary *activities* (studies of opinions, markets and investments, motivations – orientation or planning). They have gone so far on this road as to adopt without further examination the theory of infinite growth (demographic, economic, technological, scientific, cultural) for each nation-state, even when objections and obstacles, and debts that fall due, pile up on the global scale.

The state, as a consequence, *misunderstands knowledge* by absorbing it and becoming an *ideological power*. Religion often, and morality always, serve to dissimulate the projects pursued by politicians. This use of ideology cannot conceal the other aspects of state power: its stranglehold on space and knowledge (the institutionalization of both of these). The 'ideological apparatuses' of the state explain nothing by themselves. The use of ideology indicates contradictions in a nascent or developed state within knowledge, cognition and ideology; the result being that the Hegelian *brand image* no longer corresponds to the state reality, without going so far as to contradict itself, since morality (ethics) is as much part of the Hegelian construction as is law.

The ideological power of the state enables it to capture and divert certain important aspects of cognition (information, which is not the same thing, and identification of these aspects, which constitutes an ideology). And this in the manner of propaganda and advertising. A new Holy Trinity emerges: knowledge, constraint, ideology. The state, by controlling and distributing information, betrays the knowledge that legitimizes it in the Hegelian model. New categories are needed for it, those of Marxism – as we shall go on to see.

The great strength of Hegelianism, the advantage it has over other philosophies that seek to be scientifically (epistemologically) based, is to have explained what we can call the rise of the modern world towards abstraction – a development whose full scope remains to be understood.

For Hegel, logos (language, images and metaphors, at the level of common sense and understanding, then elaborated concepts and theories) oversees and organizes this transformation. This 'world' diverges from nature and the natural, from immediacy and spontaneity – irremediably so. And this movement defines a degree of freedom, or better still, the rational freedom of the *zoon politikon*.

Marx would go further in this direction, by analysing, in the wake of the English economists, how and why objects themselves, as products of labour, acquire an *abstract* existence as exchangeable. The good destined for exchange, the commodity, temporarily loses its material existence. Suspended in this way, it gives way to an abstraction: evaluation in money.

Marx pressed further than Hegel the critical analysis of these *concrete abstractions*. He alone understood the importance of this Hegelian conception, which attributes a mode of existence to the concept, to knowledge, to what is exchanged: products and goods, language and signs. The other Hegelians searched on the side of the *subject* and '*self-consciousness*'. Combining the critique of abstract philosophy with that of a political economy which accepted and enumerated facts and observations, Marx counted among these concrete abstractions labour itself, viewed globally as *average social labour*. These abstractions, like money, have a concrete existence because they govern social relations – despite being concealed beneath the appearances of materiality and immediacy. They determine the mode of existence of these, since relationships cannot possess the same reality as things or substances. As Hegel understood, these abstractions are *forms*, endowed with an effectiveness in relationships in the same way as are the logical forms of calculation and language.

Things immediately given (needs, activities) become abstractions by becoming social entities and means.

A general movement, 'from bottom to top', thus presses the ensemble towards abstraction. Evidence or proof of this is given by the effectively growing role of social knowledge (particularly mathematical knowledge) and by contracts, an elaborated legal form – written rights that lay down reciprocal commitments for the respective parties. Moreover, with finance capital that is predominant today, money attains a kind of second-degree abstraction. It tends to detach itself still further from the material object of production, from commodities, from buying and

selling, to become money that produces and reproduces itself in speculation (which some people express by saying that the *sign* acquires
greater importance than the 'real').

True, but when Marx extended and deepened the Hegelian conception in this way, he reached a conclusion incompatible with Hegelianism:
the state itself is a *concrete abstraction*. It possesses neither the existence
of a subject nor that of a substance. It is not sufficient unto itself, and
perhaps not even necessary. It also demands a foundation. The summit
does not hold up without a support, without a base. When Hegel assumes
that knowledge-power holds the social ensemble together, like the
closed fist holds a net, he is way off course. There are no relations without supports; but after Hegel, and even after Marx, the question of
support remains open. It is hard to accept, as do positivists and empiri-
cist logicians, the existence of relationships without supports, as if it was
enough for a relationship to be given mathematical form, $y = f(x)$, for it
to become entirely visible. This alignment of social existence to physical
existence, and of the latter to mathematical existence – abstraction in its
pure state – dissolves differences between reality and cognition without
establishing a real unity, except by reduction. When Hegel attributes
existence and action to the concept (to knowledge), he is trying to speak
of *concrete abstraction*; but he leaves the idea in mid-air, attaching it to
the celestial transcendence of the Idea. As for Marx, he gives it practice
as its support, which is certainly correct, yet insufficient. How does
immediate practice change into mediation? How does it bear abstraction without losing its effectiveness? What is the relationship between
practice and *logic* (form)?

To state right away our general conclusion, we will repeat a hypothesis put forward elsewhere: the support of social relations is space. We
understand by this not epistemological, logico-mathematical space, nor
the mental space of common sense and everyday discourse, but rather
social space, as this is elaborated and constructed practically by different
societies in the course of their genesis.[23] The most abstract finance capital, that of multinational corporations, cannot dispense with *sites*: of
registration and documents, investment, transfer between national
currencies, etc. It is not completely distinct from flows attaching to
terrains and territories, and yet, beyond the world of commodities,

23   Henri Lefebvre, *The Production of Space*, Oxford: Blackwell, 1991.

beyond production, even beyond signs themselves, it attains a second-degree abstraction, all the more disturbing and ominous in that it can seize on a strategically chosen site, either for investment or for political overthrow (reactionary and fascist). This obscures the theoretical problem: the planet lives under the stormy clouds of concrete abstraction, in the shadow of recent forms of finance capital, both opaque like substances and supra-real like concepts; and without agreement between nation-states, even in conflict with them. At this level the attachment of money (capital) to materiality, to production itself, is no more than sporadic (in philosophical terms, both necessary and yet contingent). It gives way to another attachment, that of the money-abstraction to its actualization: the *will to power*. The globalization of economics and politics has taken these strange forms, unforeseeable in Hegel's time, unintelligible in terms of his categories, and yet extending these. Hegel believed and said that he thought *weltgeschichtlich* – at the level of world history. Was he wrong? No. He constructed the most general concepts, he forged the keys to modernity. Was he right? No, as the future did not happen as he had predicted, and to understand it we have to draw on Marx, and also, paradoxically, on Nietzsche, analyst of the will to power.

7) Analysis and explanation can now go further than the statist critique of the (Hegelian) state. That critique was content to say: 'No, the personnel in power, bureaucrats, technocrats, high officials, "decision-makers" – all these people are not really familiar with the social ensemble. The instances that exist today, in the "real", possess neither the vocabulary, nor the concepts, nor the theory that is needed. So, let us replace them by new people who will know.'

The modern state is no longer Hegelian, in the sense that there is a *division of power*. Not in a sense that would vindicate Montesquieu against Hegel, with various powers (a triad, naturally: legislative, executive, judiciary) denouncing and pronouncing against the unitary Power and sovereign instance at the summit. Certainly not in this sense, as another triad has appeared on the scene in the last ten or fifteen years. Power, with capital sometimes below it but more often above it, is divided between the military, politicians and technocrats. Since Hegel's time, the political class has lost its assigned place: priority in the edifice and its property, homogeneous rationality. How rapidly it has disappeared, this famous rational unity between (public) power and law! And what should we think of the no less rational unity that Hegel describes between justice and morality? The least that can be said is that the unity has becomes conflictual. Paradoxically – in other words, contradictorily – politics as such is devalued as the master key to the building, but is given greater value on the strategic level, that of decision-making.

The political machines that political professionals run are themselves diversified: parties and apparatuses. They speak; they secrete ideology, rhetorical discourse. They manipulate, possessing the means required. They manoeuvre according to the needs of a political interest, that of an apparatus, itself bound up with a class or a fraction of a class, a group that has a certain weight. Politicians are supposed to decide: they correspond to the executive power. In fact, they either execute one another, or they execute their opponents. The 'decision-makers' settle matters: situations and heads. It is not always politicians that decide, they make use of 'decision-makers', straw men, back-ups. Sometimes verbally, sometimes materially: too many political corpses to count.

The technocrats correspond to the Hegelian portrait of a 'stratum' that emerges from the middle class, selectively recruited by way of competition (examinations, degrees), who in this way gain knowledge (competence and performance) and power. However, co-optation tends to replace selection. If the 'competent' and the 'experts' manage the nation like a big firm, nothing guarantees the disinterestedness that Hegel believed. The 'cursus honorum' is not enough to satisfy individuals. Virtue and competence do not necessarily go together, and today the Hegelian would be seen as naïve. The technocrats also seek instruments of power. If money leads to power, sometimes the knowledge that leads to power also leads to money. They also divide and multiply (or, if you prefer, they multiply by dividing, by generating a hierarchy). There are bureaucrats, middle and top executives, and finally managers – those close to people who have both money and power, who decide strategically. This trilogy does not function without frictions. So much so that almost everywhere the military await the occasion, the moment, when knowledge, wealth and power (the power of politicians) weaken, to replace it with power in the raw sense: violence. With the result that the answer to the enigma, the puzzle and the mystery of this construction that appears rational is not to be found in transcendental logos, the Idea, but in violence, latent or unveiled. The army, stuffed with explosives, bedecked with killing machines and explosive in itself, has more need to kill than a male full of sperm has to ejaculate. Will submission to uniform and dictatorship last a long time? No state is without its army, which prefers civil war to foreign – internal contradictions apart. When the violence presided over by the state is unleashed, waged rationally with military procedures, it goes as far as genocide. And here we are still further from Hegelian rationality.

The nation-state today exists only in the context of global strategies. These strategies are multiple: those of the most powerful states, but also those of multinational corporations, those of energy (oil, nuclear), etc. A nation-state is today simply a more or less important piece on the planetary chessboard. Hence the increased importance of national territory (space). This figures in the international division of labour. Its importance is a function of its resources, in other words, its particularities; it is the stake (objective or target) of tactical and strategic operations. At the same time, a nation-state is of no importance taken in isolation. How can it be seen, as Hegel did, as the figure and embodiment of the universal? How can the result of an often mediocre history be honoured with this status? Not every state has ten or twenty centuries of wars behind it.

Rationality takes on a different guise and form when situated in the global context of strategies: virtual violence at every level, multiple risks, settlement dates that are closer or less close.

Was Hegel right? Yes, when he showed the nation-state as a being, giant or dwarf, struggling for its life. No, when he placed this existence under the sign of absolute reason.

We could conclude that the re-production of moments, that is, of constitutive relations, does not attain and will never attain within the state the automatism dreamed of by Hegel in his rational raving. But perhaps it is still too soon to draw a conclusion.

8) The affinity that political reflection traces between state capitalism and state socialism reveals the great poverty of such reflection: a dubious method that highlights homologies and analogies instead of seeking to bring out the differences. State capitalism and state socialism differ, like all particular societies (and nation-states), in the context of their particular mode of production. Here a classification of Hegelian origin is appropriate: temporary singularities and lasting particularities have their place, then general categories, and finally, if there is need to appeal

to these, universals. To make this clear: the singular features of peoples and ethnicities, the history of each nation, its characteristics of social and spatial origin (geographic, geopolitical), the specific moments of its state, then the mode of production, a general determination, and finally the legal and formal relations, a universal aspect of every society.

State capitalism and state socialism have a common aim and interest: growth. In both cases, political leaders have maintained against all objections the assumption of infinite growth. A remarkable assumption that for them has the certainty of scientific knowledge. They obtain the growth made immediately possible by different procedures, bound up with the differences, particularities and specificities signalled above. State capitalism gives the big firms their head; in the extreme case, the state plays just an advisory role, their databank, placing knowledge and information at their service. But the rulers of the (capitalist) state are permanently in a difficult position, caught between national and multi-national firms, small and giant industry, commerce at every level and size, money and credit, etc.

State socialism has no hesitation in centralizing and planning by authoritarian means. It is closer to Hegel's 'great machine', except that it functions neither automatically nor in a satisfactory manner. Neither the knowledge of its rulers, nor that of their advisers, covers the totality – even with the aid of calculating machines, whose support for the 'great machine' is certainly not negligible.

And here is the caricature side of the situation, familiar to everyone but whose comic aspect few appreciate. On the capitalist side, the economy is in the driving seat, constantly under threat but up to now (1973) free of global crisis. On the so-called 'socialist' side, politics is alone in the driving seat. One surprising paradox among others is that Marx, appealed to by this side, had proclaimed the opposite. What is working well? Political life? No. Life is lacking. Everything works through politics, but without life. Is there ever political life that is neither caricature nor in opposition?

On both sides, capitalist and socialist, social life has disappeared, crushed between economics and politics, the former predominant here and the latter there: an enormous void, filled by everyday life, the family, so-called 'private' relationships, i.e. deprived of scope, deprived of creative capacity. A situation that conforms to the Hegelian model, which misunderstands the moment of specifically social relations and subordinates these to political rationality and economic management, with the result that these relations are impoverished and reduced to the family and everyday life, to morality and law. A constricted 'lived experience', in brackets, vegetates in the shadow of the state.

Hegelians, whether conscious or not, for whom their model of the state represents a position of balance between the excesses and defects of public authority – these same Hegelians may claim that their model also represents the common measure (the highest common factor) between that state of advanced state capitalism and that of socialism in the course of economic growth.

Shall we please them by noting other common moments: the importance of the police and bureaucracy, 'culture' given official status as ideology, crass quantitativism, growth without development of social relations, the destruction of differences?

9) The Hegelian model sins not by ignorance but by misunderstanding social classes. It is a further paradox that it should have endured despite this deficiency, maintaining prestige and influence despite (or perhaps, because of) Marxist critique. A certain recent book, ambitious and already outdated, would provide a certain satisfaction for the ironist if read in the doubtful light of its Hegelian reference.[24] Very likely, so-called Marxist critique, still in an embryonic state with Marx himself, has committed some serious mistakes. It has even misunderstood the Hegelian model, its import, its restricted yet powerful rationality. A certain left (or, if you like, 'leftist') critique mixes up and confuses everything – reaction, fascism, authoritarianism, liberalism, military intervention – under the simplifying labels of class dictatorship, violence, power. To the political schema diffused by bourgeois ideology, which presents the state as 'neutral' (which very poorly corresponds to Hegel's theoretical model), the oppositional ideology replies with polemics: class justice, class teaching, class science, etc. – in a word, dictatorship. The concept of *hegemony* attenuates and completes what is rather too summary in the concept of dictatorship (of the bourgeoisie). There is a *hegemony* of the economically dominant class, which means that this acts and struggles to control the entire society, to shape it according to its needs. The bourgeoisie has the bases of its domination in firms

---

24 C. Alphandery et al., *Pour nationaliser l'État*, Paris: Éditions du Seuil, 1968.

(production) and the market (which it is ever more familiar with, as this is dependent on it and its strategy). Now, a society, with the social relations it implies, is reducible neither to economics or politics. In a society, there are public services: education and teaching, justice, medicine. There is the organization of knowledge, and its transmission and use. The various aspects and moments of social life date from pre-capitalist times, uninterrupted by any sudden break. In modern society, there is also urban life, and the complex relationship between town and country, nature.

The bourgeoisie struggles for its hegemony, that is, to mark with its imprint and bend to its use these moments of social relations, of practice and social life. It succeeds in this only with difficulty. Its class struggle extends to the totality, far beyond the economy, the firm or questions of wages. The social ensemble is not 'embourgeoisified' in advance, prefabricated by capitalism. And the state? A means, as much and more so than an end, an instrument rather than a pinnacle, this permits the management of the *social surplus product*, that substantial part of surplus value (in non-Marxist terms, of the national income) that goes to various 'services', to society as such.

For Hegel, this management, this extension of the state to the whole of society, is taken for granted; these are integral and integrating parts of the concept of the state. A serious mistake? Only up to a point. In fact, this mistake is made even by a large section of politicians, including those coming from the economically dominant class and representing this politically. For them, power is sufficient. They tend to neglect the hegemonic role, despite this being assigned to them by their class. This was the folly of the French bourgeoisie for a long period: to despise knowledge and almost systematically erode the 'funds' required for the general management of society (except in relation to some preferential sectors: e.g. roads and primary schools for the Third Republic).

Analysis of modernity from the Hegelian point of view refutes both the full and complete rationality of this model and the opposite point of view of a dictatorial absurdity maintained simply by violence. Conducted correctly, this critical analysis starts from an examination of *social management*. The hegemonic class does not by a long way do just what it would like to do, as everyday life and lived experience partly escape it, dominated and impoverished as they might be. It is also limited even politically by the democracy that it had itself established. How does it distribute the surplus product that the state disposes of? By what channels? Whom does it favour? For what purpose, and by what tactic? And what exactly escapes it? Along with lived experience and everyday life, sex, pleasure and love escape this political undertaking. And so does everything that is defined as offence, crime or madness (drug use, forbidden gambling). Then there is poetry, music and theatre, in other words, art (to the extent that they create something new, artists escape the grip of the state, the institutional net). In other words, the errant and aberrant, the anomic, with the underlying paradox of a genuine autonomy within hegemony: only the anomic, the aberrant, has a creative capacity. Lived experience is repressed and falls into unconsciousness, from which it again rebels. It beats its path in the shadow, and if it can, breaks out by 'inventing', 'creating'. The analyst may despair at comparing the power of the state, its hegemonic capacities, with the weakness of what escapes it. And yet, the slightest breach and smallest crack compromise the solidity of the edifice, a fragility familiar to skilled politicians, and to their henchmen in the police, who pursue certain 'offences' as significant (men with long hair!). The state eradicates what it can do without, but what *society* finds it hard to do without, and what *civilization* absolutely cannot.

A remarkable accident or revelation of a higher rationality? A 'something' of growing importance, possible even decisive, increasingly escapes the hegemonic omniscience and omnipresence of the state. What? An irrationality, as some people believe? No: *space*. Too complex: too many people and places and things. Yet nothing is more 'normal', more 'essential', in short, more 'rational'.

Here again, we lay our cards on the table rather than maintain suspense: space introduces a contradiction within the edifice, in other words, more than a fissure, and different from a challenge to state-political rationalism by the irrational. Despite the efforts of technicians and technocrats, there is a risk of knowledge rapidly escaping the administrative and political apparatuses of the state, as far as space is concerned.

10) Hegel described the ennui resulting from the satisfaction of needs that have found without too great effort the object they require, of functions that correctly proceed towards their goal, of duty accomplished. He showed the mechanism by which each satisfaction is matched by a

malaise. Removed from the immediacy of natural desire, needs become increasingly artificial (abstract). To each need corresponds an object. By consuming the object, by destroying it, need destroys itself. Hence a void that is filled by another need, in turn provoking another void. What emerges is simply the system of needs. Hegel analysed the malaise, though without detecting its bourgeois guise. He 'proved' the importance of the system of needs, to a point that we may wonder whether philosophy does not conceal a diabolical *libido dominandi* – or whether *libido sciendi* does not provide a satisfaction superior to all other pleasures. What irony! The theorist of the state already announced and denounced in advance the deadly ennui: grey on grey, twilight, gloomy and cold. He embodied it in the pedantry of the philosopher – a functionary who utters philosophical discourse in the manner of the Lenten sermons of the Middle Ages: a public service.

This is what Hegel did not say: the state sullies, kills, destroys everything it touches; everything that does not manage to escape. Nothing can resist it, neither talent, nor spontaneity, nor style. Its hygiene well conceals its pollution, but prevents fertility (which the state reserves for its subjects, women). The market in cognition or art has more than one disagreeable side; it does not sterilize in the way that the state does, by the award of niggardly grants. For Hegel, the state perfects the creative capacity of knowledge; infinite in the finite, it brings time to an end by establishing itself in space. On the contrary: the state kills whatever tries to go further, and space overflows its competence, finite by essence, which thus meets its end and the principle of its self-destruction. However, we should guard against attributing it an absolute originality. Before the philosophico-political state, was there not the theologico-political state, which has left its traces? In Rome, the pontifical state oversaw a deadly ennui for centuries, a legitimized barbarism that was already countered by the art of the baroque, the strange, the informal – surrealism, non-realism or hyper-realism before the name.

The crumbling and collapse of the modern edifice may bring about that of civilization and 'culture', society and science, and increasingly the planet itself. With the result that the self-destruction of the doomed state leads to the end of the earth and the death of the human species. In this respect, the present situation has an unprecedented seriousness – an almost absolute originality – inconceivable in historical terms.

11) Nothing happens simply. Hegel described in detail the unifying movement of 'knowledge-power', emphasizing the domination of power over knowledge, the stranglehold of the political state over cognition and science. This movement runs from within to without, from the centre to the periphery. But an opposite movement also exists: knowledge demands its participation, its integration into the mechanisms and apparatuses of power.

Kernels of acquired knowledge, tied by connections at first hypothetical, then consolidated, gain official status by becoming institutionalized. This takes place in two ways: programmes and programming – philosophical consecration of the gains, epistemology. When the philosopher accepts servitude, when he becomes a functionary and bureaucrat in exchange for paltry honours, philosophy surrenders to political domination. But what does it offer? Knowledge. In other words, philosophico-political logos may find allies and accomplices even among the possessors of knowledge. Strategic projects to institutionalize knowledge involve academic organization as well as the official predominance of a particular 'discipline' that provides the central core: formerly history, then political economy, and more recently linguistics, the innovative character of these 'disciplines' having only a ceremonial and decorative role.

By their very failure, these attempts have revealed their political meaning: to align 'spiritual' production and that of 'spirits' with the re-production of socio-political relations and the production of things (objects and goods), with a view to rationally 'totalizing' the ensemble in a self-regulated (automatic) production according to a simple model, with political control over cognition and 'culture' as well as education and teaching. If state power makes a grab for knowledge, a certain knowledge is defined by acceptance of this stranglehold, an acceptance that may see itself as 'free' because it is voluntary – in the name of logos and logic. Any partial science that would be axial and central, and the science of discourse above all, continues Hegelian logos or seeks to rescue it.

12) The Hegelian fetishizing of the concept sets this up as the unalterable core of knowledge, the centre of practical power, hence of constraint and violence (justified by knowledge: concepts fight, because flesh-and-blood men fight by using them).

With Hegelianism, Western logos thus reaches a point of both fulfil-
ment and fall. This is not sufficient reason to cast the concept into the
dustbin of history. The formal opposition of the 'conceived' to lived
experience (*le 'conçu' au 'vécu'*), the evacuation of the '*vécu*' by the
'*conçu*', may collapse, and the concept regain its place; there is a concept
of the '*vécu*' as such. The content of the concept differs from its (logical)
form, with the result that it may denote this difference instead of reducing it.

The situation is reversed when Marx appears on the stage. On the
other hand, if the opposition is seen as irreducible, if the '*vécu*' and the
'*conçu*' are incompatible and there is anyone willing to lead a rebellion
of the one against the other, it is Nietzsche.

Before tackling these dramatic scenes, the preceding analyses can be
reduced to a terminological distinction. Against Hegel's unitary (totalizing) conception, we can discern, in the site and place of the (tautologi-
cal) circle that defines knowledge by the real and the real by
knowledge:

a) *Knowledge*: institutional, official, consecrated as an assured gain (by
epistemology), and thus frozen and fixed, logicized, pedagogized,
purchasable and saleable, ever threatened with 'recycling', always on the
edge of falling into the abyss of the past/depassed;[25] a strange mixed
state between being, becoming, nothingness . . .

b) *Cognition*, a process, including the *critical moment* (critical of society,
ideology and knowledge itself), aiming – either immediately or through
mediation – at their ensemble (a totality), thus extending philosophy by
extracting itself with difficulty from ideologies, by linking up with a
practice, thus as metaphilosophy. A Promethean situation. With the
result that theoretical cognition does not claim to be sufficient, though
not ceasing to see itself as necessary. It thus becomes the site of a combat.

c) *Science*, or rather *the sciences*, specialized disciplines, hence partial
but operative, forming part of the division of labour and thus the market

---

25 [In common with other French writers, Lefebvre uses *dépasser* to translate the
Hegelian *aufheben*, which combines the senses of abolishing and preserving. 'Supersede' is
often used in English, but Lefebvre's *passé/dépassé* needs preserving here. – Translator.]

for knowledge – in a state of apparent security, yet actually involved in a process of unequal birth and uneven development, sometimes in a position of priority with imperialist pretensions, sometimes in decline and subordinated.

3

The Marx File

_____

1) Hegel sought to attain, and believed he had attained, the objective of every philosopher since Aristotle, the aim of all philosophy: the perfect system. A completed and thus closed ensemble, encompassing the whole world: cohesion and coherence, thus column, pillar, axis – the precise terms and the metaphors both say one and the same thing. Dogmatism, pedantry, a ponderous spirit – these severe words also say the same thing. And yet genius, if this word still has a meaning . . .

It was enough for the Hegel file to retrace the profile of Hegelianism, as this had itself been changed by a century and a half of posterity. If we were to go into the detail of its 'influence', long volumes would not be sufficient. To a large extent, Marx and Marxism would figure in this file. The reader would find both Bismarck and Lassalle, the vaguely rational French evolutionism of the nineteenth century (after Victor Cousin, Renan and Taine), and Italian historicism (Croce). As for those who were Hegelians without knowing it, the file would never be complete, as it would have to contain statesmen of all kinds.

Only one point has real importance. The system-bloc had to persevere in its dogmatic being, or collapse at a single blow. Now, Hegelianism, like any system or supposed system, crumbled and fragmented after Hegel himself. This process brought to light lines of cleavage, fissures in the edifice that were initially invisible. Pan-logicism and pan-historicism were products of fragmentation, since they indicated right away a lack of harmony between these moments. Coherence and contradiction, succession and simultaneity, becoming and spatial coexistence, logic and dialectic, were never really connected in the apparently monolithic system. Later philosophy sought in vain, after the death of the supreme philosopher, another way (a third way, we could say) beyond this paradigm of highly pertinent oppositions, by the intervention of a third term, consciousness; this was postulated as a unitary existence in place of the Idea; it was supposed to contain both a logic and a history, an objectivity and a subjectivity. In this specifically philosophical posterity, the political (whether reflection or practice) was of little account. Hegelianism followed the fate of the philosophies it believed it had united and superseded by realizing them: a speculation disconnected from practice. Our Hegel file here deliberately omitted the history of Hegelianism. Why? In order to proceed to a confrontation between the Hegelian statue of the state and the reality of the modern state. Without further delay.

Is the same procedure applicable to Marx? Probably not. First of all, because there is no such thing as 'Marxism', whereas the existence of Hegelianism is undeniable. Contrary to even the most widespread opinion, 'Marxism' was invented by 'Marxists' who looked for a system in the thought and work of Marx (materialism, economism, theory of history, theory of determinism and freedom, etc.), and proceeded to invent one. Though Marx's thought is in no way incoherent and disparate, it does not have the form of a system. It broke with what went before, without opposing one body of doctrine to others. The philosophical works of the 'young Marx' are no less important than the economic works of his maturity or the political works of his last years. It has been said that the concept of *alienation*, which Marx borrowed from Hegelianism and which inspired the works of his youth, does not possess a 'theoretical status'. That is perfectly true: this philosophical concept hangs in mid-air once detached from the Hegelian architecture. And yet, it is a sign of supreme pedantry to reject it on these grounds and refuse it the status of a concept. It has a *social status*, not an *epistemological* one. It has played a remarkably fermenting role, inexhaustibly fertile, in the cognition ('taking consciousness' as is misguidedly said today) of practical conditions – those of workers, of women, of young people, of the colonized (and the colonizers). Do we need to go on? If this fertility is exhausted, that is not sufficient reason to misunderstand it. Marx revealed in his own fashion, in practical conditions, in the '*vécu*' of lived experience, a misunderstood triad: exploitation, oppression, humiliation. These three terms go together, while remaining distinct. They form part of the designation and connotation of a single term: alienation.

The concepts of surplus value and surplus product have a scientific and hence epistemological status; they form part of acquired knowledge. True, but they pertain to economics, a particular science; and besides, no one makes the concept of surplus value a matter of life and death, whereas countless human beings have fought, and still fight, against humiliation and oppression, which are the ways they experience exploitation.

Second, Marx's theoretical projects remained incomplete and imperfect. His so-called philosophical works do not contain a philosophy, or another 'model' of theoretical elaboration, but rather a project, that of superseding philosophy. His economic studies on accumulation, limited to England, do not give a full understanding of the cumulative process (despite revealing the concept of this, clearly distinguishing the accumulation of capital from the Hegelian accumulation of knowledge). *Capital* and its preparatory texts and appendices come to an end, unfinished, at the point where Marx draws a picture of capitalist society, with its multiple classes, class fractions and social strata grouped between and around the two poles of proletariat and bourgeoisie – agriculturalists, artisans, traders, landed proprietors, etc. At the point of transition to the concrete, to social practice, the exposition is broken off. As for the state, Marx said and repeated before Lenin that this was the key problem, the essential question. The sum total of his works contains only a sketch of a theory of the state. In the course of successive trials, by way of polemics and pamphlets (such as *The Eighteenth Brumaire of Louis Bonaparte*, 1852), a single trenchant assertion is repeated: the state must be destroyed (and not exalted and consolidated in the tradition of Hegel). How to realize this strategic objective, how to bring to reality the anticipating vision (concrete utopia) of a society freed from its oppressive state overlay? Throughout his life, as we shall go on to see, Marx sought the means, stages, moments of this action that defined the revolution. Neither the anarchistic trashing of existing reality, nor a superseding effected within the liberal bourgeois state, nor a '*vécu*' transcending rationality, humanism and liberalism, would achieve this result. It could only be projected on a different path, that of a multifarious struggle, polyvalent rather than simply economic, or simply ideological and theoretical.

Third, this incomplete, broken, imperfect character of Marx's thought paradoxically explains 'Marxism' and its successes. Collections of texts, more or less cleverly selected and fitted together, gave the appearance of an original thought, a doctrine attributed to Marx. These successive 'systems' serve as alibis and masks. In the wake of Lassalle, and along with many others, Stalin called himself a Marxist and effectively bent Marx's words and concepts to his own use; he replaced the Marxist critique of the state, reprised and emphasized by Lenin in *The State and Revolution*, with a super-Hegelianism, an unconditional apologia for the state, a theory of its strengthening. Hegelian logic was in full operation in Stalinist ideology and the practical construction of a system that imprisoned those who tried to escape from it. At the opposite extreme from this conception, Georg Lukács constructed his personal 'assemblage' of Marxist texts with a view to drawing from them a speculative historicism, uselessly open to the possible (*History and Class Consciousness*). Historicism, economism, theory of productivity and planning, theories of determinism (economic, historical, sociological), thus used Marx's texts and twisted them into a different meaning, that of an era, a country, a school or a 'thinker'.

Does this mean that we should reduce Marx to the dimensions of a brilliant essayist? No. His texts contain more than exciting suggestions, and something other than a system. What they contain is better: a vocabulary, a terminology, a *language* (as many eminent minds would say) different from current language and everyday discourse, yet unlike the discourses developed by specialists (economists, historians, sociologists, etc.) or philosophers. It is very different to speak of 'surplus value' rather than 'profit'. Marx described, analysed and explained existing society differently from how it perceives and conceives itself, the way it lives without understanding itself. The terms and terminology he used put an end to the customary representations, stereotypes, verbiage, background noises and accompaniments of this political-economic reality. Marx was not content with words; he pursued them to the level of *concepts*, and assembled these into *theories*. Why did he not complete any of the theoretical constructions he undertook? Lack of time? Lack of material? Lack of method? No. Understanding aims to attain 'an all', or even 'the All'. But the All slips from reach. The *critical moment*, intervening both in (against) the constructions under way and against (in) the object of cognition, shatters the edifice before it is complete. The real changes during the analysis. By the time of synthesis it has already changed. A scrupulous exposition can only proceed cautiously by signalling the way, showing the horizon. And so, by twisting his thought and assembling his texts, many 'Marxists' have even used Marx's own language: a different language from the everyday discourses of the bourgeoisie's scholars and 'thinkers'.

As a young man, still almost adolescent, Karl Marx criticized Hegel for his 'grotesque craggy melody' (letter to his father, 1837); and yet he 'dived into the sea' of Hegel's philosophy. Sensing that Hegelian doctrine was based only on postulates and presuppositions, he then wrote a long dialogue, proceeding to a 'philosophical-dialectical account of divinity, as it manifests itself as the idea-in-itself, as religion, as nature, and as history. My last proposition was the beginning of the Hegelian system'.[1] Shortly after, Marx began to 'turn upside down' the world in which the idea precedes the real and the divinity is incarnated in nature and history. He directly attacked Hegel's philosophy of right and the state (1842–4). Hegelianism holds a prominent position in *The German Ideology* (1845), in which Marx, impelled by Engels, threw the whole of philosophy overboard, seen as ideology. This raised serious questions, for example concerning the concept of truth elaborated by philosophers. In *The Poverty of Philosophy* this condemnation excludes the Hegelian dialectic itself, apropos its first popularization in France by Proudhon. Then a long silence. In 1857, working on capitalism and capital, Marx took up Hegelian logic and dialectic. In 1867, when Hegel's influence in Germany had fallen to the point that he was seen as a 'dead dog', Marx 'coquettishly' used dialectic in *Capital* as a method of investigation, analysis and explanation. In 1875 against Lassalle, as with his writings on the Paris Commune, he renewed with doubled force his attack on the Hegelian theory of the state.

It would be possible to publish certain works by Marx (for example, the *1844 Manuscripts*) setting opposite one another Hegel's paragraphs and their critique by Marx, as Marx himself did apropos Hegel's philosophy of the state. This would illustrate textually the dramatic image of

---

1 'Letter From Marx to His Father', *Marx Engels Collected Works*, vol. 1, London: Lawrence & Wishart, 1975, p. 18.

perpetual struggle. In a famous fragment that openly had in mind Adam Smith and economic productivism, Marx wrote that 'the criminal produces crimes', in other words, law, judges, executioners and prisons, as well as detective stories and tragedies that punctuate for a moment the deadly ennui of bourgeois society and the state. Did he not surreptitiously have Hegel himself in mind, and his theory of the self-production (of 'man' and the state) by knowledge?

It follows that Marxism coincides only very little with the history of Marxism, a moment of a history that differs greatly from that which Hegel cognized and theorized, to the point that it is perhaps no longer a 'history' in the accepted sense of this concept. Paradoxically. (How many paradoxes have we not already encountered on this journey? Does it have to be repeated that 'paradox' means a contradiction that is misconstrued, stifled, blunted?)

Marx waged a titanic struggle against (with) Hegel, like that of Hercules and Antaeus in the Greek myth. He seized from Hegel the materials (categories and concepts, themes and problems) for his systematic elaboration, first taken apart and then used fragment by fragment. The *guerrillero* Marx, for a long while accompanied only by Engels, then surrounded by uncertain and half-convinced allies ready to betray him (Lassalle), took from Hegelianism weapons that could be turned against it. He took this *material* (procedures, methods, triadic rhythms, reciprocal but poorly elucidated imbrication of logic in dialectic and vice versa), but with a radically different project, based on completely divergent propositions: a different perspective, a different path – and above all a path beyond the Hegelian achievement, that of philosophy, of thought, of history, of man in the state.

After the death of Marx, the struggle continued – the same struggle, on the theoretical level, in cognition, with (against) Hegel and Hegelianism: to turn these weapons against them, and change the arm of criticism into the criticism of arms, in other words, to eradicate from the earth the harsh reality that Hegel presented and re-presented. A strange struggle, seemingly different from the class struggle, yet actually the same. A strange battle: in shadow and against a shadow, but the shadow of a giant, and against a giant in the shadow. Considered carefully, not a moment of this lacked dramatic beauty, that beauty which André Breton, speaking of something quite different, called 'convulsive-frozen'. In the course of the century that has elapsed since then, the diversion of Hegelianism by Marxism has followed its course towards exhaustion. Reversal of theoretical propositions has replaced reversal, in a slow but sure fashion, in the space where the contradiction develops.

It follows from this that the 'Marx file' is initially hard to distinguish from the 'Hegel file', yet it has its distinct features, and even differs from it radically. Another paradox . . .

2) *'Marx is dead.'*[2] This gloomy fact, erected into an ideological and political slogan, would have its place – a cross among other tombs – in the great modern cemetery: death of God, of man, of art, of history, etc. Everything is dying around us, it seems, apart from the state, the only death that Marx explicitly proclaimed.

Marx or Marxism? The death of Marxism has already been announced a hundred times, and the good news is published in the right-minded press, whether by the political right or by a certain leftism, against the political stronghold of an 'orthodoxy' caught between these fires.

Almost half a century ago now, a certain Otto Rühle had his moment of fame by explaining Marx and Marxist thought as a product of liver disease (an explanation recently taken up, or almost so, by certain psychoanalysts: Ricardo was mentally and physically constipated, Marx suffered from diarrhoea and therefore logorrhoea). Soon after Otto Rühle, a Belgian reformist, Henri de Man, had great success with a book on the theme 'Marxism is superseded'. What Marxism? What superseding? The Frankfurt school Marxists, on the other hand, such as [Karl] Korsch, found little audience with work that was far more elaborate. We can leave this alone. Every gravedigger attacks a certain Marxism, that which they find appropriate, and attributes it to Marx: philosophism, (voluntarist) revolutionism, class subjectivism, economism, productivism, etc.

In the same years, the anarcho-syndicalist tendency, deeply rooted in the French working class, openly accused Marx's works, and real or supposed Marxists, of 'dividing the working class'. Spontaneists without having the concept, these anarchists violently attacked theoretical thought; for them, knowledge and cognition, whatever their intentions, came from the bourgeoisie. From an initial general accusation (dividing the working class) they quickly passed to more threatening

---

2 Cf. J. P. Benoist, *Marx est mort*, Paris: Gallimard, 1970.

imprecations: enemy of the people, German thinkers – or inspired by Germany, etc.

If the interpretation of 'Marxism' expressed here, which sums up a long series of previous works, is exact, then 'Marxism' exists only in the form of an interpretation. Not because Marx's thought was 'obscure' or embryonic, but because it proclaimed and proposed projects, instead of asserting, (apparently) confirming the facts and systematizing the accomplished, like Hegelianism. Facts and concepts served Marx for exploring the possible and impossible by way of theory. If he analysed capitalism, if he exposed bourgeois society as a whole, it was to show its caducity. His strategic hypothesis inverted that of Hegel, pertaining as it did to the revolutionary overthrow of the upside-down world, as opposed to the frozen knowledge that seeks to legitimize the world. Like the economic base, social relations and other superstructures, the state is transformed as a function of contradictions and antagonisms that it can neither escape by ideology nor suppress by constraint, nor again resolve by political action within the system. Is this a postulate, a presupposition? Some will say that it is. But what *cognition* is possible without a strategic hypothesis, a starting point, a beginning? By what right can anyone maintain the permanence of a relationship, the imperishableness of a concept, the eternity of a fact?

Two more remarks. The hypothesis of *becoming*, according to which nothing lasts in substance without transformation and leaps, without metamorphoses, was precisely the initial hypothesis of Hegel, taken from Heraclitus (of whom the philosopher says, in his *History of Philosophy*, that 'philosophy begins with Heraclitus') and subsequently dismissed. It was recognized ever since Parmenides that the idea of eternal becoming is not without its difficulties, that it comes up against the observation of definite 'beings', the concept of distinct and (relatively) stable realities; this was how the Eleatics replied to the followers of Heraclitus. For a philosopher who claimed allegiance to Heraclitus to move over to the Eleatic position is a serious mater. When Hegel still thought that with the French Revolution, 'man stood up and built reality with his head, in other words, with his thought', he believed in becoming and in dialectical reversals in the future.[3] Later on, he immediately sterilized and put a stop to becoming. Marx took up the

---

3 *Philosophy of History*, 'Éclaircissement and Revolution'

Heraclitean hypothesis. An underlying philosophy? An assertion not demonstrated and not demonstrable, accepted as such in cognition without explicitly saying so, compromising this and compromised by it? Perhaps, but how to proceed otherwise? A different approach would immediately sterilize thought by preventing the least step forward. The Eleatic school, in the history of philosophy, was unable to maintain its paradox: the arrest of movement for the sake of stability and equilibrium. Does its approach not lead to reducing everything to accounting, recording details, noting facts great and small while accepting the repetition of these facts, the mechanical reproduction of things, the flattening of the real?

More Hegelian than Hegel, and yet profoundly anti-Hegelian – that is how the initial approach of Marx's thought may be defined. But this definition leads on to a general attitude towards facts, findings, even concepts: it becomes procedure, precept of reflection and action: 'Take each and every thing by its changing and perishable side; show that all stability, all equilibrium, all immobility is appearance; emphasize becoming; use the germs of destruction and self-destruction that all reality bears within itself'.

Is there not then a choice, an option, an act of will, at the bottom of this procedure? Yes, in a sense, and Marx opposed himself to Hegel on the basis of this very foundation. In the beginning, there is *action* – '*Am Anfang war die Tat*', in the words of Faust. Marx in no way understood by this a gesture that displaces an object, but an action appropriate to the world: an act, not an idea like the Hegelian Idea. Is this voluntarism or pragmatism? No. Marx's strength is that he shows the logical *coincidence* of this *political* postulate with the imperative of thought and cognition as such. There is no cognition that does not insert the fact in a relationship, that does not integrate the finding in an ensemble, and that thus denies its isolation and envisages its modification, its transformation, its virtual disappearance. This is what Hegel declared of the dialectical method, when he explained it in strict terms. Not without difficulties. In fact, for all thought, all reflection, every act of cognition that is initially an act, a beginning is necessary. And nothing is harder than the beginning, as Hegel declares when he seeks this as far, as 'deeply' and as abstractly as possible: pure sensation (in the *Phenomenology*), pure formal identity (in the *Logic*), pure metaphysical origin (the Idea). When Marx explained capitalism and bourgeois society, he sought the beginning of his presentation as far and as abstractly as Hegel: in the pure form of 'exchange-value', in the commodity in general, in abstract (socially average) labour. But at the start of his critical reflection and his work, the beginning of action and thought, the initial act, are produced *practically*, in other words, *politically*, meaning by this word a terrain on which thought establishes itself and conducts its activity, hence its struggle, which leads to the critical examination of the political itself (of actual politics). Pure philosophy ends in a blind alley. It divides into positivism (fetishism of the fact, the observation) or voluntarism (activity that claims to change the world without cognition of it). Marx's approach avoids the impasse; it does not fall into this dilemma and resolves the problem. At the beginning, there is practice: the act that posits and presupposes that the world can change – because it does change – and that inserts itself in social and political practice in order to guide this change.

In the course of its history, with Hegel and others, philosophy attained the scale and scope of the world. It measured this and its problems. It became global. The philosopher who refuses to confirm the world as it is (in the way that positivism, empiricism and political realism do pragmatically) sees it changing. He wants therefore to *realize* philosophy, conceived as the project of a different world, the perspective and horizon of a higher and truer (human) reality. In what way is this philosopher going to realize philosophy? The philosopher falls silent; powerless, he goes back into himself and sterilely asserts his will. At this point, philosophy comes to an end and is superseded. As a consequence of what? Of the revolutionary postulate that raises cognition and active being to a higher level. A postulate? Yes, and even a political postulate, once again necessary so that the antecedents (philosophy and knowledge) continue to preserve a meaning and an import – and so that there are consequences, even if this continuation differs radically from what went before. 'As the world becomes philosophical, philosophy also becomes worldly . . . its realization is also its loss', Marx wrote in 1839 in his doctoral thesis on the materialism of antiquity.[4]

The inaugural approach of Marx's thought refused and rejected both philosophy en bloc and Hegelianism as a 'compendium' (summary) of

---

4 'Difference Between the Democritean and Epicurean Philosophy of Nature', *Marx/Engels Collected Works*, vol. 1, p. 85.

all philosophy, but at the same time it extended these, carrying them to a higher level. With the result that philosophical concepts, reprised and modified for this purpose, can serve in the transformation of the world, as means rather than ends. The philosophical (epistemological) status of these concepts is thus replaced by a social status, connecting them to practice. The concept of alienation, for example.

Right at his beginning, the beginning of a multiple combat, Marx accused Hegel of *Realpolitik* and almost even positivism (something Hegel detested); but this was to wrest from him the dialectic, giving this back the cutting edge of an offensive weapon. The dialectical approach was turned back against Hegelianism and against philosophy, analysed in its final duplication, determined as a requirement of a metaphilo-sophical superseding.

Marx is dead, they say. But how could such an approach disappear? Its beginning can always be newly resumed, with differences arising from the actual changes in the theoretical and practical situation, changes whose elucidation it makes possible. If there is a choice, it is between the attitude that works to close reality, to confine the accom-plished within its limits, and action that seeks to open, expand, shift these limits and shatter them. The attitude that prohibits movement, philosophically associated with the Eleatics, is expressed in constricting decisions. Such an alternative still retains a full and complete meaning today. Taken as an act that founds a cognition and a being (instead of seeking an origin elsewhere – in the distant past, in a no less distant transcendence), Marx's approach is dateless. In fact and in truth, 'Marxism' does not act in the modern world as a system already here, present like a rock. It acts like a germ, a ferment. This living being trans-forms itself; it spreads germs and ferments that diversify, that die or degenerate here or there, but prosper elsewhere.

3) Croaks are heard from the muddy ditch, and cawing from the grey sky: 'Marx is dead! Nothing that he predicted, proclaimed, prophesied, has been realized – nothing at all'. This from the political right. From the left, more precisely the anarcho-*gauchiste* left, an interesting proposi-tion has been put forward: if it had not been for Marx and Marxist theory, the proletarian revolution would already have happened. Marx as protector of capitalism. And yet, peasant revolts did not bring about land reform, machine-breaking has never transformed society. This

anarcho-*gauchisme* avoids a problem, an important conflict – between institution and organization.

If the question of inventory and balance sheet is raised, let us establish right away:

a) Marx's writings contain a certain number of *short-term* forecasts or predictions. Among others, the imminent – because already under way – concentration of capital. Its consequence being the end of *competitive* capitalism, which took place under a double pressure: that of the financial capital that arose from concentration, and that of the working class acting both on the economic level (strikes, wage increases, reduction in working hours) and on the political level (parliamentary action, subversive action, revolutionary action). Who today can deny the realization of this 'prophecy', based on the analysis of tendencies and contradictions inherent to the capitalism of free competition? Just by itself, the realization of a pronouncement on this key point would ensure the validity of Marx's analysis and explanation of capital. However, the validity of Marx's analyses was apparent only belatedly, once this transformation of competitive capitalism into monopolistic (imperialist and financial) capitalism had taken place, and moreover through various interpretations (Hilferding, Lenin, Keynes, etc.) and contradictory events.

Recently, apropos the crisis in raw materials and energy, we have read – above authoritative signatures – various declarations of the kind: 'unforeseen crisis . . . crisis unrelated to Marxist thought . . . Crisis with no relationship to the Marxist hypothesis of overproduction and underconsumption'. Now Marx's theory of crises can be summed up in the assertion that every crisis has its specific characteristics. He himself studied in his own lifetime a crisis triggered by the scarcity of a major raw material, cotton, imported from the region of North America ravaged by the Civil War. Finally, the overproduction that Marx analysed was above all that of *means of production* (machines, labour-power).

The disappearance of competitive capitalism took place, as Marx foresaw, through a double process: the pressure and action of the working class, which in 1917 undertook to replace this mode of production in a large agricultural country, and the rise of financial capitalism in the advanced countries. A connection that matched Marx's overall predictions but did not match the details of these, as he had envisaged revolutionary transformation in the advanced industrial countries, under the leadership of a working class that was highly developed, both qualitatively and quantitatively. The hypothesis of such a *political revolution*, preceded by, and enabling via the transformation of property relations, a rapid growth (economic) and development (social, qualitative), thus turned out to be partially mistaken. Incontestably, according to Marx, there would not be growth (in the productive forces) without overturning social relations. Growth and development of society had to go rationally – harmoniously – together, in a style that we might call Hegelian: *domination* over nature and *appropriation* of nature could not, for Marx, be separated. The concatenation of facts, the victory of the Hegelian type of state over the revolutionary forces, would result in growth without development (victory of the quantitative over the qualitative), along with the flattening out of the social (crushed between the economic and the political). On the other hand, this generalized growth *partially* realizes the transitional period envisaged by Marx. It makes *possible* (which does not mean *necessary*) a qualitative leap, the contribution of social forces stifled up till now by repression, by the political use of knowledge, by ideology. The growth of the productive forces has generated new sectors: computing, for example. True, capitalism has seized for itself these gains in the productive forces and the integration of science into production. And yet, the result has been a 'socialization of society' and of the productive forces themselves, whose elements (firms) are no longer isolated, separated in space – something that Marx had predicted as the work of 'socialist' society. What prevents this qualitative leap? The Hegelian type of nation-state, with its repressive power, its constraining structures, its frozen forms (formalities and formations), its 'satisfying' functions. In short, with the weight of its institutions based on productivism and quantitativism.

b) *In the medium term*, Marx proclaimed within the bounds of the predictable the formation of a different society. Characterized by what modalities of existence? Marx had little to say about the future society that would be born from a total revolution. He refused to write 'recipes for the cook-shops of the future'. Sometimes, it seems, he saw it in *ethical* terms (each person respecting all others), sometimes *aesthetic* (everyone a poet or artist). It was predictable that this future society would be characterized initially by collective, and thus social, ownership and management of the productive forces and the means of production, in other words, of the economy. Subsequently, by the disappearance (withering away) of the political state and of the political as such. Thus, by the predominance of the social over the economic (controlled) and the political (reabsorbed). This predominance of the social, and of social (collective) needs, is what defined socialism and then communism according to Marx. It implied for him diversity, the riches of social relations (true riches), the appropriation or reappropriation by (social) 'man' of his conditions and means: nature, technology, science, etc. It also implied the end of repressive and oppressive institutions: along with the state, before or after it, religion, family, nation and fatherland, imposed labour, ideology, etc. would also disappear.

What of this project has been realized? Nothing, or as good as nothing. And yet, a large part of the things whose disappearance Marx announced is already rotting rather than growing stronger.

c) *In the long term*, Marx's thought regains the upper hand. In several texts, from *The Poverty of Philosophy* to the *Grundrisse* – the preparatory work for *Capital* whose texts are not the most famous or vulgarized – Marx analysed machinery, the stages and complex process of its perfection: the combination of tools, the use of other energies than human, the material application of technology and scientific results. Marx foresaw the coming of automatic machinery and the automation of production (something Hegel had already envisaged, though without basing his prediction on a precise study of this abstract-concrete object, a study that was made possible for Marx by the work of Babbage, one of the founders of this technology). Machinery, increasingly complex, would receive from outside, in relation to its internal functioning, energies and raw materials; it would transform these by a self-regulated process into finished products, making human labour unnecessary. The infinite division of labour would be reunited, as the productive process in automatic machinery.

This long-term prediction of non-labour is one of Marx's 'prophecies', despite being in no way eschatological or millenarian in the traditional sense. Marx sensed that this decisive perfection of productive forces would bring about a revolutionary change in the world. It contained within it the most contradictory possibilities: catastrophes or miracles, or both at once. If the political and social revolution did not

take place, the upheaval of technology would be responsible for transforming the world; but if societies were not ready to accept it, to control
technology, to ensure the appropriation of the world for human beings,
then the worst consequences would result. What would people do if
they no longer had to work, yet would still have to feed machinery (with
energy and raw materials)? How would these enormous units of production be managed, dispersed as they are across the earth's surface as a
function of flows of energy and resources of raw materials? How would
they be subordinated to social needs, and what needs?

In fragments that have been ignored until recently, Marx even foresaw that an agglomeration (a city)[5] occupying an urban space would
have an 'energy balance', in other words, an exchange of resources with
the surrounding space (the countryside) and that further away. How
would these exchanges be governed? Without control of this process – a
rational regulation – urban reality risks destroying its own resources
and even itself. Foreseeing so-called ecological questions, without
however thinking that they might become the most important, Marx
envisaged a global self-regulation of productive processes, but did not
think that a regulation of exchanges at the highest level (between town
and country, for example) could happen automatically, without the
intervention of activity and cognition.

These questions and indications can be discovered today in fragments from Marx that do not form part of the 'vulgate'. Clear and
distinct they are not. They have to be read with twentieth-century eyes,
and interpreted as a function of a century of experience.

How can there be a different procedure for studying texts that have
no relationship to literature, differing from this both by their form (a
different language from the everyday, without this language being
singularized by the individual effort of the author) and by their content
(an analysis of the actual oriented towards the virtual)? Hegel had
already defined this procedure: *regressive deepening* from the beginning
(in this case the thought of Marx) and *progressive determination* of this
beginning as such, reprised each time in a different manner, without
there being a definitive reading and a fixed meaning.

---

5 Cf. Henri Lefebvre, *Marxist Philosophy and the City*, University of Minnesota
Press, 2016. Cf. also many passages in the *Grundrisse*.

4) As far as the state is concerned, there is no 'model' of political reality to be found in the work of Marx. Against this, we find throughout his work a detailed critical examination of Hegelian theory (more than several polemical remarks against this or that statesman, remarks that also aim at the corresponding state).

Why this absence? In Marx's time, the state was beginning its shattering career; apart from its existence in the texts of Hegel, there was a political entity only in France. Marx saw the collapse of Bonapartism in France and the rise of the state in Germany with Bismarck and Prussia. In England, tied to the world market and the beginnings of capitalism, the state remained weak. Perhaps Marx saw the critique of Hegelian theory as sufficient, without replacing it by a different construction? Perhaps he deemed state architectures too fragile, too quickly modified, to deserve a theoretical elaboration? Or perhaps he was never able to grasp the links between the state and the (capitalist) mode of production, having only the English example available to him?

Marx could not accuse Hegel of ignoring production and misunderstanding the productive process with its double aspect: in the narrow sense, labour, economic activities (productive forces), the manufacture of objects conforming to demand and needs; and more broadly, the production of social relations and society, the self-production of human reality.

The Hegelian philosophy of history and the self-production of his own reality by 'man' was subjected to the filter of Feuerbach's anthropology. Who lives and acts? A palpable and sentient being, a subject-object that is born from nature and never emerges from it, even if he modifies it. Hegel conceived productive activity in its full amplitude, detaching it from nature in the name of reason (the Idea). Feuerbach restored naturalism by misunderstanding activity. Marx restored the unity of (social) 'human being' by superseding Hegel's speculative rationality and Feuerbach's limited naturalism – by breaking their limits in a dialectical movement. He perceived, moreover, the new problems that emerged with this superseding: how can a 'being' of nature, born of nature, living from it and in it, dominate it? If there is not a rationality that is both higher and immanent to this becoming, what happens to 'man' when he masters nature by cognition? Marx rather left these questions in suspense in the *1844 Manuscripts*, content to characterize human alienation practically and socially.

The human being does not wrest himself from nature in order to dominate it without pains and risks. Labour itself, which Hegel – a bourgeois ignorant of it – unconditionally praises by subordinating it to knowledge, his own; this labour, alienating-alienated because divided, subjects the labouring individual, on the one hand to the technical demands of the productive process, and on the other hand to the social demands of the market (itself double: the labour market, and the market for the products of labour). First remark: neither production nor market possesses the internal equilibrium that Hegel attributes to them, presupposing a harmony between the system of labours and the system of needs. Hegelianism was bad at interpreting the discoveries of the English economists. The regulation of the market, to the extent that this exists, results from the bitterest competition, which eliminates the less well endowed and the less well placed. The market does not promote a higher rationality and an ascent towards the Idea, but rather the rise of the powerful and rich. The victims of the market and the division of labour include above all the 'labourers' themselves. Hegel's optimism does not hold up to critical analysis.

Was Hegel unaware of social classes? No, but he misunderstood their essence, and therefore their role. In the French Revolution he saw only the rational rise of the nation-state, almost completely ignoring the class struggle between bourgeoisie and aristocracy (something discovered however by Saint-Simon in the early nineteenth century). Though grasping economic production on the one hand and social classes on the other, he did not conceive their connection. His speculative triadic construction drove him into an enormous mistake. For him there were the two labouring and thus productive classes – peasants; workers/artisans – and above them two other classes: the hierarchy of the thinking class, a political class or rather a caste, and the ruling class (governors, government). Where in this construction are the means and relations of production? Who possesses the means of production, in the name of property relations? An illusion of rationality and harmony disturbed Hegel's vision. The *middle class*? For Marx, as against Hegel, this does not have a well-defined existence. There are middle classes and strata. The name changes; Marx pejoratively calls 'petite bourgeoisie' what the Hegelian philosophy of the state decorates with the fine name of 'thinking class'. This supposed class is made up, for Marx, of very diverse elements: certain *agriculturalists*, themselves a very varied group

(agricultural workers, share-croppers, capitalist or non-capitalist farm-
ers, landed proprietors) belong to it, along with merchants, the liberal
professions, civil servants, etc. Unproductive? No. Many, if not all,
produce in their fashion, even the criminal. Bound by a determinate
legal tie to the means of production? No. Only the capitalists *possess*
these means, premises, machinery, raw materials, wage funds.
Merchants? They produce in their way, as the transport of goods from
one place to another is part of their production. Through the work of his
'personnel', the merchant produces surplus value just as the industrialist
does. By the same title, he receives a share of this surplus value, in
proportion to the capital invested in his firm. The larger the scale of
commerce, the more similar it is to industry. The same holds for agricultural undertakings. But there are many small and medium merchants,
many small and medium officials, etc., who make up the 'petite bourgeoisie'. These middle classes may well have the ability to reflect, that is,
to go from uncertainty to uncertainty; they have neither the capacity to
direct production nor that of orienting the political ensemble. Their
quantitative and qualitative importance is certainly considerable, but in
no way does it correspond to the role that Hegel assigns them. Lassalle,
an inconsistent Hegelian, cheated, and his supporters along with him,
when they said that the middle classes, vis-à-vis a politically active
working class, formed a reactionary mass together with the bourgeoisie.
For Lassalle, this absurdity concealed a dangerous tactic: to hold out a
hand to the feudalists and Bismarck himself, who had arisen from the
feudalists despite outclassing them in the scope of his political views.
Lassalle forgot that the bourgeoisie overturns society by industry in a
revolutionary way, and that the proletariat, as the most authentic product of this overthrow arising from large-scale industry, aims to strip
production of its capitalist character.

It is true that the ruling personnel are drawn selectively (by examinations and competitions) from these middle classes, and ranked in a hierarchy. Here, Marx had a stroke of genius, one among so many others,
expressed initially in a different language. For the body of state officials,
whom Hegel constantly praised for their competence, devotion and
honesty (a triad of virtues), Marx immediately found the word 'bureaucracy'. That led him to a fundamental discovery, which would pertain to
what is today called 'sociology', if that specialized science had raised
itself to critical cognition. The bureaucracy, as a constituted social body,

has its own particular interests. It seeks to maintain, and even expand and extend, the domain over which it rules, to preserve its cohesion as a body and numerically. So, if bureaucrats take measures to manage society, as a function of the resources attributed to them and their sources (the 'national income' and 'gross national product'), they take this from others so as to persevere in their (social) being. And they do this within the political order. The rationality or irrationality of that order is of little concern to them. Besides, the rational and the irrational are mingled, the first turning to absurdity and the second working itself out in very well-reasoned formalisms and texts. The bureaucrats accept this situation as a premise of their action. In so far as rationality matters to them, it is the rationality of their preservation. The function of functionaries is duplicated: public management and control of the social ensemble; self-preservation of the various constituted bodies and of the bureaucratic ensemble as social body. If there is self-regulation, then, it is not the political totality that benefits, as Hegel wished, but a part of society, which cuts out a place for itself and expands this in a constant struggle. This struggle is superimposed on others, and tends to conceal these rather than to simplify them. The contradiction runs right to the heart of the state edifice, fissuring it from top to bottom.

On the one hand, the bureaucracy, with its higher stratum or caste of managers (whom Marx does not yet call 'technocrats', but whose rise he anticipated), manages the social ensemble, in other words, the state, the 'public services', education and teaching, health, scientific research, etc. For these activities, the bureaucracy has at its disposal the *social surplus product*, which it levies by various means: taxes, state corporations, etc. We know how much this question of surplus product and its management preoccupied Marx in his *Critique of the Gotha Programme* of 1875. The bureaucracy organizes and manages these services, taking into account the interests concerned, and consequently the interests of the economically dominant: the capitalists, and the bourgeoisie as a class. By the mediation of these bureaucrats, the economically dominant class *tends* (this is in no way a fait accompli, a state of things given from the start) to exercise its *hegemony*, to shape even needs, knowledge and social space, although not without resistance, including resistance arising from the self-defence of various institutions sheltered by the bureaucracy. But at the same time (and we cannot insist too much on this simultaneity) the bureaucratic-political apparatuses *tend* to set themselves above society, to dominate it instead of managing it. The rise of the whole towards abstraction, applauded by Hegel as a sign and proof of rationality, has this absurd aspect. The managers of society, ceasing to act on behalf of the dominant class, acquire an autonomous reality. In the extreme case, they are able to impose their specific interests; they end up pillaging the whole of society, including the economically dominant class (handling it despite its energetic resistance). This acquisition of autonomy, which enables the state and its apparatuses to weigh heavily on society and the social as such, is not without its inconveniences. In the absence of (democratic) control from below, the elements of the social body divide; they compete with one another for power and its advantages. Set above society, the state crumbles along its lines of cleavage, like any other system. Acute rivalry engenders violence. Either the military or politicians (possessing an apparatus) profit from this situation, disdaining the possessors of knowledge (the higher technicians and technocrats, who however often take their revenge, as they are indispensable for the management of society).

Marx explains this double dialectical movement within the state and its apparatuses in *The Eighteenth Brumaire of Louis Bonaparte*, after having already described and analysed its conditions in his *Critique of Hegel's Philosophy of the State*. In 1852, a group of political adventurers and officers seized hold of French society and set out to pillage it. A *lumpenbourgeoisie*, allied to the *lumpenproletariat*, seized the state already erected over society and took this process to its conclusion (just as fascism did later). Marx revealed in Bonapartism this tendency on the part of the state, as soon as it escapes democratic control from below. A *tendency*: Marx only ever analysed tendencies, movements, processes, in other words, becomings. Is this the Hegelian state? No, but it is what awaits it, its destination if nothing threatens it *from below*.

Marx revealed the social reality of the political state. It has, as Hegel discovered despite misunderstanding his own discovery, a social basis: the relations of production. As a consequence, the working class, bound to these relations of production precisely by the fact that it has no immediate relationship with production but only mediated relationships (contractual, since there is a contract, verbal or written, between employer and employee) with the owners of the means of production – this working class is part of the basis: the state weighs on it.

The political events in France from 1848 to 1852 illustrate this entire process. The French state, already strong under the *ancien régime*, then strengthened and centralized by Napoleon, was still in no way a modern state. The edifice was constructed on an agricultural basis; the state bureaucracy (the administration) connected a multitude of isolated units of production, the small peasants of the villages and small towns. The Restoration emphasized the artificial character of the state construction, as its basis changed: the peasantry shifted and the working class appeared; in 1848 this manifested itself and the edifice shattered. The Republic failed either to reconstitute or reconstruct it as a function of the new realities, industry and the working class. Then adventurers came along, and seized this proud prey in a coup d'état.

Weighing on the working class, therefore, is the modern political construction, both to maintain the relations of production, to organize consumption, and if possible to supervise production, to guarantee the surplus value destined for the whole of society, the various 'services'.

There is nothing stable, balanced or rational about this basis. The productive forces? They grow and conditions change. The relations of production? They relegate private property of the means of production (including land) into the realm of the irrational, even if its political weight increases. Classes? Their number constantly changes; classes disappear as such (landed proprietors in France, for instance) and others are born (the fragmented peasants after the French Revolution and its agrarian reform).

A further paradox: the Hegelian construction expresses a 'reality', a certain result of history, and on top of this a project, a hope, a perspective – that of the bourgeoisie. Something that Hegel to a certain point ignored, misunderstanding his own presuppositions, in the way of every philosopher.

To the extent that Marx elaborated a theory of the state, this starts as a critique of Hegelian theory in his early works, is continued as a polemic against Bonapartism, and culminates in an attack on the German Social Democratic Party – aiming through this at its inspirer, Ferdinand Lassalle, the 'Berlin Marat'; through Lassalle it reaches the Hegelian target, so that this final text reprises and concludes the first. Marx's constant theme: 'The present conditions of property are maintained by the power of the state, which the bourgeoisie has organized to protect the conditions of its property. The proletarians must therefore overthrow the political power' (1847).

The *Critique of the Gotha Programme* deserves deeper study, for many reasons. This text, obscured by interested parties (the German Social Democrats), first of all remained unknown, and then was not understood.

Before returning to this short and condensed text, which I have already drawn widely on, let us take one highly important remark. Does Marx allude to the Commune? He mentions this only in connection with the end of the First International. Now, he was perfectly aware of what had happened in Paris in 1871, and approved it – particularly as far as the state was concerned. As well as some bold but fruitless measures, the Communards broke the existing state, a bourgeois state that was very far from democratic, established on the ruins of Bonapartism. By demolishing the bureaucracy, the police and the army, the apparatuses set up above and against the people, the Communards showed the way. Marx's *Critique of the Gotha Programme* says nothing of all this, and it is only between the lines that the reader finds there the Commune. There were two reasons for this. First of all, Marx knew that he could not speak to the Germans, four years after, about what had been done in Paris: they were unaware of it or rejected it because these socialists were imbued with nationalist prejudices. They situated themselves, as Marx angrily said, 'within the framework of the present-day national state', thus in the Bismarckian context, going so far as to forget that the German Empire was situated economically in the context of the *world market* and politically in the 'system of states'. This was more than the national 'framework', with the result that verbiage about the 'fraternity of peoples' replaced the common struggle of the working classes against the ruling classes and their governments.

Second, we can believe a century later that this situation already disturbed Marx, that he had difficulty understanding it. What happened? In his own time, the working class of the most powerful European country organized itself politically. It drew inspiration from him, Marx, by way of a man who knew the *Communist Manifesto* by heart – Lassalle. And now this working class, already powerful both qualitatively and quantitatively, fell into the crudest of traps: nationalism, statism. What a blow to Marx! His own work was escaping him. How and why? Did he sense that the working class would not be protected from contradictions? That it would not accomplish its 'historic mission' at a single stroke, with a powerful simplicity? If Marx suspected this, he did not say so, but he closely analysed the internal contradictions of the German workers' party. Within it, the working class began to mix revolutionary verbalism with opportunist formulae – like Lassalle, waxing about the 'iron law' of wages while cosying up to the most reactionary class on the pretext that it rejected capitalism! Similarly, the German workers' party campaigned for the 'emancipation of labour' and the 'abolition of the wage system'. By what means? The establishment of production cooperatives with the support of the state. A supposedly 'free state' (Section II of the programme).

'A free state – what does that mean?' Marx asked. An independent state? A state free in its movements as a state? Dangerous nonsense. 'Freedom consists in converting the state from an organ superimposed on society into one thoroughly subordinate to it; and even today state forms are more or less free depending on the degree to which they restrict the "freedom of the state".'[6] This dissolves the programme's monstrous confusions and abuses of language. As for the state in general, it is a fiction. Modern states, established on the common foundation of bourgeois society, but within a more or less developed capitalism, will accordingly have essential characteristics in common along with secondary differences. When the German workers' party declared that it accepted the existing 'political framework', the state of the Prusso-German Empire, it seriously mortgaged the future. It ruled out in advance the essential element of the revolutionary transformation that changes capitalist into communist society, in other words, the transition phase 'in which the state can only be the revolutionary dictatorship of the proletariat'. Engels and Lenin would take this Marxist thesis to its logical conclusion. What did the revolution consist of on the political level? Three connected and successive acts: to break the 'existing' state in a particular national conjuncture; to construct a different political edifice, that of proletarian dictatorship (or rather, hegemony); and to bring the state and politics to an end by their withering away (not by disintegration, rotting, etc.). More briefly, two active verbs: reabsorb the political sphere and absorb the economic one into the social, by establishing the priority of the latter. Such is the strategic objective.

Marx goes on to ask, in revealing terms, 'What social functions will remain that are analogous to the present functions of the state?' In the

---

6 Karl Marx, 'Critique of the Gotha Programme', in *The First International and After*, London: Verso, 2010, p. 354.

society he envisages, political functions (supposing that politics did have certain 'functions') will have disappeared and been replaced by *social* functions. There is no longer a question of economic functions. The social – 'emancipated' as was said at this time – would expand once relieved of economics and politics. It would develop as such. Social functions, which would be no more than *analogous* to those of the political state, would depend on a rational (scientific) analysis of society. And, Marx added, it was not by coupling the word 'people' with the word 'state' that progress would be made towards solving this problem. Only cognition of the social ensemble could resolve it, by becoming social practice.

What social functions are these? Essentially, the levying and managing of the surplus product. The project of attributing to each worker the fruit of his labour or its equivalent, revolutionary and bold as it seems, is in fact meaningless. Once hegemonic, the working class will have to make the whole of society function, and draw from the total result of production what is indispensable for the continuation of services described as public or of general interest (if transformed in their content): education, training, health, etc., along with scientific research, art, etc. A serious question is whether armaments and an army should form part of these applications of the social product. The answer is no, except in the case of such a threat that the whole people has to arm in order to resist the operations of an opposing strategy – a class strategy.

It is appropriate here to repeat that this theory of the social surplus product has been neglected by the majority of Marxist currents. Why? Because it is chiefly (though not exclusively) to be found in the *Critique of the Gotha Programme*, a misunderstood text. Also because Marxists have been so concerned with great philosophical questions, or with specialized sciences (history, political economy), that they have left aside the social in the strict sense, also misunderstood in its specificity. And finally, because political and trade-union militancy has always emphasized (and still does) questions about production, thus the firm, wages, etc., neglecting the other moments of social reality.

Only one very remarkable thinker, despite or because of his aberrance – Georges Bataille – took up the analysis of the social surplus product in his book *The Accursed Share*. He interpreted the theory in an original and paradoxical way. For him, the real stake in class struggles is this surplus product, its levying and its use. All the more so as this surplus, this excess available to societies, makes possible everything that goes beyond the hard life of productive labour and the everyday round: wars, festivals, religious sacrifices, pleasure, luxury, works of art, monuments – in short, what economists treat as waste, useless expenditure, yet what makes life agreeable. The surplus product makes it possible to fight, and is what people fight for. Bataille illustrated his theory with pre-capitalist examples. It could be that it had truth value for societies in which the ruling classes (aristocracy, clergy) still had to take the people into account; the survivals of primitive community or military democracy, the traditions of general assemblies in villages and towns, obliging 'notables' to sumptuous expenditure in the sense of [Thorstein] Veblen's 'leisure class'. Is this still true under capitalism? Less and less, or more and more, especially if we consider armaments as waste! This expenditure has taken other forms (foundations, donations, etc.). As for waste, either it is hidden, whether public (bureaucratic) or private, or it ceases to be extra-economic and becomes economic, the accelerator of growth and production (as Vance Packard has shown).

We have to accept, however, that the class struggle is not restricted to questions of wages at the level of the firm, but covers the whole of society, affected as this is by the hegemonic management of the social fund levied on surplus value.

After Marx's critique of and response to Hegel, peremptory as it was, what remains of the Hegelian thesis of a perfect rationality in the existing state or the state in general? Philosophical architectures, like political constructions, display a *limited rationality*. The working class will go further in reason than the bourgeoisie, according to Marx, after a leap (qualitative, that is, revolutionary). It is in this sense that, for Marx, the working class receives the legacy of philosophy and makes it fruitful at a higher level. The working class will act according to its theoretical analysis, according to the indications of cognition, instead of proceeding either speculatively (like philosophers) or empirically (like professional politicians). The error or illusion of Hegelian rationality consists in its underestimating contradictions and believing them easy to resolve, as if cognition of conflicts already contained their solution. Hegel the dialectician disavowed and rejected his own dialectic. For Marx, the state summit, the supreme instance, cannot really cognize or resolve the contradictions that arise from this double irruption that puts an end to the old historicity: industry, the working class.

This class, according to Marx, has a dialectical privilege corresponding to its mission being not *historical* but *universal*. It cannot assert itself without superseding or negating itself. If it becomes 'collective subject' and thus *political subject*, and seizes the state by revolutionary means, this will be to negate both the state and politics by bringing these to their end. The process, for Marx, includes three moments. The working class asserts itself, and therefore shatters and destroys the existing society, including the state. This assertion, positive at the same time as negative, qualitative although quantitative, introduces a transitional period during which the now hegemonic class will be faced with multiple problems, those of the global management of society, which presupposes organizations and coherent actions, thus a kind of 'state' and political life. Subsequently, the social develops; the state will have withered away and disappeared, while the socially controlled economy is no longer a distinct and prior level.

Many objections can be raised to this theoretical schema. Still triadic as ever, and a bit simplistic, it does not take into account either the unevennesses of economic growth and development (glimpsed by Marx, but whose theoretical concepts and laws would be clearly formulated by Lenin) or political obstacles, wars, repressions and constant violence. Besides, what prevents statesmen from acquiring a broader knowledge than the remote vision of what they see in the far distance? The state, if we venture to speak so familiarly of such an admirable reality, does not let itself be pushed around. The hypothesis that the state fissures and crumbles by hardening has no more consistency than a metaphor. It too readily lends itself to subversive rhetoric. It seems to fuel two modern myths already mentioned; that of the Titan (Prometheus who attacked the gods) and that of the Evil Demon (who uses a vulnerable detail to demolish the edifice).

And yet, this debatable schema contains the revolutionary capacity of Marxist thought. It actualizes the concept of freedom, which a century after its expression by Marx remains the most subtle and strongest thing that Western rationality has developed, with the result that we find ourselves faced with a dilemma: either to accept this schema, or else to concede an irremediable opposition between the irrational and the rational (the *vécu* of lived experience and the *conçu* of conceptual thought).

A limited conception of freedom runs through Hegelianism, along with a limited conception of reason, underlying the philosophy of knowledge and emerging in the theory of the state. Freedom is defined by cognition of necessity (of determinism). A thesis that has the advantage of combining with the philosophical tradition of logos – subject and object, discourse and reason – the scientific discoveries of the modern age, starting with Galileo and Descartes.

Hegel develops in minute detail the moments of freedom – three in number, it goes without saying. The 'free will', individual desire that declares itself free, is only an initial moment, empty and uncertain: freedom is confused with arbitrariness. The undermined will – the 'I' as pure subjective activity – must be limited and determined to attain existence: to will something, and thus to be will. Decision, determination and knowledge go together. The 'free will' that is generally known as 'freedom' trusts to chance. This is the level at which the majority of people remain in practice, and so, even on an ideological level that believes itself superior, does so-called liberal thought. The freedom of the individual is the art of taking advantage of accident, chance or mischance. Nothing more. Contradictorily, Hegel says: 'The ordinary man believes himself free when he is permitted to act arbitrarily, but it is precisely in this arbitrariness that he is not free. When I will the rational, I act not as particular individual but according to the notions of ethics.' This first degree of freedom, however, subjective and incoherent, acquires with property an objective and already necessary existence. This contributes to leading the will that seeks freedom towards the second moment, morality. At this degree, it recognizes other wills; it is reflected in them and reflects them in itself, thus advancing towards the substantial reality that it attains only at the third moment. This unites and supersedes the two others, subjective and objective, arbitrary and substantial. Freedom is then defined as 'actuality that conforms to its concept', as the 'totality of necessity', cognized and recognized in the family, civil society and the state. It follows from this that morality and right, rational custom and law, go together, as do needs and labours. It also follows that the *system of right* constitutes the determination and realization of freedom, 'the world of the spirit generated by itself as second nature'.[7] Right and morality guarantee the individual against arbitrariness from without and against the arbitrariness of his own 'free

---

7 [Here Lefebvre is again paraphrasing from Hegel's *Philosophy of Right*, where the theme of free will is treated particularly in paras 5 to 29. – Translator.]

will'. The highest freedom consists in cognition and re-cognition, thus acceptance of the systems implicated in the state: needs, labours, right, morality. For Hegel, nothing is more rigorous than this definition or determination of freedom, yet on examination it soon reveals its ambiguity. It may be twisted in the most varied directions. Does this cognition or recognition of necessity mean accepting it, or rather struggling against it so as to dominate it and free oneself from it? In Hegelianism, Western logos postulates its lucidity and univocity, its signification, which immediately duplicates and even shatters. The discovery of astronomical laws, from Kepler to Newton, did not make it possible to modify phenomena, only to predict them. On the other hand, the doctor familiar with the determinism (cause–effect) of a disease can intervene and sometimes cure the patient. The concept of *cognition* diversifies. Not only does it distinguish itself from knowledge and specialized cognitions, it calls for new categories. Sometimes cognition makes it possible to *dominate* a connection of facts, to control and thus modify them. Sometimes it does not enable this, and is limited to more or less precise prediction, often 'probabilistic'. Sometimes cognition makes it possible to appropriate or reappropriate processes to the needs and desires of the being who cognizes and lives in society.

These concrete differences overturn Hegelian theory. As Marx very well grasped, without developing the differential concepts that he attempted in the works of his youth (in particular, 'appropriation' in the *1844 Manuscripts* where he strongly contrasts this with 'property', showing that the latter prevents the former).

For Marx, freedom is defined on the *social* level, and only on this level, to the exclusion of economic determinisms as such and political constraints as such. Who is this individual? A social being, says Marx, a node or nucleus, a (mobile) centre of social relations. Their degree of practical and concrete reality, thus of freedom, depends on the complexity and 'wealth' of these relationships. Here, wealth in social relations is contrasted with wealth in money as appropriate to property. Poverty in social relations may go together with wealth in things, in money and capital. Conversely, wealth (in relationships) often goes together with poverty (in things and money). The one does not exclude the other, otherwise any hope would have to be abandoned. Social relations include relations of production, but they envelop these by superseding them. Thus, social relationships that bear the names 'culture' or 'artistic production' go beyond the technical and social division of labour. The wealth of social relations, a complexity more than a complication, implies the diversity and multiplication of the *possibles*, for each person and for all. Freedom in Marx's sense is analysed in successive moments, enveloping and developing one another. It implies first of all a *domination* of nature by technology, by productive forces. Then, a *control* of the political processes and economic determinisms thus constituted. And finally, an *appropriation* of the whole (base, structures and superstructures, in other words, productive capacity and organization of this capacity). In the simplified illustration given above, the doctor who cures the patient dominates a determinism of natural facts, controls the result of his intervention and reappropriates the body for the individual concerned. At another degree of social complexity, the (successful) realization of an inhabited space (a city) requires the domination of multiple natural determinisms, including climate, water and site, along with control of the various flows that come together in this space – energies, information, raw materials, goods – and finally the architectural and urbanistic appropriation of the space itself. It is here and in this way that Marx's concept of freedom is born and expands, but there were unprecedented contradictions unknown to Marx: domination may lead to the destruction of the dominated (nature, among other things). Control of the economic process does not bring about appropriation, which either presupposes these two components, or superimposes itself on them.

By a stupefying misunderstanding or an inconceivable aberration, the Hegelian concept of freedom has invaded Marxist thought. So-called 'Marxists' have defined freedom in this way, conceding to the (bourgeois) fetishism of effective knowledge, accepting (capitalist) productivism! In practice, this definition leads to identifying the freedom of the citizen with the recognition of economic determinisms, with the imperatives of growth and the acceptance of political constraints. The impoverishment of the individual, 'freely consented', is seen as supreme freedom! The philosophical definition has been distorted and 'realized' in the most unfortunate manner.

When philosophy – that of the Stoics (but more than one philosopher not officially affiliated to this school was a Stoic in his beliefs) – defined freedom as acceptance of fate, and even '*amor fati*', this was in order to reserve the inner consciousness; whereas in the name of a definition of freedom that was supposedly revolutionary because it was

attributed to the schoolmaster of revolution,[8] the state reserves the right
to track the individual even in his inner reserves, his hidden resources,
his secrecy, refusing him any inner consciousness and accusing this
intimacy of psychopathic (anti-social) deviation.

To sum up, once again, for Marx, Engels and Lenin the revolution
they envisaged, the total revolution, was distinguished from political
revolutions by the promotion or rise of the social against the political
and the economic.

5) If we are to believe Marx, the result of the Hegelian triads generating
complete satisfaction by the harmony of three moments, 'needs, labours,
pleasures', is in no way satisfying. What did the actual triads consist of?
How should they be named? There is 'oppression, exploitation, humiliation', and 'ideology, violence, knowledge', or in modern terminology,
'politicians, military, technocrats'.

Complexity gives rise to perplexity. Which of these pictures of the
modern world, the dark or the light, the Marxist or the Hegelian, is
'correct' (a cautious term, reserving for other use the term 'true')? A
thorny question, all the more so given the complexity of the modern
state, its economic functions, juridical forms and political structures, has
duplicated the critical position. A *right-wing critique*, liberal, petty-bour-
geois (in the extreme case 'Poujadiste',[9] reactionary, even fascist) opposing a *left-wing critique*, of Marxian orientation.

A remark: the ingredients of the modern state are sufficiently diverse
to ensure the variety of mixture. Is it not possible that the 'knowledge'
element prevails in one place and the 'ideology' or 'constraint' element
elsewhere? That in one place there is exploitation without too great
humiliation, and in another, humiliation rather than exploitation. Here a
few more technocrats, there a stronger military, and in a third place
clever politicians? So that these general concepts become *operative* in the
analysis of conjunctures . . .

Whatever the case may be, many elements are missing in the picture
left to us by Marx: many boxes remain empty. Incontestably, statesmen
and political apparatuses, by manipulating information, have

---

8 [Apparently a reference to Stalin. – Translator.]
9 [After the movement headed in the 1950s by Pierre Poujade, a predecessor of the
Front National. – Translator.]

assimilated knowledge, including Marxism (if somewhat *reduced*). This knowledge has produced institutions, particularly those concerned with the economy, and directly or indirectly steering (indicatively) production. The process of institutionalization[10] has modified state structures, and particularly the contractual system.

In a sense, therefore, the transformations of the modern state have 'Hegelianized' it. In truth, enough combinations between the elements listed are possible, with those in which technocrats predominate being closer to the Hegelian model than the others. Is the modern state often closer to this model than at the time when Marx only had as material for his analyses the Bonapartist and Bismarckian states?

And yet, this modern state swings between two poles: a think tank or databank in the service of economic organizations and firms (national and supranational capitalist), and an oppressive and repressive apparatus, policing and military, which dominate 'civil society' and tend to subject this in order to exploit it for its own account.

The analyst sometimes ends up wondering if these two pictures – the dark and the light – are not both equally and simultaneously true. But then, should analysis not change its register radically, according to particular materials, categories and themes? Consequently, this offers an opportunity for a Nietzschean analysis of the will to power.

6) To the brutal question 'is the world Marxist?', too clear in as much as it demands a yes or no response, both answers are possible.

The 'world' that calls itself Marxist, and is generally known as communist, is neither Marxist nor communist. These labels and epithets carry with them an ideology and a mythology. 'Ideology' and 'mythology' do not mean unreal; once again, people kill one another in the name of ideas and ideologies, myths and utopias, far more than for 'realities'. Both communism and anti-communism are part of modern ideologies. The so-called Marxist or communist 'world' has its Marxist ideology, in other words, Marxism has been transformed into an ideology and the project of a 'communist' society into rhetoric. The texts of Marx, Engels and Lenin on the state and its withering away are both numerous and undeniable. These texts may be obscured, cast into shadow, but not refuted. If we conclude, in the name of history or the 'direction of history', or more

---

10 Cf. René Lourau, *Analyse institutionelle*, Paris: Éditions de Minuit, 1971.

commonly in the name of pragmatism and political cynicism, that they are out of date, then all of Marxism collapses. It still provides a vocabulary, an ideology, but no longer has (theoretical) veracity. In the present theoretical and practical situation, this paradox, brought to a peak, becomes a contradiction that is glaring yet pushed into obscurity by all means possible; Marx's thought, which elaborated the concept of ideology and sought to eliminate all ideology, has been changed into ideology; the radical critique of the state by Marx, Engels and Lenin has been changed into state doctrine. More than a metaphor, this is a metamorphosis![11]

Where has the working class raised itself to the level of collective subject – political subject – breaking the state and politics? Where and how has it exercised its hegemony (substituting this concept, refined by Gramsci, for the somewhat brutal one of 'dictatorship')? Where has it accomplished its mission, not historical but universal, a positivity reached by way of radical negativity? The working class attempted this with the soviets of 1917, and since then . . .

Malicious commentators have described more than once the homologies and contrasts between the so-called socialist countries and the capitalist ones. In the latter the state often gives signs of fatigue, but this is never so in the former: it stresses its 'socialist' character, ever more bold and far-sighted, letting nothing escape or filter out, except what knows how to follow the contours of shadow.

Unfortunately, corruption has little in common with the withering away of the state, unless it makes possible a democratic control exercised from below to watch over 'power'. In fact, the hegemony of the working class has these three characteristics: increased pressure on the opposing class, expansion and deepening of democracy, disappearance of state privileges. Corruption and degradation, on the contrary, can be used by right-wing criticism, leading either to fascism or military dictatorship.

7) The theory of coherent discourse, logic – the privileged expression of Western logos since Aristotle – has also received a surprising

---

11 A reservation about China. If it is true that Mao broke the party apparatus, a state within the state, with the help of young people during the Cultural Revolution, this is a fact of world importance. And yet, what about the state itself, planning, the organization of the territory, the reconstructed party? We know too little to give a verdict here, despite our sympathies.

promotion. Not only has it changed, it has undergone a metamorphosis, becoming socio-political practice – it aims qua activity at social cohesion in the given economic and political framework: the mode of production, the state.

Logic appears to perfect itself and develop. One might say it engenders multiple logics; who does not appeal to a 'logicity', a rigorous coherence, in their statements or projects? In actuality, the theory of coherence, applied to this or that 'object', covers and justifies an action that aims to fix this object. Action of this kind is called 'strategy'. Logics (of the social, of the commodity, of signification, of violence, etc.) need to be analysed as strategies: resources, objectives, agents.

Dialectic seems to have been defeated and eliminated. We should not conceal the fact that the 'logic/dialectic' problem has still not found a solution. What is the exact relationship between the theory of coherence and cohesion, of equilibrium and thus of stability, and the theory of conflicts, contradictions, transitions and mobility? All that can be said is that with modern 'logicism', Western logos has found a justificatory ideology, perhaps the last of its kind. It is bound up with political power by the mediation of technocracy, specialized in the study of structures of equilibrium, in strategies. Now the contradiction arrives from all sides: from the multiplicity of logics and strategies that confront one another, from actions that divide up and allocate space.

8) Is the contemporary world Marxist? Certainly not. Marx has undergone a double ill-treatment: studied almost everywhere, joining the ranks of 'classic' authors in many countries, become 'cultural', he has been reduced to a small number of quotations, the staple of students and activists.

Reduced and shrunk in this way, Marx has been blunted. Stripped of political critique, as without destroying itself this cannot spare so-called 'socialist' states and politics. Under the banner of 'scientificity' (epistemology, economic, historical or sociological science, etc.) this thought has been rendered insipid, divided into separate pieces, either by erudition (Marxology) or by interpretations, readings and re-readings, each increasingly abstract.

Restoring Marx's thought? The project is defensible, under two conditions. First of all, by taking the totality of his work in its movement, instead of excluding this or that *a priori*, as being or not being political, being or not being philosophical, economic, historical, etc. No one has the right to subject Marx's thought to subsequent concepts, theories and problems. Second, by reconnecting this thought to the '*vécu*', the lived experience of our own age, with its multiple problems that remain in shadow, including the enormous and risky problem: what is the state? What to do with the state, in the state, against the state?

To tie Marx's thought to official and institutionalized knowledge, to the *conçu* against the *vécu*, is a monstrous operation, an act of self-destruction.

No, there is nothing Marxist about the world today. No alienation has disappeared. On the contrary: different and surprising new alienations have aggravated the old ones. Superimposed on the alienation of workers, women, children, colonized peoples, etc. is political alienation (by the all-powerful state), technological alienation, alienation through space, etc. Work itself has not superseded its contradictory status: alienating-alienated, realization of social being by production, but divided, fragmented, deprived of any 'value'. We know, at the same time, that the Hegelian-Marxist concept of alienation has pursued an impressive trajectory. Stripped by Marx of its Hegelian obscurities, defined as a blocking of possibilities, it has illuminated many situations, despite not having a theoretically (epistemologically) well-defined status. The intellectual sadism that stubbornly opposes the *vécu* has tried to kill off alienation. Too late: after accomplishing its work, the concept (or if you prefer, the image) was already on the decline.

9) No, this world is in no way Marxist, neither directly nor indirectly. By an irony opposite to Marxist irony, the opponents of Marx, those he had killed, are resuscitating: Proudhon, Stirner. The demand for decentralization has revived the work of one, and the irreducible 'individual' once more appeals to the other. Alongside revolution after its successive defeats – and especially that of total revolution – rebellion, revolt and subversion have reclaimed their rights: either in opposition to political revolution, so as to obtain 'everything right now', or by completing the political revolution by the destruction of the state.

How could this world appeal to Marx? He never separated growth from development. To ensure their agreement, he placed political revolution before growth, which did not take place. In other words, the 'upside-down world' has not been reversed; rather, it has been perfected by separating growth from development and domination from appropriation. Something that Marx could not have conceived!

In relation to the modern world, Marx does not assume the figure of a benevolent and optimistic '48er, seeing salvation as coming from the people and the workers. Reason advances. If it frees itself from the idealist Idea, it attaches itself solidly to industrial production, to material labour.

No, generalized industry has shown the limits of its rationality, giving rise to a world of violence that persists. How and why? Do Lenin and Leninism offer an answer to this question? Like the existence of a Marxism, many people accept the existence of a Leninism, which makes it possible to legitimize Marxism-Leninism. On examination, Leninism fragments. Dialectical materialism? The study of the peasant question? It is Kautsky, dragged through the mud by Lenin after he had borrowed so much from him, who can claim the honour of these discoveries, given that they were discoveries. The materialism that Lenin counterposed to empiricism and empirio-criticism, with very little of dialectic about it, remained quite summary and brusque.

The law of uneven development (it would be more correct to say, inequalities of growth and development) is envisaged in certain fragments of Marx. Only Lenin formulated it and gave it its full scope, envisaging its disastrous consequences. Since then, this law has been verified, extended, diversified – a major law of the modern world, whose importance cannot be underestimated. This was Lenin's great discovery, the essential aspect of Leninism. In uneven development, the coexistence (far from peaceful) of all levels, from the local to the supranational, by way of the regional and national, generates a new problematic. Uneven development gave rise to imperialism, and thus violence, within the industrialized world. And yet, inequality by itself is not enough to explain violence; only the existence of the state, stimulated by inequalities, can explain this.

The most risky point of Leninism, which passes for its strong point, is its theory of knowledge and the party. Knowledge belongs to the intellectuals. They possess concepts, theory, scientific terminology. The working class, unable to go beyond blind spontaneity, receives knowledge from outside. By what mediation? The political party, support or subject of knowledge, transmits this to the workers, communicating it, making it accessible, while not ceasing to possess it. Now the political party, along with the state and under cover of the state, tends to set itself above society.

Experience shows this and theory can prove it. Every political party, whether knowing it or not, is Hegelian in its essence.

Marxism has thus been permeated by the Hegelian theory of knowledge, 'positively' linked to political action and by this mediation to the state; this theory has escaped Marxist criticism, to yield a theory that *deprives* the *vécu*, the spontaneous, social practice, of actual or virtual cognition. The *conçu* and the *vécu* are opposed, with political cognition ascribed to the party and blind spontaneity ascribed to the masses, incapable of lucidity and culture.

10) It is far from assured, for all that, that capitalism – the capitalist mode of production – is thereby constituted and endures as a coherent system. Nor is it assured that the bourgeoisie is definitively constituted as a *class* on the world scale and can survive. There are still opportunities for the working class to assert itself as 'collective subject', thus political subject, in the sense indicated above. Despite obstacles, constraints and violence, certain indications show that the *breakthrough* – not ideological but practical – of the working class is possible. This possibility is enough for the 'system' to be unable to stabilize itself as such or to close itself in the way that every system desires (as soon as it closes, it imprisons its own; Stalinism with the Stalinists, for example).

Some would even deny the present-day existence of capitalism as an ensemble (mode of production) and totality. 'Capitalism', according to them, is already broken up into nation-states, 'societies', whose particularities – cultural and political – dominate the general economic features. This would relegate Marxist analysis to a kind of folklore, another way of delivering the sentence: Marx is dead – unless it is another way of announcing the end of the bourgeois age and the coming of the proletarian age, with its ideas and ideologies replacing bourgeois 'values' and ideologies! Like many others of its kind, this excessive proposition remains ambiguous: maybe 'leftist', maybe rightist.

Would these theories, or rather ideologists, deny that there are such things as capitals, some invested at a particular site, others floating above national spaces and seeking a site, sums of money certified by signatures, guaranteed (more or less) by a *concrete abstraction*, gold?

These capitals 'report' to their capitalist owners. How? In two ways: by directly producing other capital through speculation, and by being invested to produce surplus value.

The result of this is not that there is no longer capitalism, but that 'capitalism' no longer forms, as it did in Marx's time, a relatively intelligible totality, a relatively well-defined 'system' despite its internal contradictions. Differentiated, spatialized, globalized, it consists of a plurality of sub-systems: national states, the 'monetary system', the world market, etc. Have contradictions disappeared? Certainly not. More complex and mutually interfering, they have rather grown sharper, sometimes even bordering on the point of rupture if without reaching this . . .

Is the modern world not 'Marxist', then, in this sense and to a large degree?

Have the relations of production been transformed? No. Private property remains the cornerstone of this society, and now extends to the entire space. The transfer of land or resource titles to the state has hardly modified the situation, any more than has state management of the means of production. State property just like so-called 'private' property removes the management of the productive forces and production from the interested parties, those involved in it, both producers and users. 'Privatizing' changes little, whether exercised by a particular individual or a state institution.

The reproduction of the relations of production is a problem today on the world scale. Against Marx's expectations, these essentially reproduce themselves. Yet there are many changes in the world: economic growth, the extension of capitalism to the entire space (apart from the so-called socialist countries), the power and unity (fragile but constituted) of the world market. What assures, and how does it, the reproduction of social relations? What changes and what does not change? It is not easy to answer this. The position of women, for example, is tending to change, which does not overturn the relations of production but should not be underestimated as a deep-going change.

A pyramidal society is constructed on the basis of property. Its pillars are industry and urbanization, property in businesses and property in land. It is based on realities that are established and even programmed: everyday life, the urban condition. And yet, in the course of this vast process, the 'socialization of society' continues to proceed: in other words, barriers fall and are reconstituted only by constraint (violence).

Let us repeat this shocking truth, which is very little assimilated: the primacy of the economic, of exchange and exchange-value, of production for the market, is what characterizes capitalism, whatever the political label and ideology that accompanies this. The bourgeoisie maintains this priority in the state and political order it promulgates. As for socialism, in principle it reverses the upside-down world, re-establishing the priority of use and social needs. It thus restores, according to Marx, the transparency of relationships characteristic of pre-capitalist societies, while freeing this 'transparency' from the direct (extra-economic) violence that previously characterized personal relationships.

It is needless to return to the fact that the objectives of so-called 'Marxist' socialism are basically only economic. Economism and productivism, drawn from Marxism and justified by appeal to Marx – not without distorting his writings – have invaded the modern world.

Is the modern world not Marxist in this (ironic) sense? It is so, no less ironically, if it is true that one formula has become universal during the 'transitional' period – that of growth. A formula that replaces to good advantage the idealist delirium of the Christians and the famous 'Love one another', likewise the no less famous motto: 'Proletarians of all countries, unite!' Today, the dominant slogan, the maxim of action, if still unconscious, is: 'Exploit one another!' The rich countries exploit, oppress and humiliate the poor, who take their revenge as best they can; regions and sectors likewise. Artisans, peasants, civil servants, intellectuals and even workers seek no less to draw the (economic) maximum from their situation, from social relations. Class, fractions of classes, groups and castes mutually exploit one another in the apparent unity of 'society', the national state. The struggle for the division of surplus value and the surplus product intensifies and sharpens. Other strata rival the bourgeoisie (with far less resources), which continues to impose its hegemony, opposing its own 'optimum' to the 'maxima' of other classes.

Does this not chime with the 'underlying' analyses of Marx, those of the (unfinished) ending of *Capital*?

11) The hegemonic bourgeoisie has partially assimilated (recuperated) Marxism, in particular, rationality based on industrial practice (production). It has drawn from it, as well as from its political experience, concepts and practices: a certain control of the market by way of knowledge and the sciences; a sense of organization that has modified traditional (competitive) capitalism, a semi-planning.

In the extreme case we find the state to be a think tank for capitalist firms, in opposition to the state as the organization of pillage. An opposition that defines a middle way, which is in fact a broad spectrum of possibilities, compromises and nuances, as has been said above.

If Marx was right to a greater or lesser extent, the greatest mistake or folly for a movement that calls itself revolutionary is to strengthen the state. But have they not all followed this road, one of failure?

This world cannot be called 'Marxist', and only in an ironic way can it be studied as such. When politicians adopt the perspective of unlimited growth in all sectors, of the power of knowledge, something that implies (organizational) gigantism, are they Marxist? Some of them believe this, others pretend to. We can ironically say: perhaps, but . . .

Yet Marx's concepts do have a precise meaning: the revolution is made against the state, and so at a particular moment the state becomes counter-revolutionary.

An assertion such as this does not incline to a form of anarchism that rejects cognition and tends to a 'wild' individualism and naturalism. It implies the transfer of *institutional* privileges to the *organizational*, something that we can ascertain will in today's conditions no longer arise from industrial practice but rather from *spatial practice*, which is superimposed on industry and increasingly overdetermines it.

This is the way that Marx's thought can be taken up on the basis of the present day, as a function of what is new in the world. A reprise equally different from both exegetic repetition and adventurous interpretation.

4
The Nietzsche File

1) Less bulky than the file for Hegel or Marx? Seemingly not. More surprising? Certainly, since 'Nietzscheanism' has been associated with literary and poetic madness, full of wild rhetoric and lacking any connection to social action and practice.

At the start of the twentieth century, a girl from the bourgeoisie who took a lover and intended to 'live her own life' would quote Nietzsche.[1] In those days, in France, 'Nietzscheanism' stood for a kind of anarchistic leftism that would give birth to rowdy children.[2] In Germany and Austria, in the 1890s, Strauss and Mahler respectively dedicated to Zarathustra and Nietzsche musical works in a heroic and heavy style. Later on, in France, the 'reception' of Nietzschean doctrine (if this word can be used) would run in diametrically opposing directions – Gide and Drieu La Rochelle, for example, left and right. Nietzscheanism then meant an elitist attitude, the (supposed) formation of a new aristocracy.[3]

On the subject of Friedrich Nietzsche, it is necessary to distinguish between posterity and influence. In the first case, his work entered into

---

1 Cf. Daniel Lesueur, *Nietzschéenne!* (a novel), Paris: Plon, 1908.

2 Cf. Raoul Vaneigem, *Revolution of Everyday Life*, London: Rebel Press, 1983. A book that conceals its genealogy.

3 A section of this chapter was published in Pierre Boudot, *Nietzsche et l'au-delà de la liberté*, Paris: Aubier Montaigne, 1970. French writers from the 1930s through the 1950s have happily complemented the work of G. Bianquis, *Nietzsche en France*, 1928.

what he himself would have called the genealogy of certain men, thinkers, poets, men of action. In the second case, one misunderstanding followed another, and the influence spread in a chain of ignorance; a 'proper reading' of Nietzsche would have dissuaded many would-be disciples! The same could be said of Marx (but is there one proper reading and other bad ones?).

Certain filiations particularly deserve to be studied, in several different lights. For example, the relationship between Nietzsche and Georges Bataille, or between Nietzsche and Hermann Hesse, or between Nietzsche and Robert Musil. *The Glass Bead Game* predicts what happens to a society when an esoteric knowledge claiming to be absolute possesses prestige and seeks power. What does happen? It is held by a caste that resembles a monastic order; this order, dominant in one region (Castalia) but not the whole country, comes into conflict with the state and 'reality'. This knowledge is refined and perfected, becoming truly total (mathematical, linguistic, musical, historical, etc.). The result: a no less total failure. The Hegelian thesis of the primacy of knowledge turns back against philosophy and the philosopher. Hermann Hesse, however, retained from Hegel his elitism, the role of logos and of linguistics as the primordial science, and he attached to music, as did Nietzsche, a value equal to and rivalling that of knowledge. As for *The Man Without Qualities*, this great book is pervaded by a very Nietzschean irony. A response to Stirner, and still more individualistic than 'the ego and its own', the man without qualities has them all, but does nothing with them and can do nothing with them, in the Europe of 1913.

Anyone who has the full Nietzsche file to hand and browses it attentively will find it full of surprises. He will note that General de Gaulle, the famous and influential French statesman of the mid-twentieth century, attributed to Nietzsche a fearsome importance and responsibility, despite committing an unbelievable blunder about the poet-philosopher's thought. For him, Nietzsche and Germany were one: Germany had adopted Nietzsche, who reflected the Germanic spirit. 'The Superman,[4] with his exceptional character, the will to power ...

---

4 [Translation of Nietzsche's concept of the 'Übermensch' as 'superman' (or, still worse, 'Superman') has led to frequent misunderstanding. Nietzsche created a noun from the common adjective 'übermenschlich', which means 'beyond (normal) human power'; he certainly looked to the advent of a superior type of person, but his concept implies neither maleness nor domination of others. Lefebvre clearly understands this,

appeared to these passionately ambitious men as the ideal they sought to achieve.[5]

The fact that a statesman could utter such stupidities and make such blunders has certain consequences; first of all, an already confirmed lack of respect, followed by suspicion, about the 'thought' of this man and of statesmen in general – to the point that it seems not impossible that German statesmen committed the same capital blunder in relation to Nietzsche.[6] There is a strange and unforeseeable irony: a Wagnerized Nietzsche (which would certainly not have pleased him!), a mythical image of the poet-philosopher, long possessed prestige and influence.

Based on very varied misunderstandings, there has been an anarchistic Nietzsche and an elitist Nietzsche (therefore 'rightist' and even quasi-fascist). More recently, the return to Nietzsche, pursued impartially by historians of philosophy, has restored textual truth: Nietzsche's writings had been mutilated so as to 'twist' them in one direction or another. Nietzsche's sister, Elisabeth, was guilty of falsification after her brother's death: reactionary, anti-Semitic (under the influence of her husband), she did not hesitate to modify the meaning of texts, by way of montages, suppressions, etc. Once historical truth was restored, Nietzsche continued to undergo certain insults. Rationalized, systematized, dogmatized 'à la française' (following the tendencies of current French thought, i.e. a Cartesian logos and cogito in full crisis, philosophers seeking to save face and make a name for themselves), Nietzsche has lost the aspect of his poetry that is scathing, offensive, sometimes haughty.

The renewal of his 'influence' (a suspect word, bearing in mind what Nietzsche said of it) has led in France to a curious renewal of philosophy. Whereas under Hegelian 'influence' the professional philosopher became the (servile) servant of politics, the philosopher of Nietzschean affiliation claims to be opposed to power of any kind. To a certain extent

---

and though he uses both the noun 'surhomme' and the adjective 'surhumain', it has seemed preferable here to render both by 'superhuman' – except in this quotation, which Lefebvre introduces precisely to show its author's misunderstanding of Nietzsche. – Translator.]

5   Cf. A. Philomenko, 'De Gaulle, un philosophe de la guerre', Études polémiques, 7, January 1973.

6   The complete file would contain Nietzschean references on the part of certain theorists of the Third Reich. On this subject, cf. Henri Lefebvre, *Nietzsche*, Paris: Syllepse, 2003 [1939]. (The date is important; this was the first book written to show that Nietzsche was in no way responsible for his interpretation by fascism.)

he no longer survives; he revives. He finds the mark of authority (of power and the will to power) even in language. Sometimes he goes so far that, after killing God and 'man', he even kills meaning, truth and finally Identity (that of self with self, which makes it possible to name and to grasp what is named). This philosopher in turn professes great contempt: contempt for what is not great. Like Nietzsche, he places civilization (ill defined, we have to say) above society and state.

Does this modern philosopher remain one? If he is interested in Nietzsche only in terms of philosophy (or because linguistics has again become fashionable, a science that in Nietzsche's day was called 'philology', including by him), this interest does not go far; it leaves our modern thinker quite calm in the midst of those categories he believes he has superseded, but which he preciously preserves. If the modern thinker follows through, if he understands the basis of the 'will to power', where does he end up? This question will find a response below (an attempted response). It may be that the situation of this philosopher is uncomfortable and his valour fails him. Why? Because Nietzsche condemns and rejects the whole of philosophy. As did Marx. Marx rejected and refuted philosophy because it lacked connection with practice, and could not *realize* its idea of man. For Nietzsche, philosophy is made up of myths that no longer have the beauty of the myths of mythology. Philosophical representations contain some myths of origins and the original. Philosophy represents beginnings to itself: those of the world, of man, of consciousness, of thought. It arranges things so that the question contains its response: Being, God, Soul, Nature, etc. The secularized myths of philosophy can be listed: primordial Being (seen from below: Nature, Matter, 'Ground'; or from above: God, Transcendence, the Idea) – dualism (Good and Evil, Thought and inert Matter), etc.

Denounced by Nietzsche's renunciation as an easy option, philosophy ends up with the gestures of Orpheus or Narcissus. Orpheus turns away from his path, turns towards a life that is forever lost and so loses himself. Narcissus, obsessed by the mirror in which he discovers himself, learns that he is himself only a reflection and dies of this. Philosophy and philosophers no longer have any other resource: either the gesture of Orpheus, a return in vain to the original – or the gesture of Narcissus, death in contemplation of self. In both cases, philosophy meets its end. It can do no more than generate the illusion of height and the illusion of depth in philosophical mental space. It seeks sometimes the effect of transparency, sometimes the effect of opacity (substantiality). Philosophy ends up being buried by its own failure, the failure of the human species: forcing it to go beyond 'man'.

2) If we look carefully, Nietzsche does not fit into these categories: philosophy, the quest for a system, the teaching of a knowledge. How to describe this 'frightful' genius, as he presents himself: 'What I have to do is frightful in every sense of the word . . . It is not the individual I defy, but humanity . . . An unspeakable fatality remains attached to my name' (unsent letter to his sister, Turin, December 1888). Nietzsche belied and dismantled every discourse, those of religious minds, scientific minds, political minds, by showing their wellsprings. In a language that has nothing in common with his own, as it is not very poetic, but that corresponds to the operation of his thought, we could say that he was the Great Decoder of the Western world. He deciphered all the messages, all the languages, of Europe. Nietzscheanism is the attitude of those for whom discourses no longer hold a secret; the locks have been forced, the drawers opened, the strongboxes broken. Everything that there was in the archives of churches and states is here on the ground; anyone can read and trample on these inept writings. This, however, changes only the fate of writings, not of things. Deciphered, decoded, writings that sought to be enigmatic will no longer have the least attraction.

Did the Great Decoder have a code? Did he keep there his secret, an ultimate secret? Would this be the no-code that escapes all deciphering, therefore lacking faith or law, home or place, and thus the end of ends?

Nietzsche mercilessly pursued anatomy and dissection (biological terms), analysis and process (intellectual and juridical terms), the decoding (the term of a rather affected modernism) of Christianity, of Greco-Latinism, of the European logos. He appealed from this to an Orient of poetry and music, to divine lightness against the heaviness and boredom of the West.

Since then, in the lineage of Marx, the trial of the bourgeoisie, of capitalism, has been conducted with a double or triple error. The same crass truths about the bourgeoisie have been repeated ad nauseam, and these truths have become boring. They were boring from the start, because they were moral: the harshness of the bourgeoisie, its egoism, the injustice of bourgeois society, the inequalities of capitalism, etc. For Nietzsche, those who condemn bourgeois society in the name of justice, charity and truth do not go far enough.

The so-called human sciences, in a nascent state around the end of the nineteenth century, left aside the question of the brutal origins and harsh conditions of capitalism, in other words, the accumulation of capital (a theory that has certainly become topical again today, apropos the Third World and socialism in 'backward' countries). Given the limits of their theories and of polemical blind alleys, there has been a return by way of society to the 'primitive', to ethnology and anthropology, thus bypassing modern society after having diverted its study towards a moralizing rhetoric and a politicized historicity.

Nietzsche avoided these errors and elisions, neither turning away from them nor around them. If he had little to say about capitalism and the bourgeoisie, this was because he despised and condemned them en bloc, not deeming to see there an 'object' worthy of interest, and also because he included them in Judeo-Christianity. The whole of the West, since its beginnings – since the defeat of Greece – had been drifting towards what it became. The orientation of Europe was decided in the sixteenth century. The West did have other possibilities. After Reformation and Counter-Reformation, monetary wealth and state power were combined; the die was cast. Some superior types, like the universal creator (Leonardo, Michelangelo) or the 'virtuoso' (the man of *virtù*, of bold intelligence: the Prince, Cesare Borgia) would disappear forever.

For Nietzsche, the critique of the 'modernity' he saw being born around him in about 1880 formed part of a wider critique: of the history that began in Greece and Rome, and ended with the European barbarism of the nineteenth century. If he hardly spoke of capitalism, Nietzsche did not believe this meant restricting his polemic and reducing his thought. On the contrary.

Throughout and always, whether discussing religion or the state, economics or politics, Nietzsche dismisses from the start representations and ideologies, justifications by knowledge. To use once again this too modern word, he casts the *codes* currently used into the rubbish tip after revealing and formulating them. He eliminates the conceived and the perceived, the better to illuminate lived experience [*le vécu*]. He proves to those who suffer, in a hundred ways, that suffering has to be endured in the name of general interest or truth. To the humiliated, he demonstrates that humiliation and the virtue of humility is their destiny. But if 'I' focus *my* attention and *my* lucidity on 'my' suffering, on 'my' humiliation, then everything changes. The affective result becomes fundamental; the subjective accidental comes to the fore, without this lucidity implying a concept of the 'subject' or of 'emotion'. This is a poetic fact that succeeds the moral justifications of suffering, the ideological legitimations of humility: lived experience grows steadily broader, nocturnal and deep; it proclaims itself, demands a voice and seizes this. It speaks in terms of poetry, song, music, dance. It enlivens another metamorphosis: pain is transformed into joy.

There is thus in the work of Nietzsche, in relation to the generally accepted conception of knowledge (a conception ritualized by Hegelianism), an inversion of meaning, a reversal of perspective. As with Marx? No. With Nietzsche, turning the world upside down is not objective and practical. The revenge of lived experience is also the revenge of the subjective. Hegelianism, and later the thinkers in the Marxist lineage, theorized the 'illusions of subjectivity' in order to reject them. For Nietzsche, the subjective has right on its side, more radically than do the conceptual and the objective. When he speaks of the men of antiquity, of the Middle Ages, of the Renaissance, Nietzsche never ceases for a moment to think of himself, to reflect on himself, with his suffer-ings, rebellions, humiliations. He experiences in his own flesh the whole of Judeo-Christianity, the enemy of the body. In his thought, he experi-ences the fervour of the great figures of the Renaissance, and in the fascination with death, a fascination over which it is necessary to triumph in order to continue to live, he recognizes the tragic sense of the Greeks. Is not the great mutation, the 'transvaluation', initially this: the assertion of the *vécu*, of the subjective *moment*, by abandoning the cage of the Cartesian cogito, the philosophical subject enclosed in itself? Each moment of *my* unique life irredeemably disappears. If it ever returns, if it is reproduced, this is a prodigious chance. Its value *is* infi-nite. 'Is'? No. Each moment 'is' derisory, but if I attribute to each moment an infinity, that of value, then I finally live it. Experience: I can and must value it infinitely.[7]

So Nietzsche becomes a poet through dominating knowledge by poetry. The reversal of the situation, this act that can be described

---

7 Cf. letters of 19 June 1882, September 1881, etc.

'dialectically' but in no way depends on a theory of dialectics, does not repudiate or deny knowledge. What it rejects is the priority of knowledge, adhesion to a 'representation' of the real in the name of knowledge – to an ideology – but it does make use of knowledge. As philologist, psychologist, sociologist, historian, Nietzsche in no way abandoned knowledge and the sciences. He reverses their priority by subjecting them to lived experience. With him, poetry becomes a means and a way of cognition.[8] He does not abolish knowledge in the chasm of non-knowledge. He studies the natural sciences, physiology, physics, the chemistry of his day, even logic, to find arguments for and/or against certain theories ('eternal recurrence') intermediary between philosophy and poetry. Western Logos, along its route, made certain statements whose importance, truth and infinite value have been shouted on the rooftops. 'I think, therefore, I am.' But no! When I think, I am not, and if I think, it is because I am not: I am seeking being. The thinking 'subject' is revealed as a discoursing, questing, suffering 'subject': a subject of non-being. As for Hegel's repeated assertion, Hegel for whom being and knowledge were identical (with the result that everything that is realized, even by force, has the right of reason on its side), Hegel who placed at the centre the Idea, Self-Consciousness, Knowledge – what a madman, and what madness! Consciousness, in the universe, is in no way universal: it results from an accident, a chance, an encounter (fortunate or otherwise) of circumstances on a small planet – a conjuncture not a necessity, an accident not an essence. Perhaps a monstrosity. Perhaps a sickness of 'being', a sickness that condemns the conscious being to suffering so as to acquaint itself with misfortunes that the 'unconscious' ignores: finitude, death, repetition, vain struggles and so much more. Besides, the consciousness of a 'conscious being' consists only of outcrops, emergences, evanescences: it is a *surface* beneath which is depth and on which is light, a surface analogous to that of a mirror that reflects and 'is nothing': precious, marvellous and vain.[9] The inaccessible opacity of depth, and the vain transparency of the heights, only leave for consciousness the place of surface or mirror.

---

8 [On the distinction Lefebvre makes between *savoir* and *connaissance*, see note 1 to Chapter 1 above. – Translator.]

9 Cf. 'The Philosopher: Reflections on the Conflict Between Art and Knowledge', in *Philosophy and Truth: Selections from Nietzsche's Early Notebooks*, ed. Daniel Breazeale, Amherst, NY: Humanity Books, 1999, particularly sections 54, 64, 139, etc.

To be defined in this way, however, in their value and not in their illusion of truth, knowledge and consciousness need cognition, full cognition, of philosophy, philology (which for Nietzsche means linguistics,
rhetoric, the stylistics and history of language), the critical history of art,
etc. What experience teaches, what human pains conceal and what
poetry declares, is that it is necessary to 'be cognizant of the most powerful of passions'. Knowledge can then be disavowed – relativized – without being contradicted, in favour of a broader conception or vision. To
put consciousness in its place in the universe – a tiny and deceptive
reality, but an infinite value for the concrete 'subject' – a force is needed.
What force? That of cognition. Only then, and only in this way, does
consciousness stop placing itself at the centre of 'reality' and taking its
uncertain reflection for a 'substance'. It also ceases to destroy itself by
considering itself as insignificant. Naïve and vainglorious optimism is
succeeded by a pessimism. A nihilism? No. The problem no longer
centres on reality – studying it, reading it – but instead on metamorphosis. Change the real! Change life! Which does not mean 'live better,
produce more', but create a different life. Changing the real means trans-
figuring it, in the way that light transfigures things without modifying
them materially. As art transfigures what it touches, creating 'something
different' with the elements of the real. As tragedy creates a joy with
horror, blood and death.

3) 'In some remote corner of the universe, scattered in the blaze of
countless solar systems, there once was a star on which intelligent
animals invented knowledge [*connaissance*]. This was the most arrogant
and mendacious moment in "universal history", but it was only a
moment. A few sighs on the part of nature and the star froze, the intelligent animals had to die. Such is the fable that someone could invent'.
    This is the start of a short and decisive text from 1873: *On Truth and
Lies in a Non-Moral Sense* – a text that not only heralds Nietzsche's later
views, but contains a theory of language, a theory which, as the reader
soon perceives, heralds and surpasses the most modern elaborations of
linguistics, semantics, semiology or semiotics, with the result that an
understanding of it would have avoided many an error or extrapolation.
This writing was also overshadowed, hidden under a bushel, ignored,
lost among Nietzsche's sketches, drafts and projects, the works of his
youth.

What then happened between the moment when Hegel placed knowledge at the centre of man and the universe, with no reservation or scruple, combining logocentrism, Eurocentrism and anthropocentrism in the same philosophy of the Idea, and the moment when for Nietzsche the earth, man and consciousness were no more than fortunate accidents, perhaps errors of material nature in the infinity of space and time?

Many scientific events happened, and particularly the work of Darwin, the theory of evolution. *The Origin of Species* was published just a few years before Marx's *Capital*. The scientific and intellectual world echoed with the terrible blow that Darwin dealt to theology and traditional philosophy. A new figure of man in the world came onto the stage. At what moment did Nietzsche become acquainted with the theory of evolution, and conceive a kind of unity between this theory and the thought of Schopenhauer (which placed unconscious life and nature at the origin of human reality, rather than the Idea)? It is hard to be precise, but we should not overlook the fact that this 'research' governed a period of Nietzsche's thought, running from *Human, All Too Human* to *Dawn* and *The Gay Science* (1878–82).[10] For Nietzsche, Darwin continues Hegel: '*Ohne Hegel kein Darwin*' ('without Hegel, no Darwin'). However, the latter so greatly changed the meaning of history and development as to remove from it any Germanic character, even while the Germans remained Hegelian and optimistic, quite misguidedly.

Darwin's great work and theory were hailed by Marx and Engels as inaugurating a new epoch in science. Had they measured its consequences? If Darwin was right, then 'generic man', the 'species being' on whom Marx established his thought, correcting Hegel by way of Feuerbach, no longer appeared as the favoured child of Mother Nature, who had borne and suckled him, carrying him in her arms to raise him to the summits of thought. This naturalism, this optimistic materialism, which still privileges the human being and very likely comes from Spinoza, collapses. 'Man' is for the Darwinists no more than a product of chance; species, in their struggle for life, generate forms fit for this struggle through the disappearance of others.

The human species seems strange, which for classical theology and philosophy means that this species is strange to nature, to matter, to life,

---

10 Cf. on this particular point, section 354 of *The Gay Science*, 'On the Genius of the Species', also section 357.

pertaining therefore to a theory of transcendence. The theory of evolution returns the human species to the ranks of nature. It may be 'specific' among more general groupings: vertebrates, mammals, etc. Its specific characteristics are, however, rather hard to define, and anthropology is hard pressed to establish itself as a science. What characterizes man? Speech and language? Upright stance? The skull? The jaw? The hand and work (for Marx)? Self-consciousness (reflection)? Laughter? Knowledge? The theory of evolution suggests a different interpretation of 'man'. The human species signals the 'end' of nature. In what sense? Finality? Exhaustion? Error? A failed species? Schopenhauer's philosophy of the will to live aggravates these questionings without giving an answer. What is knowledge according to Schopenhauer? A kind of uncertain state, midway between the blind will to live and the renunciation of life, between the assertion and the future self-destruction of the human species along with the world.

Between Hegel and Nietzsche,[11] in just a few decades, the sciences changed and advanced, with major consequences of a 'philosophical' order. But there is also something else. First of all, what Marx saw as two failures of the revolution: in 1848 on a European scale, and in 1871 in France. Who benefited from these events? Imperial Germany, which anticipated imperialism. The war reparations imposed on France stimulated German industry: this was its 'take-off'. In just a few years, Germany made up for its economic and political backwardness. By filling this gap, it lost its theoretical spirit and replaced this by the heavy erudition of *educated philistines*. The Iron Chancellor triumphed on all fronts. Did not Nietzsche witness the ostentatious rise of the *will to power*? For a few years, he failed to discern its *political* features. Like Schopenhauer, he still called it 'will to live'. Gradually, not without occasionally letting himself be impressed by political grandeur, he perceived that the quest for power governs social relations, as much as and perhaps more so than the quest for profit, money and honours. He perceived, accordingly, that the connection between this will to power and Schopenhauer's biological-naturalist 'will to live' was a philosophical

---

11   Hegel and Goethe died in 1831 and 1832 respectively. Marx began to write and intervene politically around 1842, in his twenty-fifth year. His last major writing dates from 1875. By that time, Nietzsche had already published several books, including *The Birth of Tragedy* and *Untimely Meditations*. The 'theoretical' text cited above dates from 1873.

operation in the worst sense of the word: speculative and abstract. 'There is no will but in life, but this will is not the will to live, indeed, it is the will to dominate. Here is what life formerly taught me, which enables me, Oh Sages, to resolve the enigma of your hearts.' So Zarathustra would speak. The subject, the foundation of consciousness, is to be grasped neither as 'thinking' nor as 'willing' this or that, but as subjecting others, seeking to dominate: *libido dominandi*. Grasped in the social and political conduct of the human species, and above all in the state, the will to power illuminates nature and life. Not the reverse. As Marx had said (though Nietzsche did not know this), the later explains the earlier, the result explains the principle, the final development makes it possible to understand the process.

Fundamental to his experience, which Nietzsche realized only with horror – he had already fled Germany before the war of 1870 – was that the Bismarckian state, an imitation of the Napoleonic state, would serve as a model for Europe, a Europe that 'works with a feverish virtue on its armaments, presenting the look of a hedgehog in heroic mood', he ironically wrote in a letter of 21 February 1888. This is what led to Nietzsche's thunderous declarations, first against the state, and then against Germany. These declarations are contemporaneous with *The Gay Science* and *Zarathustra*. The evolutionist, almost Darwinian period, which produced (along with other ancestors on the genealogical tree, in particular La Rochefoucauld, Chamfort, Stendhal) the cruel aphorisms of *Human, All Too Human*, came to an end when Nietzsche discovered that the secret of 'man', if there is one, cannot appeal to and appear in the name of a biological theory. Meaning or the absence of meaning are revealed in a reality of historical order, as Hegel had declared, but the meaning appears only by taking the opposite view to Hegelianism. This would lead further: towards the superhuman.

Die fröhliche Wissenschaft ['The Gay Science'] begins and ends with poems, the latter ones being an appendix to the book and entitled *Lieder des Prinzen Vogelfrei*, 'Songs of Prince Free-As-A-Bird'. In the first song, the Prince who sings like a bird takes aim at the whole of the West, and launches a challenge to logos by way of Goethe, parodying the end of Part Two of *Faust*:

> *Weltspiel, das herrische,*
> *Mischt Sein und Schein*

> *Das Ewig – Närrische*
> *Mischt uns – Hinein!* . . .

> [The World-Sport, all ruling,
> Mingles false with true:
> The Eternally Fooling
> Makes us play, too!]

The sections immediately preceding this reveal Nietzsche's deep thought, among them the famous section 377 of *The Gay Science*, '*Wir Heimatlosen*' ('We with no homeland', a section interlaced between the verdict on Germany and that on Europe; cf. 356, 357, 362, etc.). We homeless ones are also without fear; '*Furchtlosen*' in the title of the fifth and last section of the book.

Zarathustra boldly goes further and strikes harder: 'A state? What is that? Well! Open now your ears unto me, for now will I say unto you my word concerning the death of peoples. A state, is called the coldest of all cold monsters. Coldly lieth it also; and this lie creepeth from its mouth: "I, the state, am the people." It is a lie! Creators were they who created peoples, and hung a faith and a love over them: thus they served life. Destroyers, are they who lay snares for many, and call it the state: they hang a sword and a hundred cravings over them.'[12]

To attack the state, in the late nineteenth century, meant for Nietzsche to attack Germany. He was not only homeless (*heimatlos*), a wanderer, a traveller who preferred the sunny South and its cities to the lands of the North. He would go towards the South with the mistral ('*Mistralwind, du Wolkenjäger*': 'Mistral wind, who chase away clouds') and adopt its way of living, its values: the Gay Science. He wished to find health, '*die grosse Gesundheit*' (section 382). He rejected his homeland of Germany, which had forgotten life and accepted the weight of the state, along with that of ponderous culture and pedantic knowledge.

Nietzsche's correspondence confirms the sincerity of these increasingly severe verdicts, starting with *Dawn* and *The Gay Science*. A letter to Overbeck of 18 October 1888 sums up his charge sheet against the Germans, who have on their conscience 'all the great misfortunes of civilization'. Each time that Europe, seeking its path, has glimpsed a

---

12 *The Gay Science*, Chapter 11, 'The New Idol'.

wider horizon, the Germans intervene and spoil such possibilities. When England and France discovered a scientific way of thinking and acting, in the eighteenth century, Germany launched Kantian philosophy into circulation. Germany defeated Napoleon, who alone had the capacity to make Europe an economic and political unity. Today (1888) the Germans have the empire in their heads, hence the resurgence of particularism, 'at the moment when the great question of values is raised for the first time'. No moment was ever more decisive, 'but who would suspect this?' The Germans are leading Europe and the Western world on the path of decadence. As for the Europeans who set out on the path of progress (economic, technological), they are unaware of their decadence. They will fail Europe, as the Greeks after Pericles failed Greece and fell into an impoverished life, into 'the desire to perish, the great lassitude'.

Nietzsche himself, like so many later poets and artists (then so many tourists), fled to 'backward' countries not because they were 'backward', but because they preserved a bit of the civilization that the 'modernized' countries were losing. Despite poverty, social relations there were 'richer'.

A few incidental remarks. First of all, consider the remarkable simultaneity and striking correspondence between Marx's critique of the German Social Democratic Party's Gotha Programme and Nietzsche's critique of German statism! Even the dates correspond. Around 1875, Germany and Europe – in which Germany was dominant – took a bad turn: the pressure of the state was both so strong and so rationally (ideologically) justified that it crushed all action and all thought, even that which sought to be revolutionary (the action and thought of Social Democracy).

The Nietzschean critique starts from the same place as that of Marx: Hegel and Hegelianism as theory of the state – statist principle and practice as application of the political rationality, particular to Europe, that Hegel had theorized. The same starting point, but in diverging directions. The poems of the Bird-Prince are so different from the writings of Marx and Engels as to have nothing in common, even in their respective critical intention. Marx and then Engels negotiated, if somewhat reluctantly, with the politicians and thinkers of the German 'left' (with the exception of Dühring). Despite and against everything, Marx and then Engels continued to bank on the German working class, which led the world in terms of its organization and consciousness. Nietzsche, at the same time, despaired of Germany as a whole, democrats and socialists included. The Bird-Prince broke his bonds; he took flight for the South and the gay science, that of life and health, enjoyment, poetry and love (what irony!). While Marx and Engels, revolutionaries and in their own way outlaws, would be betrayed by their own, the Bird-Prince who sought love, madness, pleasure, the gay science, would find nothing of this.[13]

Second remark. The grandeur and decadence of the Roman Empire was an obsession for entire generations of educated people in Europe, Hegel included. Every political analyst sought a way to avoid a decline like that of Roman power for his country, his kingdom and his king. Hegel saw here a verification of his dialectical law concerning the relationship between quantity and quality: *beyond* a certain limit, what is formed *within* this limit breaks.

It was Greece that gave Nietzsche the themes and problems of his meditation, in as much as his thought was oriented to a retrospective that he saw as different from history. To the philosophy of the Greeks before and after Socrates, to their political thinkers (Aristotle and Plato) and their moralists, Stoics and Epicureans, Nietzsche put the problems of European logos. As Marx prescribed *methodologically* in the *Grundrisse*, thought moves from the present to the past to examine it, before moving from the past to the present to reproduce it (explain it historically). The first and fundamental procedure is defined *regressively*; the *progressive* procedure then follows secondarily, interspersed with stimulating questions. As Hegel had seen and said, but without doing it, since his history reconstructed (generated, reproduced in its broad features) the time of historical genesis.

Nietzsche questioned Greece about Europe. Ahead of his time, he felt European because he no longer felt German. But Europe, its logos and its practice (economic and political), disturbed him. The Greeks lost themselves after a period of magnificent ascent. They committed suicide in wars that had initially aroused their agonistic (polemical) spirit. Europe could not be compared with the Roman Empire, victim of its greatness but threatened by barbarians from outside. Europe resembled

---

13 An allusion to the sad affair between Nietzsche and Lou Salomé, an unhappy attempt at courtly love (1882).

Greece, except that in Greece it was the city-state and not the nation-state that dominated. Europe resembled Greece in its bold spirit, its conquering reason and its internecine struggles. At a time when every hope seemed permitted, the Greek city entered into decline and Greece into decadence: not by the decline of an empire, but by the decadence of a civilization, which is far more serious. What then of Europe?

Third remark. In this late nineteenth-century Europe and Germany, understanding and communication were disappearing at the highest level, that which makes for civilization and high culture. To be understood, references, quotations and erudition were needed. In relation to Nietzsche, as to Marx, incomprehension and misunderstanding took extravagant dimensions. Nietzsche knew this, just as Marx did. 'Disciples' are the worst authors of misunderstandings, and this is shown in Nietzsche's correspondence as in Marx's. What ponderousness, what threatening barbarism there was in this Europe that Germany dominated with its industry and its army! What a decline already in relation to the times when Florence, Rome, Paris and Vienna, each in its turn and with its particular style, could claim the title of the 'new Athens'.

The Germans, between 1880 and 1890, were already so imbued with their political greatness, so pervaded by state ideology, that they saw no direct connection between Nietzsche's attacks on Germany and his critique of the state. He was seen as a renegade from German culture, an anarchistic enemy of the homeland. And yet, if he polemicized against the Germans, this was not because of a German state that preened itself by exhibiting its power, but *on the contrary*, because the Germans let themselves be contaminated by 'the foreigner', that is, by Bonapartism and the Napoleonic state. Almost everywhere, the procedure of 'nationalists' and chauvinists was pretty much the same. In Nietzsche's letters, he complains at seeing himself confused by his readers with the 'anarchist Dühring' (as Dühring, whom Engels treated as a mere reformist, was called by the nationalists). (Cf. a letter of December 1885, sent from Nice to F. Overbeck.) Among the few buyers of *Zarathustra* were Wagnerians (as they wanted to defend their idol) and anti-Semites, who associated the author with his sister's husband, a well-known anti-Semite; whereas Nietzsche constantly protested against this accusation and said that Europe could not realize itself without the Jews, as yeast in a dough that risked rotting before it had risen!

The Germans, therefore, were unable to receive, assimilate and conceive the critique of the state. They took it as rejection of 'society', of the 'homeland', along with God and morality. Were they alone in Europe? Certainly not. In France, at the same time, there was no less misunderstanding, and no one went as far as Nietzsche.

4) Nietzsche laid siege to the Hegelian fortress from all sides. He waged his decisive assault against the three great towers that held up the system: the theory of history, the theory of language and the theory of knowledge.

The attack on history began very early. The very title of *The Birth of Tragedy* (1869–72) amounts to a manifesto. For Hegel, who wrote about tragedy in Book Three of his monumental *Aesthetics*, the Greek dramatists, following the model established by Aeschylus, dealt with a fundamental opposition, 'that between the state, the moral life in its spiritual universality, and the family as natural morality'. Tragedy belongs to a history of conflicts that leads to their resolution: the harmony of the three spheres – state, family and individual.

For Nietzsche, tragedy was *born*. It does not translate a wider rational process. It is not (and nothing is) the effect of anterior causes, pre-existent conditions. It does not 'express' a rational historicity at one of its moments. Attic tragedy was born from a profound conflict, insoluble because inexhaustibly fertile, that led to no synthesis and came to light in a unique and unpredictable conjuncture. It had a birthplace, a cradle, which was Attica. 'We shall have made a decisive advance in aesthetics when we understand, not as a view of reason, but with the immediate certainty of intuition, that the evolution of art is bound up with the dualism of the Apollonian and the Dionysian, just as procreation depends on the duality of the sexes, their constant struggle broken by temporary reconciliations' (the first lines of *The Birth of Tragedy*). Just like the two sexes, and the gods whose figures express profound truths better than do concepts, the forms of art are irreconcilable; they do not form part of a totality, a spirit of the age (here, that of Greece). What a contrast between sculpture, an Apollonian art, and music, a Dionysian one! And likewise between art and science! In Greece, art was supreme over science, and the primacy of the latter led, with Socrates, to the death of art. The conflict of opposites stimulates creation as a conflict *experienced*, not *conceived*, with the result that this creative conflict differs from Hegel's dialectical contradictions. Despite being still and always a matter of contradictions and antagonisms (since every German is and will remain Hegelian, Nietzsche ironically wrote a few years after *The Birth of Tragedy*, mocking himself), the essence and meaning of these contradictions have changed radically; they are no longer thought, they are lived; their place lies between the moments of the 'experienced', and the *conceived*, or rather representation, follows later. They are situated in the struggle of two worlds: dream and intoxication. The realm of Apollo has the beautiful appearance, surprising yet pacifying, of a dream in which sufferings become a play of lights and shadows. The realm of Dionysus has intoxication, in which individuals lose their limits, breaking the fragile '*principium individuationis*', with the result that subjectivity disappears into dance, orgy, cruelty, voluptuousness. Dream and intoxication (Apollo and Dionysus) are opposites like the sexes: conflict and desire. The conflict never gives rise to a 'synthesis'; there is never a third term. Fertilization yields a different being, which however repeats one of the generators, which 'is' male or female, 'is' dream or intoxication, and thus belongs to one or other of the 'worlds', without the opposition ceasing. Without it being possible to speak of alienation in the Hegelian sense.

Dream and intoxication, like love, metamorphose things instead of confirming them. They are not subject to the 'real' and do not affirm it by knowledge. They change it right away. Anyone can experience them. This experience reacts on the past and makes it possible to understand the meaning and import of the great Greek myths. A procedure that already has nothing in common with history and historical science in the usual sense.

In a text well known for its preliminary remarks to his critique of political economy (the Introduction to the *Grundrisse*),[14] Marx signals an enigma, a fact irreducible to economism and historicism: the 'eternal charm' of Greece, of mythology and tragedy, even when the mode of production has completely changed. He wonders how the Greek gods could retain a meaning after modern metallurgy had replaced Vulcan's forge, or the world market replaced small-scale exchange under the patronage of Mercury, god of commerce, etc. Later, Marx and Engels were forced to pose similar questions about logic and law that had survived across epochs, modes of production, changes in the base,

14   Karl Marx, *Grundrisse*, London: Allen Lane, 1973, pp. 110–11.

structures and superstructures of societies, and consequently defied economic and historicizing explanations.

Nietzsche replied to the question left in suspense by Marx, and that Hegel had not even conceived, since for him Vulcan the smith was already the knowledge (know-how) that would later develop into metallurgy.

In *The Birth of Tragedy*, Nietzsche's violent attack on Socrates – accused of having diverted into conceptual knowledge the Greek spirit that had been capable before him of inventing a remarkable way of living – was aimed at both Hegel and nascent modernity: the man of technique and knowledge, the theoretical man who knows much and lives little. If Socrates already contains Hegel and modernity, this is because time should not be conceived in the manner of Hegel and the historians. For Nietzsche there are filiations, genealogies, rather than geneses; there is no history in the sense of a quantitative and qualitative development.

The attack on Hegelian history and historicity was continued in *Untimely Meditations* (1873). Why this anti-historicism, which Nietzsche reinforced by targeting a survivor of the Hegelian era, David Strauss, the liberal historian of the beginnings of Christianity?

a) Historicism is not confined to a discipline more or less bound up with a philosophy. It invades the whole 'culture', which loses any style and ceases to transmit a civilization, by overcharging it with memories and philological erudition. From here, historicism contaminates education, which ceases to educate (for life).

In 1873, Hegel, dead now for forty years, had almost disappeared from the horizon, and Hegelianism was no longer the fashion. Injustice? Misunderstanding? Hegel was no longer spoken of, but imperial Germany was Hegelianizing from top to bottom. The virtues so praised by the German scholars and men of learning (exactitude of references, specialized activity) were, for Nietzsche, mere ponderousness and pedantry. The more they studied Greece, the further removed they were from Hellenism! Scientific barbarism placed itself in the service of the state, which supported it. A state power that uses history as propaganda destroys it as knowledge and consequently maintains it in a false position. The moral virtue and intellectual honesty that are proclaimed change like all morality into their opposite, hypocrisy and lies. Knowledge self-destructs by simulating veracity.

b) Art seeks to break these chains and emerge from this vicious circle (above all, music, poetry, tragic theatre). Fetishism of the 'iconic' past, exemplary and monumental, destroys the creative capacity. Yet this subversively reappears, against 'things' – reality, the state.

c) Historicism comes up against unbridgeable obstacles. Should it manage to define a rational process across incidents and accidents, convulsions and wars, then the problems of origin and end are impossible for it to solve, bound up moreover with arbitrary periodizations (in Hegel, for example, with an ill-determined prehistory, history and post-history).

As far as *origin* is concerned, this is always lost for history in the night of time; every study and historicizing procedure presses it further back, whether the object is a particular living being, a species, 'man', life, the earth, religion or a particular religion, etc. The same with meaning and finality. This is duplicated – for example into phylogenesis and autogenesis. Historicizing reason (which justifies itself by history and conceives history as its own genesis) postulates origins and ends, causes and meanings, explanatory connections (causes and effects). Thus Hegel postulated (or presupposed) beginnings: for consciousness this was sensation, for practice it was activity directed by a logic, in his philosophy of art and history it was the Orientals and Chinese! He postulated a finality: the state. As for the motor of history, he presupposed knowledge and reason, opening the way via nature, life, the body and peoples.

No, Nietzsche would reply ever more strongly. The motor, in as much as we can speak of one, is neither reason nor knowledge, nor even practical interests and well-defined political goals (even if these interests and goals always play a role). The motor is the will to power: the quest of authoritative power for its own sake.

d) Bravely, because unwittingly, history and historians get into a series of contradictions, whose import they fail to perceive – even Hegel, whose logical theory of (dialectical) contradiction is not exempt from (logical) contradictions, in other words, incoherencies. Historians and historicizing thought postulate *becoming*, and even philosophical becoming without boundaries or limits, neither backward in the direction of origins, or forward towards the end, which avoids a number of awkward questions. They accept an evolutionary schema of time, the concept of a generative development, with the result that a coherent sequence of causes and effects accounts for the genesis of diverse 'realities'. But what is it that they discover? *Repetitions*. Besides, if the same causes are not repeated with the same effects, how can there be cognition of history, acquired knowledge? The repetitive attracts historians, as it answers their call for an explanation: same causes, same effects. And yet the repetitive destroys the temporal schema, that of a generative development. The ironic result is that historians repeat themselves because history is repeated. History as a science is thus refuted in two ways: in the name of an *immobilism* (which discovers everywhere the same causes, the same effects, the same forms and structures, constancies, invariances, repetitions) – and in the name of a *mobilism* (which accentuates conjunctions and conjunctures, unique situations, in a word, differences).[15]

Either we then accept that the state, as the fruit of history, the final constancy, puts an end to a history that implied it since the beginning through the rationality included and diffused in each 'moment', or we accept that it is necessary to go further, beyond this 'end' that is only a 'mean' – an intermediate period. Towards what? Ten years after *Untimely Meditations*, Nietzsche would reply: towards the superhuman.

e) This theoretical situation corresponds to a practical situation. 'Real' history is bogged down in state reality. Formerly, wars had a meaning, or rather it was possible to endow them with one (for God and faith, for the king, etc.). Modern wars are no more than 'explanations' between states, without anything new arising from the political confrontation between wills to power (Nietzsche almost speaks of these as *imperialist* wars, attaching this concept to that of power rather than to the economic quest for maximum profit). In practice, this society cluttered with memories, commemorations, icons and monuments, now only has in its knowledge the mirror of its wretched reality. It can no longer represent to itself a genuine future. Politicians, almost by definition, lack both thought and imagination. All they know is to continue the lines of the past; they lack perspectives. The Nietzschean perspective is not confined to relativizing the past and the present by showing that a 'perspective' (a value) even determines the past. It opens up a future: a perspective is an avenue, a

---

15 Cf. Henri Lefebvre, *La Fin de l'histoire*, Paris: Éditions de Economica, 2001 [1970].

way and a horizon. Politicians always live and think and act behind the possible, in accordance with what is most aged, most well defined, in the 'real': as Hegelians, whether they know it or not. This is how at the moment of attempting a great adventure and bringing into the life of its peoples a great idea, Europe, politicians and political thinkers erected the nation-state as an absolute, imagining that they were operating with and for eternity! The struggle, even the wars, for Europe (such as those waged by Napoleon) had a meaning. A struggle between states, and particularly between European states, has no meaning, no acceptable reason.

It is quite hard to reread *Untimely Meditations* (1873) a century later if we ignore both the subsequent works of its author and subsequent events. The idea of Europe does not appear in 1873 with the force it would have ten years later in *The Gay Science*. During these ten years, Nietzsche had gained a European experience, by living in the south of France and in Italy, and discovering a different way of life, closer to the 'great health'. This is what the title of *The Gay Science* refers to. What to do against power? Go elsewhere; seek a different path; do what one can to break the machine, to derail its cogs. How? By poetry. Is that possible? How can this be foreseen in advance? Let us try the adventure, gaily. Moreover, there is nothing in common between the Nietzschean perspective on Europe and the projects that were based and would be based on those economic and political 'realities': United States of Europe, Common Market, European Community of this or that. The Nietzschean project was founded on a 'historical' knowledge (Greece, the possibility of a Greater Greece in the time of Pericles, the ensuing decadence). It was still more deeply founded on the 'non-historicity' of so-called historical becoming, in which moments only recur as 'depassed'. The return of a game or a nexus of forces in action is always possible and therefore highly probable: such conjunctures can be recognized in situations extremely distant in space and time. The analogy between ancient Greece and present-day Europe therefore has a meta-historical meaning.

In any case: 'This long, dense succession of demolition, destruction, downfall, upheaval [that] now stands ahead ... Why is it that even we look forward to this darkening without any genuine involvement and above all without worry and fear for *ourselves*?'[16]

16 *The Gay Science*, 343

Nietzsche's courage, from *Untimely Meditations* onward, is not that he protests in an anarchistic way against the abuses of power. His thought goes further. Not only does he challenge the political being of the state, he challenges the *politicization* of the 'real', of culture, thought and life. And this is not only because this politicization, being tendentious and malicious, distorts information, distracts knowledge, denies truth. No. It blocks the way of the possible, it closes openings. No politics, being *Realpolitik* by its means and ends, can escape from the 'real', from the accomplished. Now, there is a cut and a break between the real and the possible (between realism and utopia, if you like). The 'real', which the Hegelian conception saw as harmoniously united with the possible, works as an obstacle. It bonds 'rationally' together with the state; and the state builds its fortresses on the road to the future, keeping this under the fire of its guns. It obstructs the passage.

What is then for Nietzsche, from *Untimely Meditations* onward, the freedom of spirit that he constantly demands (above all in *Human, All Too Human*)? It is a matter of demarcating himself, as a 'free spirit', from the freedom of opinion proclaimed by democrats and liberals. For them, the first great freedom of the spirit is to escape from religion, from authority of the religious type, from the dogmatism of theological ascendancy. Alright, Nietzsche says, and this freedom even needs to be taken to its logical conclusion, not resting content with saying 'I am an atheist', but proclaiming 'God is dead, so I am alone! Alone in the world! No more finality! No more truth! No more anthropotheology and ontology! I am alone! Alone with myself! In the unending and goalless dialogue of "I" with "me". No witness! No judge! Even alone, without accepting either god or devil, good or evil, I cannot dispense myself from decreeing a hierarchy between acts, evaluating them, placing them in perspective.' Along with God dies the act of setting up as a father or manufacturing a father for oneself. No one can ever be stopped from seeking a genealogical tree, but the theological-philosophical justification of paternity has disappeared along with the related philosophy. Here is the culmination of Feuerbach's anti-theology, his theory of alienation taken to its final term: man rises when he ceases to 'flow off' into a god.[17]

The free spirit resembles neither the 'classic' libertine nor the 'classic' honest man. He frees himself from religion, but this is not in order to

---

17 Cf. *The Gay Science*, 285

have his little 'personal opinion' in his own mind. Freedom of opinion is no more a form of freedom, for Nietzsche, than the arbitrary will is for Hegel. The freedom of the free spirit has a political character, in the sense that it does not accept any politics but passes this through the sieve of criticism. No state, and no state decision, finds grace ('grace of state') before this free thought. Even at the risk of being seen as cowardly, the free spirit will have the courage to denounce the absurdity of violence, rivalries and wars. When bodies that contest with one another and fight resemble each other, what is more absurd than their battles? This 'free thinker' rejects any appeal to history to justify and legitimate the actual. His freedom obliges him to challenge and combat. He will leave his country, not to turn his back on it by shaking the dust from his shoes, but so as to see it better, just as the traveller leaves a town to see it as a whole and measure the height of its buildings; to see it better, and thus to see and tell his truth, and sometimes to momentarily dissimulate this in order to have it burst out with greater force. The Nietzschean free thinker has the bravura of a hero; he is a fighter, a warrior.

5) For Hegel, theorist of logos, how is there no theory of language? This theory exists, it figures in the *Phenomenology*, where logic and history presuppose that cognition of language is acquired. This cognition naturally has *three* moments, since language has *three* aspects: one immediate and positive, a second, mediate and negative, and a third, positivity re-established at a higher level, transcending and integrating the two former.

First moment: the initial interaction between subject and object, in other words, between the nascent consciousness, still infra-real, infra-linguistic, infra-perceptive, and the real perceived '*hic et nunc*' (the here and the now), gives rise to a third term to which reflection can attribute neither objective reality nor subjective unreality, but which retains the fundamental characteristics of both these conditions. This third term is 'perceptible' (resonant) without being a 'real' object; it is a relationship between consciousnesses, without being 'unreal'. By way of the sign, each consciousness emerges from itself towards the outside, and simultaneously receives in itself other consciousnesses and objects. There is alterity rather than alienation, as this consciousness-of-self in the nascent state grasps itself by designating and naming the other. At this degree, it is established in a relative identity, 'consciousness-of-self', freeing itself from identities by way of the changes and diversities in the perceptible: initially the 'here and now', perceived space and time; then things themselves, trees and what makes them trees, leaves and what makes them leaves (with the result that designating them with a sign – the word, graphic – we already reach the level of the real).

Second moment: signs and their concatenation, languages, and even non-verbal signs (in architecture, for example, which Hegel deals with at length in his *Aesthetics*), are cold, frozen, motionless. What is an isolated sound, a 'syllable' or a 'pure' sound, perfectly defined as such by the tuning fork? Signs are mortal, and do the work of death. Languages serve as cutting and breaking tools, which fragment nature just as weapons put an end to the living. Hence the use of signs in magic and ritual formulas, imprecations, sorcery, invocations of all kinds. The *negative* moment of language is characterized, philosophically, by a vain *abstraction* devoid of content. This is the mortal moment, which dies and which kills. Discourse is continued indefinitely, words link up in an empty formalism, rhetoric, verbalism. Discourse then leads to the 'bad infinity'.

Third moment: the positive is re-established at a higher level in the *concept.* The concept retains from the negative moment the capacity for action, in other words, subjective activity, which attacks the object, breaks it, fragments the totality, and thus analyses and uses it. Along with the negative it is removed from the perceptible substratum, but it regrasps the implicit content of the perceptible. The concept retains from the first moment immediate acquaintance, hence a grasp of what is general and what is specific (different) in each 'real' object (already from the start the reserved element for formal knowledge). To this extent, the terms of language acquire their meaning: the copula (to be), the substantive (subject) and the attribute (quality, objective property, relationship, etc.). Signs – the reception and concatenation of signs – thus constitute the body of knowledge.

For Hegel, therefore, (ordinary) language serves as a solid ground for science: a growth pole, an epistemological means, however you put it. *There is nothing arbitrary about the sign*, the abstract character of signs has nothing arbitrary, because formal abstraction and objective knowledge are not separated. If the sign is the bearer of some 'non-thing', this character does not just imply a limitation of arbitrariness; it is a definition of the abstract, which enables the sign to enter into a *system*: knowledge (and not the discourse of language) of this system coincides at the summit with the political moment: the state, which for Hegel was in no way arbitrary.

If we now examine what Marx says about language, we note that he has serious reservations about the third Hegelian moment, and is content with an addition to the second moment; that he fully accepts theory, in other words, the connection of language to logos (to reason).

A very well-known passage from *The Holy Family* rebuts the Hegelian extrapolation of the concept into the Idea (the absolute Idea as unity of concept and reality: of conceptual form, belonging to discourse and logic, with its content, its determination). When Hegel, after elaborating the concept of the tree or the fruit, declares that the idea of the tree or the fruit gives birth to the 'real' tree and fruit, Marx says this is speculative magic. Hegelianism allowed itself to present the Idea as *final cause* of the world. Against this, in the first chapter of *Capital* Marx expounds the language of the commodity. The exchange of goods (the objective products of social labour) generates a different effect from the exchange of thoughts (subjective products of social relations) – different but comparable. Objects, having become commodities, are the bearers of an *exchange-value*. They are linked in relations of exchange (commerce). Practical (everyday) discourse thus has these two aspects: the formal, subjective side, which tends to the negative, in other words, to verbalism, and the objective side. The world of the commodity has its positivity, its language, its logic (the laws of commercial exchange, like those of logic, are rules of *equivalences*), which coin and money, the signs, make it possible to evaluate. As for cognition, this comes on the one hand from a critique of the discursive knowledge that is born from practice, seeing itself as definitive and bearing a fine name: political economy, on the other hand, comes from analysis of the everyday itself, of what happens when someone buys or sells cloth, sugar, wheat, etc. For Marx, right at the start of *Capital*, theory simultaneously deciphers the obscure language of commodities (hieroglyphic, Marx says) and the everyday discourse of the people who work, buy and sell, and remain in the empirical and the discursive. There is no logic of signs and signifiers as such, of coin or money, but rather the logic of a certain social practice, fashioned initially by money, then by capital. *Theory invents a language, that of revolution*, by decoding both the empirical language of capitalism and the empirical language of oppressed, exploited, humiliated and alienated people (deprived of their own truth).[18] Yet this higher cognition differs only in degree, in level, from other cognitions and from formal knowledge.

Let us turn now to the Nietzschean theory of language. This is found in texts that for a long while were dispersed and hidden from view.[19] Reflection on these texts would have helped contemporary scholars, specialists in linguistics, semantics or semiology, to avoid many illusions. It is worth comparing them with the texts of Hegel and Marx; from this starting point, immense perspectives unfold on the whole of knowledge, on Western logos and its boundaries.

Nietzsche takes the opposite course to Hegel. The (obscure) background against which questions stand out is perceived by each in a diametrically opposing manner. Intellect? For Nietzsche this is born from dissimulation; it develops its forces as the art of the lie. How can we believe in the advent of an honest and pure instinct for truth in the human species? Consciousness, like the eye that rules it, glides over the surface; it has no more thickness or substance than a mirror; it reflects. What ugliness, what heaviness, when modernity has no other reference than language! When it makes itself noticeable by words of its own, instead of referring either to joy or enjoyment, or to the (disappeared) transcendent. And what predilection ensues for a dismal rigour, for boredom!

To the question of whether language is the adequate expression of realities, Nietzsche answers in the negative without any ambiguity. Proof: there are many very different languages. In one language, a certain 'object' is in the masculine gender, in another in the feminine (*le soleil*: *die Sonne*; *la lune*: *der Mond*). Why is a tree in French masculine and a plant feminine? What arbitrariness in transposition! What is a word? Saussure would say that the word 'dog' is a (signifying) *sound* corresponding to a (signified) *concept*. Nietzsche denounces in advance the falseness of this analysis, which already presupposes the concept (dog). *The word is only the representation in sound of a nervous excitation.* The object 'dog', for its part, is simply a sequence of impressions. The same with 'the stone' or 'the snake'. Words and language only denote

---

18 Cf. Henri Lefebvre, *Langage et Société*, Paris: Gallimard, 1970 [1966], pp. 336ff., and *Marx philosophe*, Paris: PUF, n.d.

19 An essential text is 'On Truth and Lies in a Non-Moral Sense', written in 1873.

relationships (between things and human beings); they express these relationships *metaphorically*. The result is that metaphor and metonymy have in no way the character of 'figures' of discourse, of a second degree or second code that already implies a coding/decoding at the first degree (denotation, connotation). They have nothing 'rhetorical' about them, but preside as good or bad spirits over the birth of language. There is already metaphorization in the fact that a nervous excitation (tactile, auditory, visual) is transposed into an image and then into a sound. *Metaphor* should be taken in the strong sense: a leap from one sphere to another, the capacity to change one being into another: *metamorphosis*.

The word is only erected into a concept by identification of the non-identical. We should recall Hegel's jokes about Leibniz's discovery of difference: no leaf is identical to another one. In truth, establishing this refutes the Hegelian theory of identity, which accepts difference only in a subsidiary way, in relation to a repetition of the identical: A is A, the leaf is leaf, the tree is tree, the fruit is fruit, etc. 'As certainly as one leaf is never completely identical with another, as certainly was the concept leaf formed thanks to the deliberate abandonment of these differences', Nietzsche remarks. There then arises the representation of something that would be 'the leaf', a kind of original form 'according to which all leaves would be woven, designed, coloured . . . by clumsy hands, to the point that no example was completely successful'.[20]

What can be said of 'the leaf' can also be said of a human 'quality', honesty for example. What then is truth: 'A moving multitude of metaphors, metonymies, anthropomorphisms, in short, a sum of human relationships that have been poetically and rhetorically elevated, transposed, decorated, and that after long usage seem to a people firm, canonical, constraining'. The initial metaphors and metonymies are lost in conventional and constraining schemas: the social and political 'values' of which the truth forms part, in other words, what each person must accept and declare to form part of a society.

The Nietzschean theory of language thus establishes a connection between discourse, social relations and the constitutive 'values' of these relations. Language has nothing in common with the expression of an ideal truth or a given reality. It is not the instrument of cognition, but a schema in the service of an *order*, in other words, a *power*. It makes it

---

20 Op. cit.

possible to construct a pyramidal order of castes, to create a new world in relation to nature, a social world of laws, privileges, prescribed conventions. Regulative and imperative, 'the great edifice of concepts shows the rigidity of a Roman columbarium'. What then is this famous order, this proud state? A cemetery, which 'exhales in logic the severity and coldness that is specific to mathematics'. The space of concepts and the space of society correspond. As for art, only the pedantry of the theorist sees it as a second and derivative activity, an 'expression'. It is at the base, or rather, at the foundation, of societies. Every society, every civilization, does work comparable to the work of art. Aesthetics, like rhetoric, is revealed as fundamental. The *architectural spirit* of man builds marvellous constructions: societies, states. This powerful constructive spirit produces colossal domes with a material as fragile and subtle as the spider's thread: the concept.

Nietzsche did not invent the familiar perspective that views language and discourse as everyday facts, collections of banalities, by taking the science of language as the kernel or centre of a higher knowledge, as the 'epistemological foundation'. On the contrary, he sees language (more exactly, languages) from a *socio-logical* point of view, as an essential moment of social life, its foundation if not its 'base', a moment some-times symptomatic of disturbances, sicknesses, either among the people or among the 'elites'. In short, from its very birth, from the cradle (in both time and space: at the start of the human species and in each indi-vidual), language cannot be defined by knowledge, whether virtual or actual. It is a *power of metamorphosis*, which is blocked by knowledge as a definitive acquisition (episteme). Metaphor and metonymy, present from the first act of naming, constantly make a different world arise and reappear from the perceptible and from nature, the world of society, with its 'values' and regulatory conventions: the world of *lived experience*.

Language, in its background and foundation, is *poetical* in the strong and broad sense of the term; it is creative. Social practice and communi-cation do not simply produce objects and works. They do not simply combine pre-existing materials. They create: the new arises, dies, reap-pears, repeats, changes, differs, from one metamorphosis to another. Between people (individuals), things, words, there is no correspondence that pertains to or is the basis of a knowledge; yet there are relationships and even unity across language, unity of a poetic order: on the level of

'values', implicit or declared, accepted or rejected, rather than on that of
a knowledge common to all. If there is a fatal moment of language, it lies
in the political use of discourse. If there is a higher 'moment' of language,
this is to be found in poetic usage, in the discourse of poets. While the
philosopher for Hegel, the revolutionary thinker for Marx, take up and
bring to the highest level the characteristics of language (the philosopher bringing them to the concept, the revolutionary theorist to political action bound up with the working class), for Nietzsche it is the poet
who seizes words from the 'columbarium', from the magnificent and
funereal palaces of societies. He restores to words (to discourse) a 'positivity' that has nothing in common with either knowledge or practical
action: poetry, in which are reborn both the nature ousted by discourse,
and the power of metamorphosis captured by this same discourse. Thus,
if the poet speaks of the sun or the city, he is speaking of the same object
as other people, yet it is not the same object. He speaks of the body and
it is a different body. He transcends language as mortal, conventional
and constraining, by rediscovering rhythms (of the body or of nature).
The texts that Nietzsche devotes to language go incomparably further
than Saussure's overly famous *Course in General Linguistics* with its
dogmatic conceptualism. As we know, philosophers have ascertained
three positions: nominalism, conceptualism and (Platonic) realism. The
majority of them believe they are forced to choose, as constructors and
champions of a system, to be either nominalists, conceptualists or realists. Philosophical knowledge (*connaissance*) is defined by one of these
terms, thus by an attitude and a theme that are taken to an absolute.
Nietzsche, however, attributes to each attitude a degree, a level. He
presents an empirical nominalism, on which are superimposed a socio-
political conceptualism, then a poetic realism. Empirically, leaf, dog,
man are concepts that denote only uncertain and variable traces (memories, sensations, images), and do not dispense us from indicating this
individual, this leaf, this dog, this man. With the result that the relationship 'signifier/signified', which is seen as central and has been the object
of so much attention since Saussure, is neither unambiguous nor well
defined. The majority of words, being polysemic, imply 'values' that
permit a meaning to be chosen. However, on the level of the effectiveness of discourse in communication, in other words, the socio-cultural-
political level (as we would put it), the concept has a reality that it obtains
from language as a social fact. It thus has an institutional significance;

right, law, truth itself, wield this practical existence in a social architecture made up of conventions and 'values', those of castes and classes. At
a still higher level, there are realities both symbolic and concrete, accessible only to the musician, to the poet, and consequently true by a different truth than that of experience or of socio-political concepts. The sun,
for example, is both a symbol and more than a symbol; a glorious body
that reveals the world, telling of the cosmos, centres of energies and
sources of heat, cycles and returns, tragic deaths and resurrections. The
sun says to the poet what the musician and music also say, likewise
tragic theatre and tragedy. The sun confirms for the eye what dance and
heartfelt song teach those who have ears to hear. The sun thus has a
triple existence: *empirical* (at this level it is taken as the object of science),
social (regulator of time and space for human activities), and finally
poetic (symbolic and mythic). It is this last that has the greatest importance (value). Between these levels and degrees of language, all kinds of
transitions, substitutions and metaphors, transfers and metonymies are
at work. On many occasions, Nietzsche notes the importance of visual
metaphors (vision, perspective, point of view, etc.) in rational (social
and political) language.

This is where *metaphilosophical* thought comes in, responding to
questions of the philosophers yet without being itself a philosophy.

Let us admit that an order had to be imposed on the chaos of sensations, the confusion of sentiments. Let us admit that this had to begin
with the *inter-dit*.[21] Time comes to an end with history itself. And yet
this period is extended. Why and how? At the level of social and political practice, discourse is not innocent, language is not inoffensive – no
more than is knowledges. And we again encounter and discover the
question of power. Philosophy has produced and reproduced the
discourse of power without ever dissociating itself from it otherwise
than in appearance. Only the poet transcends this discourse.

6) Does the Nietzschean critique of knowledge aim at destroying this?
Does Nietzsche take the side of non-knowledge against knowledge, of
discourse without law or faith against reason? No, certainly not. Rightly
not. We have to insist on this, to repeat it. Such an interpretation distorts

21   [*Dit* = said, *interdit* = forbidden, *inter-dit* implying something 'said between' or
sub rosa. – Translator.]

his thought by precipitating it into absurdity. The fetishism of the absurd, the cult of the irrational, replace the fetishism of logos only for a thought that swings between fetishes. Poetry does not forbid understanding. On the contrary: by starting from lived experience, it reaches a cognition qualitatively different from knowledge; this cognition of 'living' and the 'lived' reprises the other spheres (empirical, socio-logical, socio-political) by giving them a new meaning. It differs from abstract knowledge in nature, in essence, and not simply in degree. Cognition reveals the cruelty of lived experience, the implacable relations of force that make it what it is. It reveals the bitterness of combats, which have nothing in common with struggles of ideas, writings and scribes.

To make possible the transition from one sphere to the other, we have first to delimit the sphere of knowledge: to show the limits of socio-logical logos and discourse. This knowledge, with its political use and its logico-linguistic scaffolding, has a domain: political society. It tends to eliminate residuals, differences and the body itself, the entire lived experience, by malignly confusing them with ignorance and misunderstanding and misuse – even with stupidity, that old alibi of men of knowledge – whereas this knowledge is itself misunderstanding and misuse; even, in the extreme case, foolishness! Poetic meditation rejects these reductive procedures of knowledge, and especially of political (state) knowledge. If some people speak naïvely, no one writes innocently. Here we can see the connection, the link, and more still, the fundamental collusion, between knowledge [*savoir*] and power [*pouvoir*]. All writing, except poetic writing which recaptures speech, is reductive, a mortal moment of language.

The Nietzschean reflection on non-knowledge and knowledge (or, as is sometimes said, on the unthought within thought and the unperceived within the perceived) is pursued in two opposing directions. Sometimes, in modernity, we see a violent enterprise aiming at the conquest of non-knowledge, its annexation, its resolution into knowledge: this is the reductive enterprise. Or else, on the contrary, reflection (or meditation) uncovers (unveils) the meaning of non-knowledge, develops (unfolds, opens out) the non-known and reveals the constraining action that has placed it in this situation. This rather particular deciphering presupposes other methods than the logical.

Does not the ambiguity of psychoanalysis result from the fact that neither Freud nor his disciples made a clear choice between these two paths? Whereas Nietzsche had shown the two perspectives and opted for the second.

The perspective and poetic practice of Nietzschean cognition runs directly against the Hegelian construction of knowledge. In relation to Marxist theory, there is divergence rather than opposition. In the name of a supposed 'theoretical practice', the Marxist conception of cognition has been aligned to that of Hegel, not without muddying the tracks. In taking up the Marxist theory, we should recall that, for Marx, the critique of classical philosophy and the critique of specialized scientificity (polit-ical economy, first of all) expand into a critical theory of intellectuality. The latter, despite its ambitions and pretensions, results from the divi-sion of labour. Within a science, or a laboratory, or a team, there can be a technical division of tasks, with complementarity. On a wider scale, the social division, in other words, the market (capitalist or not), imposes its laws. That is the social status of acquaintance. If the philosopher seeks to transcend the social division of intellectual work, he succeeds only incompletely, at his own risk and peril. Only radical critique, which banks on the critical moment, manages a certain superseding.

Knowledge as such, simultaneously separate (from everyday life, from the people), erected (into distinct institutions) and merged (invested in production and various activities, including political ones), becomes a *property of capital* (not of a single capitalist or of capitalists as a class, but of the society in which capital exerts its hegemony). The aim of theory and action is therefore to seize cogni-tion from capitalism, from the bourgeoisie, from its state, from the state in general, from political use, which presupposes first of all that specialism is rejected as a criterion (as superior to the non-specialized, to the everyday, to global cognition), and subsequently that we redis-cover somewhere, in the concept or in the social, an intellectual *subject*. How? By class struggle waged on every site, on every level, in every domain, Marx replies.

We could also reply in a Nietzschean vein: 'By changing the meaning and centre of cognition, by employing analysis to reveal what is hidden in all the activities of society where cognition is twisted by hegemony, where it exerts its power over knowledge, with knowledge. By decoding the messages of both non-knowledge and knowledge. By understanding non-knowledge as such, without reducing it. By revealing the underly-ing values so as to bring them to light, sometimes to take them into account, sometimes to reject them, after passing them through the sieve of an attentive but friendly critique'.

If Western knowledge – logos – is bound up with material growth (economism, productivism, quantitativism), the question raised above and Nietzsche's reply to it are completely valid. However, this dismisses logos, which Marx and Marxist thought fundamentally accept as a social gain, liberating it from its capitalist and bourgeois trammels.

It is not certain that the 'de-centring' of logos can consist simply in a work on language (and a literary practice). In the Nietzschean line of argument, it is necessary to go further. To replace the fetishism of logos and its rhetorical unconscious by the fetishism and rhetoric of desire? This half-baked project again does not correspond to the Nietzschean perspective.

Here too, recourse to the Hegelian thesis makes it possible to get our bearings and locate the Nietzschean perspective. Remember that, for Hegel, *need* has a positive existence, a rational being; it corresponds to an object, to productive work. No need exists in isolation, or returns to the immediacy of natural desire. Needs, therefore, constitute a rational ensemble, a system that enters into the workings of the systems of civil society within the state. The system of needs and systems of work correspond to one another. Each need defines a satisfaction: it consumes an object, one that is reproducible (the conditions of this producibility pertain to political economy). In so far as they go beyond the immediately natural, needs are *abstract* and *social*, one going together with the other (today we would say that they are sophisticated). As for desire, it fails to emerge from the immediacy described in the *Phenomenology*: desire to desire and be desired; it destroys the desired object, devours and brutalizes it; it destroys itself, with no other trace than its ravaging, in a burst of mad enjoyment. Thought and desire lead towards a bad infinity: romantic rhetoric, ceaseless verbiage, irrational delirium.

Marx? Against desire, he chooses need. Although he puts it in brackets in order to analyse exchange-value, need and use are connected. The Marxist critique of labour does not extend – with Marx – to the critique of need, despite touching on this here and there. Despite certain reservations (in the *1844 Manuscripts*), there is no disagreement on this point between Hegel and Marx, who accepts the rationality of Western society (limited because bourgeois, but nonetheless real). Over the last century, Marxist reflection has avoided this reef. A surreptitious division may be noted: should needs be limited (the position of certain Trotskyists), or expanded indefinitely (the position of the productivists), or should their artificiality be combatted (the position of moralists, humanists and naturalists).

With Nietzsche, a different perspective opens. Desire and lived experience (misunderstood and not knowing itself) pertain to poetry. The initial desire and final result, we might say, of an explosive expenditure of energy. A certain energy (quantifiable, though this is not so important) is focused at a centre, on a 'subject'; but this energy exists only by acting, producing an effect. The living or thinking being expends it in games and struggles, as well as in work. They waste it frenetically. Needs? These are calm investments and rewards of vital energy. What shapes them? Language, the socio-political architecture, the political power and ideological pressure that are exerted on desire. And work . . .

As for 'profound' thought (in scare quotes, as Nietzsche ironizes and mistrusts as soon as the conscious being emerges from the surface, the scintillating mirror, the poet alone being able to soar), Nietzsche's thought seems to be as follows, at least until *The Gay Science*. Initially the 'profundity' of the body, of explosively accumulated energy, of physiological phenomena, is shapeless; accidents play a predominant role. Two procedures enable a certain order to be introduced into this initial and fundamental chaos: language brings the logic that simplifies, and judgement and appreciation bring the ethical or aesthetic value that makes choice possible. Then a social life can 'function'; need rules, whether determined or free.

Grand Desire gathers the energies scattered into various needs and activities, determined by logical conventions and moral evaluations. Grand Desire differs from initial desire in the way that altitude differs from the deep shadow beneath the surface. Initially, desire is unconscious and expended without consideration. Gathered and condensed, creative energy is not wasted, does not produce just any chance object, is not lost by destroying at random. Grand Desire is the desire of the superhuman; it is *already* the superhuman, its presence and its birth. It plays, but the rules of its game are in no way puerile. It destroys, without barbarity. It reaches the highest consciousness, that of overcoming (Überwinden); in other words, it is destroyed, consumed, transcended. Grand Desire includes cognition; it combines this with art, and above all with the art of living (since in high civilization, that of *The Gay Science*, one learns to desire; cf. section 334); it advances far beyond what we know (we human, too human!).

7) The concept (or rather, the concept-image) of the *will to power* has a certain relationship to the mortal struggle of consciousnesses according to Hegel. Nietzsche repeatedly said that every German is in some part Hegelian, and consequently has their share of violence. In the *Phenomenology*, self-consciousness is born from reciprocal action between consciousnesses in the embryonic state; this painful birth does not happen without struggle. Emergence above the immediate, nature, the 'unconscious', into abstraction and reflection (self-consciousness), implies a struggle to the death, in the course of which (more exactly, at the end of which) each 'actor' comes to be known and recognized by the other, and consequently reflects (recognizes) themselves. A game of mirrors? A play on words? A sleight of hand? Not at all. And there is nothing erotic in Hegelian thought. Conflict is necessary for emergence. Master and slave confront one another arms in hand. Knowledge benefits from this, but the philosopher learns only later, perhaps too late.

Does the class struggle, as seen by Marx, continue the Hegelian concept of the mortal struggle of consciousnesses? Yes and no. No, as for Marx these struggles have precise historical conditions, in antiquity, the Middle Ages, or capitalism. The struggle is not a phenomenological moment of consciousness in general. No, as the confrontation takes place between classes and not between speculative 'subjects', master and slave. No, as the struggle does not have as its reason and end recognition (of self in the other, of the other in oneself, of oneself), but ownership of the means of production and the social surplus product. And yet, *yes*, as the class struggle waged to the end educates the consciousness of the subjected, changes this into cognition, and sooner or later overthrows the situation to the benefit of the workers.

The Nietzschean will to power differs from this 'struggle to death' of consciousnesses in as much as it is not a moment. It is permanent, and not superseded in the course of a history. Knowledge itself serves the will to power. It is not overthrown; if the slave rebels against the master, if he risks death once again in order to conquer, it is because the will again becomes stronger than the memory – the *ressentiment* – of defeat, and that he has invented 'values' that impel him to combat rather than to acceptance. The struggle does not lead to a mutual and reciprocal re-cognition, but to a victory over yesterday's conquerors, or to a defeat of the rebels, often to a contagion or contamination of the conquerors by the 'values' of the conquered. The oppressed, the conquered, are not thereby deprived of the *Wille zur Macht*. They are simply the weaker, sometimes just for a while. Women, for example.

Nietzsche attempted an ontology of the 'will to power', contained in the book that falsely bears this title, as he planned to call it *The Innocence of Becoming*. This ontology is only very little removed from a rationalization or theorization *accepting* the 'given', the 'reality', that are envisaged.

It is true that the will to power expresses the vital energy that acts in the body. This energy is accumulated and expended in various ways, most commonly with violence, except in cases where it is contained and maintains its tension, refining this and thereby attaining the levels of concentration at which it finds plenitude and joy: in poetic creation, in pleasure (the will assumes a tension that by successive degrees and measured rhythms mounts the slope leading it to the summit, moments of relaxation and expenditure, the surging burst, deliverance, self-destruction, perhaps orgasm).

The theory of the will to power, accordingly, relates to an energy that is fundamental yet complex. What it faces is exclusively other wills to power, other energies, diverse in their unity and reciprocal relationship. It reigns on the socio-political level: in the struggle for state authority, we can recognize the will to power in what might be called a pure state, since it sees only itself, but this recognition intensifies the struggle instead of superseding it. In the state, the will reveals itself, unveils itself, strips itself bare. But it is also found elsewhere, in all relationships, between man and woman, children and parents, as between oppressors and oppressed (bosses and workers). For Nietzsche, all that profit contributes to the will to power is a pretext, a stimulant, a means. The same goes for logic: *identity* represented, named, taken responsibility for and imposed, serves the will to power, in a way privileged by language.

The will to power cannot be attributed simply to established authority. This resembles pleasure in its capacity for destruction (abuse, immoderation, mad ambition, etc.). What defines the *Wille zur Macht* is more the conquest of power than power itself.[22] In the course of this

22 Georges Bataille confuses these when he writes, in *Inner Experience* (New York:

conquest, the will to power prodigiously invents: masks and disguises (virtue, disinterestedness, charity), and means (the 'values' that enable it to establish itself and to command and organize things).

The concept of the will to power thus brings with it a conception of the world: an interpretation, a global perspective – what for a long while would be called a philosophy. How should we describe its genealogy? It is most commonly related to the influence of Schopenhauer on Nietzsche, the vitalist philosophy of 'wishing to live' that did indeed inspire *The Birth of Tragedy*.

If Nietzsche's works are not taken in isolation, and the later are used to illuminate the earlier, in other words if ten years of life and creation through to the explosion of joy of *The Gay Science* and *Zarathustra* are taken into account, we open up a very different perspective. Nietzsche reveals the subterranean currents of European consciousness, opposed to logos, cast into the shadows by the official rationalism of philosophy and state: courtly love, itself the foundation of *The Gay Science*, Augustinianism, with its triple '*libido*' including the '*libido dominandi*', and finally the great heresy that opposes the crushing paternity of the law, criticizes the primacy of logos, the word, and awaits the advent of the spirit (the heresy of Abelard and of Joachim de Fiore).

This is the fundamental point, by which Nietzsche is descended from other ancestors than the Greco-Roman or Judeo-Christian philosophers. Poetry redeems. It manifests the power of metamorphosis that is revealed in appreciation, judgement, evaluation, as well as in play and art. With poetry, physical and vital energy is superseded (in the Nietzschean sense). Vital energy – the will to power – is superseded not by killing itself off but by overcoming itself and asserting itself in a different sphere: poetry. This is born at the moment of redemption. The poet, like any creator but better than other artists, renounces and denounces the will to power, overcoming it. The superhuman transcends the human, and first of all the *Wille zur Macht*, which has made men and the inhuman relations between them. Does Zarathustra withdraw into solitude so as to put to death his will to power, to deny his will to live in the way of a Schopenhauerian ascetic? On the contrary, he

---

SUNY Press, 2014) that the classical idea of sovereignty, bound up with that of command, is compromised by engagement with the order of things, as it becomes their reason and is no longer independent. He Hegelianizes Nietzsche!

exalts his being, finally revealed, and his dialogue with the sun expresses this revelation and exaltation.

The Nietzschean analysis of the will to power does not claim to annul sexuality and its problems. It does not put them in the foreground. The theory tends to consider the sexual domain (*libido sentiendi*) not as a sphere of causes and reasons, but as one of effects and consequences. What a human being has undergone elsewhere (by the effect of power, of the abuse of authority, privations and humiliations), in all other spheres, is translated into the sexual domain by complementary and supplementary frustrations, which are effects at least as much as causes.

8) As for Nietzscheanism, there is no such thing. There is a Hegelianism, but there is not just one Marxism; and there is not a Nietzschean theory (of the will to power, or of the superhuman, or of eternal recurrence). There is a *Nietzschean practice*, identical neither with the Hegelian practice of knowledge (theoretical practice) nor with political practice (in other words, dialectically and in principle anti-political).

Poetic practice, or rather *poietic* practice, values lived experience to the detriment of the conceived and perceived, overvalued by Western logos. It transcends the will to power by an act that does not metamorphose the real into the surreal, an artificial and impotent operation, but rather the human into the superhuman. The superhuman, far from pressing the taste for power to the extreme, on the contrary redeems themselves from it, so inaugurating a different light, a different horizon, a different world.

Does this perspective imply a more precise *project*, tending to make the impossible possible? Perhaps. The destruction of reality, of the 'subject' in the sense of Western logos ('the cogito'), of identity that serves an authority, norms and values established by authority, in short, *radical* subversion – this perspective can be seen as a 'project'. But it is insufficient. It emphasizes a great risk of death: nihilism. The superhuman is not satisfied with helping the self-destruction of modernity, of the state, of the people (classes) in power. He seeks to draw something else from dissolution: an affirmation. Instead of demolishing point by point, place by place, or simply denying and contradicting the existing order, he wants to *found*. What? An ethic? Certainly not. An aesthetic? Not that either. A way of living that would supersede ethics and aesthetics. Founded on what? Perhaps on an agreement between Dionysus and

Apollo, irreducible yet inseparable. To become heroic in the course of a vain combat, to work out that consciousness (gaining consciousness) can demolish authority as a spiritual force, is not the Nietzschean madness. No more than referring to something 'deep': desire, the unconscious. Nietzsche adopts neither the Western attitude, critical ratiocination, nor the Eastern one: sovereign detachment, renunciation and contemplation, bound up with an ontology. Instead of this, struggle. But what struggle? The one he has waged with his weak means, and the tactic of engaging as cleverly as the powerful, undoing the game of power and playing with it (dodging the blows). And so arriving at a strategy that connects with certain means (poetic writing) or even certain forces. One that does not include violence, but does not exclude it: the simple 'use value' of things, apart from their value in exchange, wealth and power.

'*To the realists*. You sober people who feel armed against passion and fantastical conceptions . . . aren't you too in your unveiled condition still most passionate and dark creatures, compared to fish . . .?'[23]

9) What is there in common between the Nietzschean theme of *ressentiment* and the Hegelian concept of *alienation*, which Marx detached from the Hegelian system and took over in order to elucidate social practice?

'Man', for Nietzsche, does not live as a being of need or desire, but rather of *ressentiment*. This term has a far stronger meaning than the trivial one: to resent something (a sentiment, an impression). A past situation, which the subject seems and believes itself to have emerged from, has left its traces. In the 'unconscious'? Perhaps, unless these traces constitute the 'unconscious' itself. They do not coincide exactly with memory: *ressentiment* differs from recognition. The initial situation is re-lived, repeated; it returns and its remembering makes it obsessive, pregnant, determinant. Simultaneously, the 'subject' allows itself to be attached to the situation and actively does so; it turns away from the present and revives the past. It flees the actual, unable to *live* it. Its *vécu* is located far back, 'deeply' back.

Did Nietzsche anticipate psychoanalysis? To a certain point, indeed, but his theory goes deeper. What produces *ressentiment* is not some

---

23 *The Gay Science*, 57

mental event, a lack, a pain. It is always or almost always a *humiliation*. It is in this way that Nietzsche pursues an in-depth excavation of the concept of alienation. The *ressentiment* of the being alienated by humiliation has something irreparable, irremediable, irreversible about it. Why? Because it amounts to denying one's humiliation, finding a singular pleasure in it; and above all, drawing from it a virtue: humility. People make themselves humble, virtuous, in order to accept humiliation and change it into a disturbed happiness. They seek the humiliating situation, or something similar to this. They offer themselves as victims, prey, objects, to the will to power that has trampled them.

Humanizing and optimistic rationalism accepted that a total de-alienation would erase the initial alienation, and could be accomplished by a reverse process to this alienation. For Hegel, the absolute Idea reabsorbs the initial alienation by which the world emerges from its womb; it even reprises the world as a kind of test, charged with knowledge. The slave can conquer the master and supersede (in the Hegelian sense) the situation of defeat. Similarly for Marx, productive (industrial) work, managed and reorganized by the working class, will supress alienating and alienated labour, divided and imposed as a foreign force.

Nietzsche no longer believes that concrete alienation – humiliation, severe deprivation – can disappear without indelible traces. The oppressed, the subjected, will have generated within themselves 'values' that enabled them to live, by concealing from themselves or even (which anyway comes to the same thing) accepting the conditions of their life. Abasement becomes a *raison d'être*, with compensations, complications, explanations, justifications; it marks out a place, the site of a hierarchy; as if by chance, every humiliated individual has others below him that he can belittle: women, children, animals, outcasts. The offended party comes to define himself in his own eyes by the moment of humiliation (the homage paid to the powerful, loyalty, devotion, etc.). In conditions of modernity, men of *ressentiment* proliferate. Everyone resents everyone else. Those who want power to revenge themselves on the existing power do not escape this destiny; they maintain it. In the same way as there are 'men of *ressentiment*', there are also women. Perhaps all women: instead of blaming morality and religion (which pretend to protect them) for their misery, they attack men, 'males', diverting the question.

Taken together, the offended and humiliated[24] establish a vicious circle, a deadly ring, a tourniquet; they increase the repetition of the resented experience, directly or otherwise; it is the only thing that they speak of. Who? Women in particular. Believers. The 'subjects' of a monarch or any government: of a state. Workers? Perhaps. Slaves, always, if the masters have known how to handle their domination. *Ressentiment* provides the secret of accepted slavery, preferred to death.

Culpability is therefore a *state*, rather than the consequence of a definite act. This *state* ravages the West, under the sign of the State. The sense of being at fault, original or derisory, mortal or venal, is linked with *ressentiment* as a source of anxiety that demands explanation. Occasions for culpability are not lacking: wars, harmful activities, and so many others. But the foundation – the fundamental character – of this culpability escapes Europeans, so enabling religious spirits, philosophers or politicians to exploit a feeling that is unaware of itself as *ressentiment*, a poison of consciousness.

The problem for Nietzsche, moreover, is not so much to diagnose or explain the sense of culpability and its poisoned source, *ressentiment*, as to show the way to curing it. The aim is health, the great health that overcomes the great sickness, the nihilism to which *ressentiment* leads. What is the path to rediscovering health? Return to nature? No. On the contrary, to overcome both nature, that is, the will to power, and the test of becoming, *ressentiment* and culpability. Instead of a historical time strewn with victories and defeats, aggressions and humiliations, the Gay Science illuminates the innocence of becoming. It does not follow a path prefabricated by a providence or arranged by a hidden rationality. It proceeds by chance. There is neither responsibility nor culpability for the individual in general, which in no way dispenses us from drawing up a charge sheet against certain individuals: the powerful.

10) At the same time as Hegel and Marx, a certain Kierkegaard placed a stumbling block on the path of becoming (of progress): *repetition*. Søren Kierkegaard introduced the paradox in a manner that is rightly seen as mystical. Kierkegaardian repetition (that which Job on his

---

24   Nietzsche's correspondence relates his enthusiastic discovery of Dostoevsky (belatedly, in French translation).

dunghill requests of God, after he has lost everything, that which Kierkegaard demands for his shattered love of Régine) exorcises time, that diabolical marvel, by invoking the Eternal. God can bring back the dead, suspend time, wind it back. And that is why God can restore what has been lost: original innocence, worldly goods (Job), the beloved (Kierkegaard). At the centre is transcendence. The paradox of repetition is likewise introduced by this.

As early as the war of 1870–1, Nietzsche proclaimed that history, reason and knowledge were drowning in an ocean of mud and blood. First repetition: the violence whose necessity seems obvious to the men who take decisions – and whose absurdity seems no less obvious to those who experience it.

But it is particularly on the basis of poetry, music and theatre (tragedy) that Nietzsche highlights the repetitive. We could study here how in his prose and his poems he uses classical procedures, all proceeding from repetition: rhyme, alliteration, recalls, syllables and key words. His poetry does not imitate music; it does not seek to be musical, it does not bend language to the laws of another art; it brings into language what has been achieved in music. Music is based on repetition. Everything in it is repetitive, not only its themes (the Wagnerian *leitmotiv*, the theme of the fugue, etc.), but also 'notes', intervals, timbres, rhythms (measure), etc. And yet, in relation to music, everyone speaks of freshness, movement, rushing, streaming, constant invention and even temporality. No repetition without difference, and no difference without repetition. As for tragedy, it goes even further in repetition: it resuscitates the hero by way of a prepared and rehearsed text. The tragic act, the mortal moment, the holocaust, is recommenced in a place devoted to this rite. It is relived with a difference: tragic joy.

Nietzsche puts the repetitive at the centre of his reflections. Instead of becoming? Not exactly. The problem is precisely to understand how there is becoming in repetition and repetition in becoming. For Nietzsche, the ancient image of the Heraclitean flux comes up against the repetitive, but the repetitive cannot be taken in isolation, as 'pure' repetition. Taken by itself, arbitrarily isolated, it makes becoming incomprehensible. Now, there is time (and even a multiplicity of times: rhythms, lineages, cycles) and a prodigious diversity of creations of becoming. But there are repetitions within time. This is the paradox that seems to elude science. Nietzsche, without disavowing science, places himself on the border between the conceived and the experienced, and thus between science and non-science: on the crest. This non-science is the *vécu*, joy and suffering, ever repeated, ever new. Divine laughter, the dance of the gods, the Gay Science, transgresses the *vécu* better and more than does sad science. This is poetry. This is the intoxication of becoming and of repetition. 'Return with all your torments' – that is how the *yes* to living is uttered.

Do we want to begin with knowledge instead of beginning with the critique of knowledge, with music, tragedy, poetry? That is possible, despite being the opposite path to that of Nietzsche. He never *systematized* the elements of his thought, on the so-called philosophical level. To *systematize* him is thus to traduce him. Here and now we are going to traduce Nietzsche, lucidly, the better to show him by his wrong side, as we might say, and the better to display him. For Nietzsche, difference is essential, although this term does not fit exactly. How can the importance of difference be *demonstrated* against those who challenge it – rationalists, people of the state?

The repetitive is the identical, and it is the very principle of logical identity: A = A. This formal principle implies a repetition, as close as possible to absolute repetition. And yet this second 'A' cannot repeat the first absolutely and in a total fashion, simply because it is second. Formal logic is involved here, and the series of numbers, in other words, mathematics: one plus one equals two. *A repetition generates a difference:* the smaller the difference, with the least content, the minimum is the residue. So it is transparent. And yet, from one operation to another, one repetition to another, an infinity is created. The infinite set of whole numbers (a set within which every difference is minimal) makes it possible to generate other infinite sets (fractions, transcendental numbers, etc.), and to extract the concept of infinite (transfinite) number. Between infinite numbers the differences are maximal. Pure logic is logically superseded.

The repetitive is the generation of numbers, and therefore of sets, of space and spaces. The infinite is generated on the basis of repetition, by concepts that today are almost fully elucidated: series and recurrences, sets, the transfinite, the power of continuity, the numerable and non-numerable, the set of sets. The greatest difference (infinite/finite) is perceived and grasped in this way. But the repetitive overflows the field of numbers. It extends to gestures, to practical acts that are reiterated. *Linear* repetition covers an immense field. On condition that we accept what it is not possible to accept: the repetitive *generates* the differential, but conversely, the differential is *produced* by repetition, in the course of a specified time.

Knowledge, therefore, and repetition itself (memory, reiterated operations, logic, etc.), is knowledge of the repetitive, just as work consists of repeated gestures. Does this field, this immense domain of the repetitive, come to a close? No. The repetitive is also the double, doubling and redoubling. Thus duplication and duplicity. Thus symmetry and dissymmetry, the mirror and mirror effects, mirage effects, echo, reflection, image. And why not the mask? The deceptive reflection?

The repetitive is again revealed in memory. Thus with all cognition: cognition means re-cognition (reminiscence). The bitter counterpart is *ressentiment*. Does not language itself have to be attributed to the linear repetitive, the repetition (in combination) of articulated sounds? Do not mental realities have to be located here: 'self-consciousness' (doubling, duplication, duplicity) and its basis or foundation in the body, the 'unconscious', with their reciprocal interactions, calls and recalls?

But the repetitive divides in its turn: linear/cyclical. *The cyclical is rhythm*. Rhythms: those of the living being. Who says rhythm says repetition. On the (moving) boundary between the linear and the cyclical, there is 'the unconscious'. Every living body receives information, from the cell to the human being, and it decodes only a tiny part of this plethora of messages. The theory of messages and codes, redundancies and variations of information, belongs to the theory of repetition. The living body has a *double character*: massive energies are distributed and expended according to cycles and rhythms, energies that are fine, informational, relational, situational, linear messages both coded and decoded. The double character of the living body is a function of the double character of repetition: *linear and cyclical*.

This is not all: not yet the All. If reflection examines the world, it discloses the cycles of the seasons, of life and death. (Dionysus and his powers; the path through tests, tragic demises and resurrections.) If reflection examines the cosmos, it reveals light. (Apollo, dream and clarity.) Energy, the foundation of being, spreads out: the law of energy is to be expended. It is dispersed by squandering itself. The energy game is played by way of the cycle 'leakage/concentration'. Energy establishes centres, nuclei, foci. Around these, spheres and systems. And this from the tiny particle through to galaxies, from the micro to the macro. Always a tension, a will to action, thus to power, which spreads, whether generous or brutal. The sun has the triple existence already recognized: empirical, socio-political, symbolic (poetic). Likewise, the small focus of the living body, the subject (the brain and its periphery). Here is the famous subject: a centre. *Not a substance*: a small centre of impulses, desires, in a word, of energies, which expend and disperse themselves, not without leaving traces.

Here, reflection shifts while dancing on the edge that separates knowledge from non-knowledge. On one side of the divide (it is ironic that, starting from knowledge, and generating it by the repetitive, reflection ends up living as non-knowledge) we have knowledge generated (generating itself) by repetition. On the other, we have the *vécu* indifferent to this genesis, but receiving from this difference another dimension, which itself has to be cognized and recognized. Living: joy, bodily pleasure, anxiety, trance and dance. Tragedy (the resurrection of heroes, denial of time by a re-presented repetition). Music (the upsurge and resurrection of joy, inseparable from pain). Death (which is repeated with life). Finally, history (with its problematic: uncertainties and certainties, memory and knowledge, tomb of time past and recall to light, encumbrance and yet solicitation).

Knowledge banks on the least difference, and art, in contrast, on maximal differences irreducible to those induced within any kind of ensemble, system or logic. What then of the future in the Nietzschean perspective? It is the totality of the cyclical and the linear, evolutions and revolutions. The same and the other. The identical and the different. And their reciprocity, their generation. Hence the obscure and the intelligible. Mythical thought and rational thought. The world and the cosmos, Dionysus and Apollo: subterranean labyrinths and hillsides in the light of day. Philosophy? Freed from the metaphysical (metaphorical) apparatus, the secretion of bureaucracies (ecclesiastical, political), it is here: reprised entirely, but on a different level, in a different light, with different obscurities. On a different trajectory, in a different project. Totalized and totalizing in a new way: from logic to music, from mathematics to poetry, from first faltering steps to creative works, which does not exclude reflection, rejecting the ec-static,[25] pleasure close to pain, trance, death, to the inaccessible. Becoming? It is this: a change in which

---

25 [As also in his discussion of Heidegger in *Metaphilosophy*, Lefebvre hyphenates 'ec-static' to emphasize its literal meaning of 'standing outside oneself'. – Translator.]

everything changes, except the totality of changes. In a relationship that is paradoxical, but elucidated by what it implies and contains, what it degenerates into, by what it is generated: the repetitive. To be or not to be? No: '*Werde das du bist*' (become what you are).

Yes. By saying this 'yes', we have accepted the worst hypotheses: the terrifying one of eternal repetition of the same, in other words, the accidents that have made us ourselves, the circumstances that have produced our mediocre too human existence, but also, and by the same token, the marvellous one of the superhuman, which is born at this very moment, bringing the meaning of becoming.

Two great lineages of philosophical thought converge here (intermingling with others, empiricism and rationalism, materialism and idealism, nominalism and conceptual realism, etc.): the Eleatic and the Heraclitean. The ancient and modern Eleatics may deny the importance of motion; they cannot deny its existence without changing the celebrated paradoxes of Zeno into dogmas. As for the Heracliteans, they have to acknowledge the importance of at least cyclical repetition. (Heraclitus already accepted it, with his 'great year'.)

The theory of universal becoming cannot refute the repetitive by relegating it to the merely apparent. The theory of the intelligible unmovable may appear to reject flux and chaotic movement, but it has to admit that becoming creates forms, determinate 'beings', genera and species that are named.

What leaves room for the intervention of thought, the practical gesture? *The repetitive*. Every action assumes a repetition, as it is itself repeated: gestures, aims. Philosophy has elucidated this feature of practical (technical) activity. According to Hegel, it is the analytical understanding rather than dialectical reason that is involved in practice, in work. For Marx, likewise, dialectical thought only discovers itself, and only discovers the real and its contradictions, by confrontation between the real and the possible, at the level of the totality. On the contrary, this in no way excludes the production of something new by the ensemble (totality) of reiterated gestures, repetitive acts, mechanical and technical interventions (which according to Marx form part of the productive forces that transform nature).

If this is correct, how can we be surprised by the importance of the repetitive in the modern world, with its objects, products and gestures? The satisfaction of having generated by repetition the knowledge of this world and in this world does not suppress the unease. And we understand better why Nietzsche did not persist in constructing a system out of repetition, but created Zarathustra to overcome the nihilism inherent in modernity. We have sketched this system above, to show what the poet Nietzsche did not say. In itself it would be only one system among so many others that modern thought has elaborated since Hegel. Every systematic mind draws a masochistic pleasure from the prison in which it confines itself, by carefully drawing the bolts. Nietzsche, for his part, opens them. 'With a hammer', indeed, but also with his blood.[26]

Modernity slips into repetition (and into consciousness of the repetitive, simultaneously revealed and masked by ideologies: pan-mathematism and pan-conceptualism, the fetishism of the combinatory and the structure, 'design' and models, etc.). The modern era thus savours to the dregs the taste of repetition. The history from which it long believed it proceeded denied repetition or granted it only a weak part, in the name of a becoming both fetishized and rationalized. This monumental history collapses, like systematic philosophy, itself monumental, along with the justifications and legitimations that many people believed and still believe they can draw from it. Modernity has this double aspect: everything changes and nothing changes; everything shakes and everything stagnates. Is not the most crippling repetition that of tyranny? Revolution, in the name of liberty, has generated a resumption of the ancient despotisms, in an aggravated modern version. But repetition is not confined to the spheres of power and the state. It is massive, by the mediation of techniques.

The importance of the repetitive, which Nietzsche revealed through a critique of history, historicism, evolutionism and the (Hegelian) philosophy of becoming, also through a rigorous analysis of poetry, music and tragedy, is thus being regularly confirmed. On all sides.

Critical analysis of everyday life shows the involvement of cyclical repetitions (hours, days and nights, weeks and months, seasons, needs) and linear repetitions (the gestures and actions of work, of family life, of social relations). Similarly, analysis of economic phenomena and, more widely, of the *reproduction of social relations* of production). This reproduction fundamentally banks on the generalization of the repetitive: if

---

26 Among the more recent, we have already cited above: Yves Barel, Michel Clouscard and Jean Baudrillard. We could also have included Herbert Marcuse, Marshall McLuhan, Jacques Monod, etc.

everything is repeated, then social relations automatically continue, by becoming automatic, by forming part of the general automatism. To the point that it is not just philosophy and knowledge that can be defined in terms of the conflictual relationship between repetition and becoming, nor modernity as (ideological) illusion, but the *entire society*. Everything weighs on one side towards reproduction, towards quantified repetition; and everything (everyone) comes to demand the new, the breakthrough, the qualitative leap forward, which does not come about.

Hegel thus foresaw a state that generated its conditions of formation and equilibrium, a self-generating and self-reproducible system. Marx, on the contrary, foresaw in the name of the proletarian revolution a leap forward of becoming, a new 'generation', without repetition but without loss of the past. Nietzsche both denounced the danger of a repetition that would kill all difference and made the demand for a complete break that transcended the past.

Here we see clearly the radical difference between Hegelian and Marxist supersession, which preserves antecedents and preconditions at a higher level by 'raising' them (more so for Hegel, less so for Marx), and the Nietzschean supersession, which denies, rejects, disowns, belies, refutes, casts into the abyss. Optimistic *Aufheben* and tragic *Überwinden* confront one another, and with them difference and repetition (reproduction).

How to choose, and is this necessary?

11) The discovery of imitation (*mimesis*) as a mental and social phenomenon cannot be attributed to Nietzsche. He did not even think of making explicit, still less of systematizing, a theory of mimesis[27] or 'mimicry'. He showed its importance in a critical analysis (critical in the Nietzschean sense: sarcastic, rather than ironic or humorous). A Hegelian admires imitation as the rational power that stimulates the reproduction of a human, social or political type. As for the Marxists, and even Marx himself, they neglected such phenomena, leaving aside the theory of identity and change (metamorphosis), in other words, of repetition and difference, of imitation and creation.

---

27 For an explanation of the concept and an attempt at a 'system', cf. Eric Auerbach, *Mimesis: The Representation of Reality in Western Literature*, Princeton: Princeton University Press, 1953.

Nietzsche revealed the importance of mimesis in nature. No leaf of an oak tree is rigorously and absolutely identical to another, and yet all oak leaves resemble one another; the concept of 'leaf' that retains only these resemblances and changes them into identity does not have the truth that the stubborn champions of knowledge attribute to it. And yet, such concepts make it possible for empirical consciousness, practical activity, to have their sphere, and for humans to dwell in a socio-political construction (architecture). In the course of evolution, from the time a species of plant has existed until it disappears, each individual re-produces that from which it is born. Between oak leaves the differences are minimal, internal to the species (characterized as a balanced 'system', each plant and the whole set of plants belonging to the genus constituting a whole). The oak and the oak leaves, its branches and its bearing, differ from the palm tree and its attributes. Here, difference makes a leap and becomes maximal. We could say the same when a new species arises, which confirms the distinction (difference) between differences *induced* within an ensemble, by repetition and mimesis, and differences produced outside of such an established system, when this system breaks up or metamorphoses.

In society, the mechanism of mimesis is a double one. It proceeds by direct *identification* with the type or model: the enslaved, the subjected, the oppressed, the people of *ressentiment*, identify with the strong man, the conqueror, the possessor and master. They re-produce him within themselves, with no intermediary. Thus children imitate their father, or subjects their prince, or soldiers their leader. Often mimesis proceeds indirectly, starting from an image or *symbol*, whether or not issued by a superior power: in an established church, each person indirectly imitates a saint, or rather, the image of one, and directly imitates the dignitary placed one step higher in the hierarchy. The analogical and the symbolic differ, but have the same effect: mimesis. This is how the comedy of the world goes, in which the best actor is the one who acts most 'sincerely'. Words serve as instruments for this comedy, more concrete (real) than discourse. Moralists (La Rochefoucauld) had long denounced the comedy of the world, but without studying its foundations and roots.

In both cases, the mimetic process includes a simulation and yields simulacra: copies that are more or less accurate. According to Nietzsche and his followers, simulation is one of the mechanisms by which individuals insert themselves into a socio-political reality, and conversely by which society uses both discourse and schemas, symbols and images, to integrate individuals.

The phenomenon thus has an enormous amplitude and a decisive weight in the re-production of the summit of society by the base, without which the socio-political structure would collapse. The complexity of mimesis is increased by the fact that creation begins with imitation and cannot begin otherwise: the future creator makes their debut by choosing a father or a master (Wagner, for Nietzsche) from whom they then take their distance, executing them if need be. As a path of creation when a metamorphosis (a difference) is produced, mimesis may also block the way by sterilizing the procedure, leading instead to repetition. The 'mimesis' phenomenon thus covers the entire socio-political field, including ethics and aesthetics, as well as fashion, education and various 'influences' (justified or not by representations, that is, by ideologies).

Some strange realities derive from mimesis, halfway between appearance and metamorphosis. The mask, for example. As a simulacrum, it duplicates the face and conceals it: the 'I' becomes an other for itself, what it wants to become. Military uniform, generator of a mimesis supported by power, is a successful mask. Apprenticeship in a role made possible by a mask leads to duplication, or metamorphosis, or repetition and return to the acknowledged identity. 'Larvatus prodeo', I advance masked, is the motto of every innovator; the mask serves as shelter, alibi. One can get lost in a role, but only loss of identity makes change possible.

The enemy is then identity, which attaches logic to mental, social, political reality. It makes possible fixation. Whoever says 'identity' also says logic, tautology, system, vicious circle, circularity, repetition, re-production of self and other. Sterile mimesis, difference induced within an ensemble and reduced to the minimum. Mask and mark, identity proceeds from trapped discourse and completes its work. Whoever says 'loss of identity' also says mutation, metamorphosis, transvaluation, poetic creation. Between the two there is a distance, a dangerous journey. What is the risk? Bewilderment, madness, suicide. Certainly suffering and dissatisfaction. Identity brings the satisfaction of achieved 'being', in ownership. The Dionysian way is not at all rest, it is not the way of rest. The superhuman, maximal difference, is only achieved by undermining identity and bridging (overcoming) minimal differences. Discourse itself dissolves, and poietic practice invents a language.

Between *On Truth and Lies* written in 1873 and *The Gay Science* of 1882, Nietzsche discovered the world of identity behind that of mimesis and mask, as already described by the (immoral) moralists. Initially, he did not yet demand the possible/impossible, the superhuman, but already he could not tolerate the world of image and mask, the comedy of the world, the world of words and rhetoric, in short, social life according to the values imposed. Gradually, slowly, the horizon of metamorphosis, of absolute difference, opened before him. In dread, with a nameless anxiety, he discovered that aspiration to the greatest difference, to the superhuman, was not possible without accepting the most terrible identity, 'eternal recurrence'. If there is metamorphosis, in other words, happy conjuncture and marvellous change, instead of a limitless linear concatenation of causes and effects, reasons and consequences; if there is transmutation, then the same chance can re-produce any moment of the world: metamorphosis can bring about the repetition of a fragment of becoming. The leap into the space of difference (in science fiction terms, we could say into hyperspace) contains the absolute risk of total repetition. If a break with the accomplished is established (not a decentring in knowledge but a decentring in relation to knowledge by diving into the enigmatic depth of the *vécu*, above or below the surface and its mirror effects), who knows what will happen on the other side of the mirror? Collapse, fall into the abyss, breakup of self-consciousness, the opening of the possible excludes no possibility; the best and the worst go together.

Here again, if there is a Nietzschean dialectic, it differs radically from that of Hegel. There is no synthesis between the terms in play. What is born either reproduces what it is born from (keeping the identity of one of the terms, in a minimal difference), or else, leaping across an abyss, it transcends, at its own risks and perils. The tragedy of consciousness overflows the comedy of the world. The deepest contradictions brought to light may serve metamorphosis, which differs from them by an abyssal distance. Simply to cure those who suffer by removing their contradictions in the manner of psychoanalysis is to betray them.

The Nietzschean aspiration thus implies a fundamental rejection of the 'real' as constitutive of the Ego (the 'subject'). Does Nietzsche take up in his own way the philosophical opposition of subjective and objective? No. His thought (his perspective) does not involve philosophical categories. These terms belong to the identification that imprisons the possible. Beyond this realm of identity, of masks and images, of mimesis, beyond the realm of shadows, the sunny horizon beckons.

Yet there is in the vision of 'eternal recurrence' a sense that can be expressed in philosophical terms of identity by return (repetition) and return of identity. What sense? That of nature and consciousness, of health and reflection, of innocence and cognition: a totality.

12) The meaning of the 'gay science' is not exhausted in the repercussions detailed above. These almost systematized analyses simply have the aim of preventing a certain thought, which in modern times believes itself to be radical, from indefinitely repeating the journey Hegel–Marx–Nietzsche, while failing to emerge from nihilism. Recommencing the path at its point of departure shows that no one in Europe has overcome nihilism. A failure on Nietzsche's part? Very likely. Until now, neither he nor we (Europeans, men of modernity) nor anyone has escaped from the realm of shadows.

Another meaning of the 'gay science': there is nothing new without a provocation, a challenge (often dangerous and even increasingly so). No challenge without an aggression, an attack, and therefore without a double risk: putting oneself in play (in question, a banal formula) and engaging with those who are stronger than oneself, so as to bring them into play (into the stake). The Nietzschean radical 'negative' acquires this guise and thus manifests in a movement (not in representation of movement) the contradictions inherent to the real. Otherwise it is simply an extension of learned discourse.

Not everything that seeks to produce a meaning succeeds. Writing and literature are insufficient. Writing, always mimetic, plays its role in reproduction more than in creation. Who does produce a meaning? The person who risks. Over the years, those who have produced meaning died from it and brought it to birth by their death: Socrates, Christ. Madness, a different form of death, can have the same effect. The break with knowledge and power, the great redemption that inaugurates the leap into the possible, implies a break with philosophy as well as with everyday life.

13) Above society, above 'culture', something exists (certainly not the state) that we can call *civilization*. 'Culture'? Educated philistines believe they possess this as their public and private property. Society? This is a

collection of social logics, in other words, of tautologies, circularities, 'systems' great and small.

Civilization is made up of values, in other words, of meanings, which live and die. It is within society that these values and meanings take shape and acquire their form. In the best of cases, such as Greece for example, or the Renaissance in Europe, a great civilization finds shape and strength: light, dancing, vigour.

An 'elitist' conception? Yes, even if it gives the peoples, thus the masses, their share. There is no hierarchy of values, and so no higher values, that are not both accepted and resented by a people. The elite – the philosopher, the poet – can only give form and force to what is germinating within the people. And conversely, peoples and poets can also put an end to higher values, killing philosophers and poets along with other heroes after engendering them: Socrates shows this, and Jesus still more so.

Nietzsche's thought and perspective do not escape an ambiguity that we can see as fertile: as a philosopher, thinker and poet of a certain elitism, and thus appropriate for 'intellectuals' who like to be marginal and set themselves apart, to make by their own means a life of hedonism or democracy; and, on the other hand, a philosopher of unflagging struggle against the state, against any manifestation of the will to power, against the logos that challenges the socio-political. 'Elitism'? Why not? Perhaps liberty, that of the free spirit, has these two aspects today. To confront death while denying the death instinct, to affirm life, is this not an ambiguity that transcends the traditional dualities and duplicities? Lucid, loving pleasure and joy without fear of suffering, playing without displaying, without promulgating a philosophy of play or a rule of the game, creating the total beyond the philosophy – this is the 'gay science'.

14) A theory generally considered as Marxist, although it was Engels and Lenin rather than Marx who elaborated it as a theory of knowledge, declares that consciousness and knowledge are reflections. The majority of philosophers of knowledge have rejected this theory, except those who explicitly seek the warranty of Marxism; the theory of reflection is seen by philosophical opinion as crude. Indeed, Lenin wielded the metaphors of copy, photo and mirror rather brutally.[28] This theory,

---

28 V.I. Lenin, *Materialism and Empirio-Criticism*, passim.

however, suits Nietzsche very well. He adopted it (without reference to Marxism, of course) both in the 'theoretical' fragment of 1873 and in those fragments from a decade or more later designed to show the 'innocence of becoming'.

If thought and consciousness cannot be defined as a substance (the position of Descartes and many philosophers after him, including Hegel), if thought is not a 'being' supplementary to 'Being' – in other words, if there is a difference between being and thought and yet thought corresponds to being – what can it consist of except a reflection? Reflection in the sense of thinking does indeed mean 'reflecting', unless this is merely a metaphor.

But what is a reflection? Where does the mirror that reflects come from? Since a reflection has neither thickness, nor volume, nor weight, and is therefore 'unreal', what does a faithful reflection of the real consist in? Such a reflection, therefore, can only be understood as a form, that of a reflecting surface (which distorts the 'real' in a determined manner).

This is what Nietzsche says, turning as we have already seen the theory of reflection against the naïve thesis of a reflective fidelity.[29] Consciousness? A surface? Reflecting and reflection? Acts of the brain, along with language and logical form, but also of whole bodies, hands, sense organs, limbs, muscles, sex. Because consciousness reflects, action metamorphoses the 'real', not being subject to any 'real' substance, either outside or within. The reflection of cognition leaves open space for symbols, for poetic invention, for conceptual images.

15) Zarathustra declares a return and recourse to the body, the body as source and resource, combining the force of poetry with 'theoretical' declarations. As a return and recourse rather than a call for rescue, the body receives a completely different status compared to that which it had in a philosophy and society pervaded by Judeo-Christianity. Philosophy and religion have betrayed the body, especially in the West; European logos persists in reducing it, breaking it, mutilating it. Below thought, the seat of this thought but with a key and radical difference, there is the body. In what does this difference consist? If we insist on pursuing the interpretation of Nietzsche's poetry by translating it into prose, we have to say that this imprescriptible difference is not definable,

---

29 Cf. in particular *Nietzsche on Philosophy and Truth*, sections 121, 122, 123, etc.

because it intervenes and acts at every moment, including in the reflective consciousness that seeks to grasp it – an inexhaustible difference, at a distance both infinite and finite, between the 'I', the 'ego' and the body, which can be spelled out in a thousand and one ways, all necessary and none sufficient. Is the body the site of pleasure, this state or situation that has only a remote relationship with the situation of the person who knows and thinks? Yes and no. Philosophical hedonism does not get very far. The body suffers and enjoys, suffering has as much meaning as pleasure, sometimes more. It proclaims a possibility, a productive crisis. A site occupied by 'affects', 'impulses'? Yes, but by many other things as well. The reason for acts that make for meaning and value yet have neither meaning nor value, such as the act of learning things, adhering to them? Yes, but these philosophical words only say what the body is in relation to philosophical knowledge.

For Nietzsche, the body contains depth; indeed, it 'is' the depth beneath the mirroring surface. For poetry (or *poiesis*), height, luminosity, the Apollonian sphere. For consciousness, for knowledge, the surface. For the body, the deep layers that the ray of analysis illuminates by piercing them like a dagger. The body, this misunderstood, unknown thing, brings with it limitless riches: rhythms, repetitions (cyclical and linear), difference. From one age to the next, from the child to the adult and the drama of ageing, it supersedes itself, precipitates the past into memory, enriches or impoverishes the entwining of its rhythms, develops or otherwise the ever new relationship between needs and desire and consciousness and action.

A return to hedonism? An adhesion to materialism? No. Irreducible to philosophy, the Nietzschean recourse to the body does not see the body as machine; it opposes to this the body as energy, the body of poetry, music and dance. The negative determination, better than a definition that seeks to be positive by using philosophical language, makes it possible to enter into the Nietzschean perspective. The poet who speaks in Zarathustra wants to put an end to the separation between the mental, the social, the natural, and consequently to the dissociation between the word and the flesh. He seeks to change at the root the relationship of body to language, by no longer overvaluing language itself as abstraction. For Nietzsche there is no *concrete abstraction*, as with Hegel and Marx. He rejects this quasi-concept, which allows all moments to be given an analogous status, by bending them either to the side of the abstract or to that of the concrete. The 'concrete' is the body. The abstract, and hence language – logic, for its part, is incorrigible and unable to renounce its formal abstraction without destroying itself – must be converted into the concrete, the body. There is nothing in common here with the 'corporeality' of the philosophers.

The status of the body? In as much as it can be described retrospectively in relation to logos, it has been perceived by some as the place and product of sin (the Fall, dereliction), and conceived by others as a kind of carnal reserve, the irrational basis of the dominant rationality, useful as a use value that persists through exchanges and exchange-values.

Today, in a Nietzschean orientation, the contradiction is deepening. The whole weight of society falls on the body, adding to the pressures and constraints of the moral tradition the injunctions of performance, the proliferation of mutilating images, metaphorization into the visual. Photography, cinema, the mass media, proceed to a dismembering of the body, a massive substitution of the body by the image, a shift from the physical to visual abstraction, a social transfer of energy to the spectacular. All this serves power, which manipulates concrete existence in this way. The fetishization of discourse and language provide the pretext for doing away with the body, with the result that the undermining of logos in the wake of its abuses of power can lead to its consolidation via the prestige of images of writing and of writings. To this degree, the alienation of Hegel and Marx acquires a changed character and significance. The deterioration of life threatens its vital foundation, the body. 'My children are here, Zarathustra has grown ripe, my hour has come. This is my morning, my day begins: arise now, arise, great noontide!'

Anything that affects the integrity of the body is attributed either to an obscure cause, the death instinct, or to a higher reason, the exigencies of knowledge and the modern world. In this way, the bourgeoisie is excused, and above all Judeo-Christianity and European logos, Greco-Latin in origin. A blind eye is turned to the tactical and strategic operations that attack the foundations of life, rationality and logos itself; that are proceeding to its self-destruction in the exacerbated modern world.

The body (living and total) establishes connections: desire and sense of value – movement and activity and object. This connection operates by way of play, dance, music. By theatre? It did in the past. Perhaps modern theatre, as discourse and spectacle, no longer has the virtues of its antique forerunner. The gap between 'signifier' and 'signified' inherent in discourse is aggravated into fractures and lets each of the two elements of the sign go its own way, unless the body, speech, voice and gesture re-establish the link.

The 'subject'? Philosophical interrogation – coming from the philosophers but calling for a reply – is duplicated. On the one hand, there is the abstract subject, which has to be attacked and dissolved. This is no longer the rational, Cartesian subject (thinking subject), nor the subject of knowledge, the Kantian subject, seat of the categories. Nor the 'subject' of linguists. It is the *subject of power*, with its investments and disguises (*investissements et travestissements*) and its myths: the Father and the Paternal, Property and Patrimony and possession, the Superego and the Supermale, etc. At the summit, the absolute abstract Subject, the state. This sanctifies the empirical existence of the lesser 'subjects of power', and of those who subject others. In this domain, myths are completed by fictions: the 'I' of thought is linked to the 'I' of the citizen (political and legal fiction), to the 'I' of the witness and the 'I' of the judge (moral fiction), to the 'I' of discourse (grammatical fiction), etc. This empirical existence has its functions in its own domain: the relational, the situational, functional discourse as such. It can be an amusing exercise to deconstruct these. Zarathustra does not deprive himself of this pleasure; all 'subjects', including the superior Man, constantly complain of the difficulty of being, the loss of identity, leading to a litany of discontents and complaints on the part of the 'subject'.

Fundamentally and irreconcilably opposed to power is the *concrete subject*: the body. This conceals unsuspected treasures (and not just pleasure or erotic games, a fallacious interpretation, nor simply what psychoanalysis interprets as a symptom). It does not contrast with the abstract as the 'untamed' to the sophisticated (another fallacious interpretation of a far broader indictment). The body when denuded is not just an object of scandal. (Modernity, stupefied by the absence of the body, has tried every escape route, every false exit, for want of having understood *The Gay Science* and *Zarathustra*.) Sex, whether masculine or otherwise, is a part of the body with no right to set itself up as an appreciation and value. No more and no less than has work (or knowledge). Perhaps it is wrong to localize the erogenous in an organ or zone of the body? Doesn't the whole body feel erogenous (the presence of creative Eros), before the signs of non-body and extra-body are deployed.

Should the body be ascribed a new status? This way of putting the question remains naïve. What status? Philosophical? Philosophy does not go beyond an essence: corporeality. Theoretical? Epistemological? With pure theory (the theoretical man) and epistemology, logos tends to sanction the eviction of the body.

A 'status' is not enough to repudiate the fragmentation of the body, the localization and dissociation of its functions (gestures, rhythms) by the division of labour. The *mosaic body*, counterpart or counterpoint of a mosaic knowledge, the body in pieces, only rediscovers its integrity when its 'status' is changed – its theoretical or even social status.

Psychoanalysis has sought to determine a status for the body, as a discipline that is specialized yet bound up with a (clinical) practice. What a failure! The space-time of the body, as depicted by psychoanalysts who seek to discern this, is reduced to the silence before and after speech, to the mortal difference that emerges from one hiatus (between impulse and discourse) and produces another hiatus (castration). This is the space-time of death. Nothing is more opposed to the Nietzschean affirmation: to the transmutation of decadence, nihilism, into a 'yes' to life, and therefore to the total body. The total body presents itself at the same time as virtuality and as actuality. For the psychoanalysts, it has no existence as a totality. For many, the body is duplicated into an organic order and an impulsive order. For these and some others as well, the unity of the body is represented only in the symbolic and the imaginary. The body of the 'subject', and that of the 'other' as the site of the ensemble of signifiers, never join together. Disarticulated in principle by verbal expression, fragmented by sex, the body only rediscovers its unity by abandoning itself to a mortal ec-stacy.[30] For some analysts, only the mirror (material and sensory effect, thus immediate and localized in immediacy) reveals its non-fragmentation to the subject fragmented by sex and discourse. The body as totality (the 'clean' body, site and 'subject' of appropriation) presents itself only in the body of the mother, first of all, then in the fantasy of identification with the 'other'. The image of the total body figures the illusory plenitude destined to be fissured by the death drive and arising from inadequacy. The object that is privileged among all others, the phallus, enables the (masculine) object to pass from being to having, even though the law as fundamental division, foundation of the

30 Cf. Freud, Chapter 7 of *The Interpretation of Dreams*.

law of the father, obstructs him from this. The result is that castration, the paternal speech that executes (kills) the body-in-motion, intervenes sooner or later; the phallus, meeting place of law and logos, but also site of their separation, arouses the vain fantasy of their reconciliation.

Nietzsche calls for subversion, revolt, the revolution of the body. A status? No. At most one could say that the body, in Nietzsche's texts, is described or inscribed at several levels, like language. First of all, the empirical, the body-object. At this level, the body studies itself, analyses itself, scientifically but also in an everyday way. This level includes the functional, the relational, the situational. Then, the socio-political level, the body-subject as foundation of judgements, 'values' that are often negative (blame, humiliation) and metaphorizations (by language, with the growing primacy of the readable-visible)? The body does not govern production and yet this is done with the body and for bodies. At this level, the body plays a role not of transgression but of transmission of knowledge and re-production of social relations, even though these weigh on it. Finally, then, the *poetic* level, that of unity regained via the test of dissociation. *Poetic speech* (and in no way original or terminal speech, that of a god, true by its essence) seeks the unity of the body and the display of its riches. Poetic speech exorcises death (the 'death drive') by the tragic, instead of giving in to this. It manages to conquer the dangers of discourse and writing, renewing both poetry and music by the rhythms of the body, by the repetitive and the differential as in the body.

According to Nietzsche, *poetic practice* means *appropriation*, as a possibility both near and distant. This concept or appropriation, speculatively conceived by Hegel (the restitution of the Idea in the state), is only weakly determined in Marx. The poet Nietzsche opens the horizon of appropriated desire and body; first of all, for the individual to appropriate their own body, and for the human species to appropriate the total body, nature and conquests of multiform activity, hence space. This does not exclude the symbolic and the imaginary, without banking on them alone. And it does not exclude the ideological, starting with the philosophically sanctioned separation of soul and body, spirit and matter (without going so far, like Hegel, as to fetishize the identity of the real and the rational).

Poetic practice is revealed in music and dance, works of life and vitality. 'Glorious body?' No. Concrete body, presence and site of presence, but virtuality as revealed totality.

16) By way of poetry, Nietzsche introduced into Eurocentric logos some explosive assertions. True? False? True and false? Full of meaning? Absurd? These terms and categories are no longer suitable, but they can be used to expound Nietzsche's assertions. These bear first of all on finitude. For philosophy, for Hegel, reflection leads to awareness of the finite: things, life, human reality. In Hegelianism, the struggle and war between states has the function that each moment, each individual, recognizes their finitude by experiencing it. The state survives in the milieu of these struggles of nations, it alone asserts itself here. Outside of the Idea and the state, the infinite for Hegel is only a 'bad infinity' (unbounded, undetermined).

For Nietzsche, 'we' are *infinite*. As for Spinoza.[31] Through thought, knowledge, consciousness? No: through the body. Each body, and thus our own (yours, mine), because it is in time and space, contains the infinite. Infinite space (the cosmos) and time (the world) imply one another and refract, each in its way, the infinite universe. A living body is at the same time a macrocosm (human bodies in relation to cells, molecules and atoms) and a microcosm (in relation to the galaxy). The infinite 'is' everywhere, before the finite. There are both qualitative and quantitative differences between a little living body on the earth on the one hand and the sun on the other, but each draws cosmic energy and focuses this in order to expend it. Time and space, maximally different yet indissociable, are joined at every place and every instant (every 'moment', to distort the Hegelian term). Music expresses this infinity, that of the body, of desire, of silence, which (finite) language does not manage to declare. Each place and each instant relate to the totality of space and time. The living body (yours, mine) has a double and elusive origin: the germ (maternal-paternal, referring to a genealogical lineage) and the species, life as a whole, the earth, referring to the entire cosmos. Each series of assignable causes and effects becomes lost in the night, which arouses ontological nostalgia, nostalgia for the origin. Each series refers to the other, the genealogical lineage to cosmological becoming and vice versa. The palpable and the unfathomable go hand in hand. The unfathomable is the bottom, the depth, chaos. The palpable is the surface, skin, the glance, the mirror, the

---

31 Cf. Nietzsche's letter of 30 July 1881. His analysis of cosmic energy, time and space, in the texts published under the false title *The Will to Power*, correspond to this appreciation.

meeting of time and space in a moment (place and instant). On the one hand, height, space. On the other, the abyss, time. In 'us', in the body.

It follows that 'infinity' is the initial, original fact. What has to be explained is where the finite comes from. In infinite time and space there is no finite.[32] Are the finite and the infinite not just effects of perspective for the '*Dasein*'? Better to affirm the poetic priority of the infinite over the finite: the primacy of joy. The *finite* in the sense that 'common sense' has it, in other words, things that are clearly distinct and separate, that can be counted and used, is no more than appearance. Philosophers have understood this, and they have even named the conviction of a unity of things 'dialectical'. They have not carried this discovery to its final conclusion. The finite is only appearance, but appearance is not separated from the 'real'. Universal energy is concentrated in countless centres and foci, expending itself in places and moments, diversifying into countless phenomena. Phenomena relative to these centres and foci repeat themselves, and all expenditures of energy differ. Space and time are only discerned by being encountered in a 'here and now'. The body thus contains the unity in constant becoming of the infinite and the finite: it has the infinite within it, it *is* of the finite.

As a consequence, necessity is both as true and as false as chance, and repetition as true as difference. On the (inaccessible) scale of the universe, the formidable necessity of space-time reigns. Difference dominates, since universal energy is expended in ever new fulgurations. On our own scale, chance and repetition dominate. Just as each thing can be analysed into time and space, and resolved into effects and cause – so that scarcely one line of effects and causes is self-sufficient and can be isolated – so does each 'body' resolve into a conjunction of chances. 'Ego' is born of a chance encounter, and if 'ego' still lives, this is a matter of chance: a shock, a virus, a gust of wind, could have carried it away – not counting various other chances. In the finite, chance and the repetitive go together. A conjunction of chances may always reappear. If I conceive time in the manner of historical time, a cold and rigid line, a thread stretched from the past to the future, I immediately have to restore the reappearance of figures, i.e. cycles and linear concatenations that are repeated: the species and childhood, life and death, sleep and waking, work and rest, or again, the violent and the peaceful, the adventurous and the contemplative, etc.

---

32 *Nietzsche on Philosophy and Truth*, section 120.

Chance and the conjunctions of chances that realize partial determinisms, along with the repetition of particularities, impose once again the formidable image-concept (vision) of eternal recurrence.[33] The body, emerging from becoming (space-time), immersed in chances (good and bad), is situated at the centre of poietic vision and practice: concrete reason, centre and reference. Not stable, not condemned to an ungraspable becoming, but producer of its own becoming, and besides, set on encounters that the will learns to divert and evade for its own use.

17) 'Loss of identity'? This is the tragedy of the situation. Alienation? An alienation effect? No. This judgement is no longer sufficient. 'Loss of identity', the condition for metamorphosis, can be rejected. Then identity, and thus repetition, has the upper hand. When 'loss of identity' accepts itself as the dangerous path of a metamorphosis, hence a difference, Dionysian intoxication rules. Life in the highest degree makes use of two procedures. Dionysian intoxication, sought in isolation, leads to lawless adventure, to drugs, eroticism, abandonment to the madness of the moment, and at the same time to the disintegration of the self and the pursuit of transcendence.[34] Memory and cognition make it possible to brake, to control metamorphosis to a certain extent, at the risk of preventing it. Apollo by itself contains the danger of a different dissolution. Unity in the contrast and confrontation of these two powers is the path chosen by Nietzsche.

18) We have been able to show the principled antagonism, as radical as possible, between Hegelian philosophy and Nietzsche's metaphilosophical thought. It is a pleasant exercise, then, to sketch the intersection between the Marxist (revolutionary) project and the Nietzschean (subversive) perspective. The common ground is opposition to Hegel. Shared, therefore, are:

a)   atheism, the idea of nature (matter, energy) as the basis of all existence;

---

33 The modern myth of the monkey at a keyboard can serve as an illustration of and (debatable) argument for this hypothesis. The monkey hitting random keys on a word processor will eventually, at the end of an unspecified time, 'produce' the whole of Balzac. And so on.

34 Cf. the entire work of Georges Bataille.

b)   a critique of Hegel's political theodicy: the state and the re-produc-
     tion within the state of history, the past, 'moments' and social
     relations;

c)   this implies a critique of language (of logos bound up with logic
     and language), as well of Hegelian historicity;

d)   the rejection of Judeo-Christianity (in Marx, from his text on *The
     Jewish Question*, and in the whole of Nietzsche's work, above all in
     Beyond Good and Evil);

e)   the idea of the senses and the body becoming theoretical (cf.
     Marx's *1844 Manuscripts* and Nietzsche's *Zarathustra*, not forget-
     ting *The Gay Science*), which implies the rejection of any system;

f)   the project and perspective of production (creation) of a totally
     new 'reality', even while retaining 'moments' of the past/depassed,
     which includes the destruction of the actual (more pronounced
     in Nietzsche, less violent in Marx);

g)   the idea that the essential, the 'creative', is found neither in the
     economic realm as such nor in politics as such; which implies the
     rejection of both the state and politics in favour of *relations* that
     Marx   calls   'social'   and   Nietzsche   calls   'human',   then
     'superhuman'.

After this table of agreements, here are the divergences:

a)   for Nietzsche, the words 'God is dead' have a tragic repercussion,
     far wider than atheism and naturalism;

b)   for Nietzsche, rationality (historical in Hegel, industrial in Marx)
     is not just limited but illusory, and along with it therefore truth
     in the sense of the philosophers;

c)   Nietzsche's idea of *creation* (by poetry, by metamorphosis)
     differs from Marx's idea of *production*, even though both derive
     from the body and its activity by generating relations
     (connections);

d)   for Nietzsche, *civilization* is far more important than society, and
     infinitely more so than the state. It is defined by way of individu-
     als and individual actions; by evaluations (values) and a hierar-
     chy of values, far more than by the level of growth and social
     development or by the productive forces (viewed quantitatively
     and qualitatively);

e)   poetry and art as paths, instead of knowledge as Marx still main-
      tains, hence creative work above product;

f)   superseding [*dépassement*] is seen as destruction (Überwinden)
      rather than elevation (*Aufheben*), which includes, as already
      said, tragedy and radical subversion, heedless of the result. The
      past is appreciated as *decadence* and not as resource, maturation,
      preparation of the possible; the divide between the past, the
      present and the possible is thus far deeper for Nietzsche than is
      the political break with the state for Marx.

For Nietzsche, therefore, there is not a transition but a perilous leap. The
past, the actual (Europe, capitalism and the bourgeoisie), the existing
world, is destroying itself. For Marx and Marxists, these have to be
helped to avoid catastrophe or hara-kiri. For Nietzsche and Nietzscheans,
it is better to drive the decadent to suicide.

Nietzsche's work can be presented as a 'right-wing critique' of a reality (the West and the Westernized world, European logos, the bourgeoisie and capitalism, productivism and economism, etc.) to which Marx
had applied a 'left-wing critique'. This is an unfair simplification! A few
years after the acme or apogee of Marx and his work, Nietzsche arrived
at the moment of initial disappointments. With Marx already on the
decline, he drew the consequences. The old 'world' continued, renewal
was delayed. Why? How to attack the 'real' that had consolidated itself
and rigidified according to the Hegelian model?

It can be said that the 'problematism' of Marxism, even its 'aporetic'
character, is replicated by the Nietzschean 'problematic'. To break class
society by class struggle? Help the working class to supersede by negating it? Destroy the state after undermining its political apparatuses?
True, if this is possible and as soon as it is possible. But this then raises
the question of *power*, hardly broached by Marx and eluded by official
Marxist thought.[35] Now, Nietzsche brings this question to the full light
of day, in complete lucidity. He detects these relations of force, these
powers with their implications of oppression, exploitation, humiliation,
where they are not perceived, where they are lived without knowing it.
The most frightening consequence is this: human beings too often end

---

35 As far as Stalinism is concerned, the least that could be said is that everything has
been done, and is still being done, to dodge the problem.

up loving and worshipping those who have power over them, imitating them and identifying with them, experiencing pleasure in humiliation.

Logos (Greco-Roman and Judeo-Christian, revised by Descartes and by Hegel on the philosophical level, made more sophisticated on the political level by the modern state) becomes a complicated instrument with a single aim: the re-production of the relations of production. Marx stopped short in the face of this situation and these problems. Nietzsche contributed a radical critique of power, going further than the Marxist critique of the state (itself neglected).

A neo-Nietzscheanism would quickly become elitist. A Nietzschean or pseudo-Nietzschean system would rescue the old philosophy that quickly put itself in the service of the state, forming part of the play of powers. Nietzsche's thought, therefore, does not escape from ambiguity, from the realm of shadows. Today (1973), under Nietzschean influence, a certain elite sees it as inelegant and outdated to talk of capitalism, the bourgeoisie, reproduction or Marx. Nietzsche, or rather a simulation of Nietzscheanism, can thus recover. Understanding of poietic practice refutes and prevents this recuperation by the elite, by knowledge. For Nietzsche proclaimed the end of declining (decadent) Western values and the genesis of new relationships between the body and consciousness, thus between the body and language, the conceived and the experienced, the serious and the frivolous, knowledge and non-knowledge: life and death.

A Nietzschean orientation calls for catastrophe. A Marxist orientation seeks rather to limit the damage. What catastrophe? That of the end of ends (various deaths: God, 'man', history, capitalism, the state, and subsequently the human species and even life on planet 'earth').

Conclusion and Afterword

1) *Who to choose?* A rather naïve and crude question, which asserts that everyone has to choose and even has already chosen, although they can modify this choice of pilot, direction and horizon. Let us summarize the perspectives.

Hegel? Meaning and reality, in complete agreement to the point of being identical, arise from the accomplished: the historical past, the acquired, and thus for Hegel the true. History? Already finished.

A solid thought to which anyone might attach themselves. A model of reality and an exemplar of coherent discourse, the Hegelian system generates a mimesis, comfortable or fascinating depending on who it is that seeks this attachment. Even if unaware of it, systematic minds, who place cohesion and order above all else, are Hegelians.

Hegelianism is a stable bloc, a certainty, to be taken or left. What is there to add to its detailed, pedagogic and political study? Details, improvements, minor perfections, which satisfy the great majority of those with a penchant for the established order, for fitting into the given space. And moreover, with at least as many openings as differences.

Remark: in Hegel's time, his philosophico-political system had something utopian about it. Its logical realism subordinated every feature (moment or member) of social production to a harmonious totality, a finality that was diachronic (in time) and synchronic (with the end of historical time). By what right? All Hegel had to legitimize his construction were analyses of the French state (monarchical, then Jacobin, then Napoleonic), still incomplete, and the Prussian state, still in its infancy as a modern state. From these realities Hegel was able to discern the essential features; by emphasizing these, he honed the concept of the state, a positive utopia in the early nineteenth century (in opposition to the negative utopias of the socialists: Fourier, Saint-Simon). The fact that, a century and a half later, the state utopia is realized practically throughout the world, and still in opposition to other utopias, negative (Fourier) or technological (Saint-Simon), gives cause for reflection. Is this not a serious, if not a decisive reason, for giving Hegel the laurel wreath, as the sole philosopher to have succeeded in transforming his doctrine of utopia into a model?

Marx? Meaning reveals itself in the future. Marx sought to unite the real and the possible, science based on the past (history) and opening towards the future. Neither Messianism nor knowledge established as such, Marxist thought presupposes the meaning of the possible and supports this with naturalist arguments: everything that exists is born, grows, dies. And society too. An analogous paradox: Marx describes the genesis, analyses the actuality and explains the becoming of a *concrete abstraction*, commodities and money, presenting the laws of exchange of goods (products) as natural laws, in a way that offers the only hope of a breakthrough, the only chance, by way of the harsh reality of established fact. What opens the path of the possible? Who beats the path to the future? Labour and the workers. This path is marked by a number of ends that give it its meaning, including the end of bourgeois society, the end of the state, the end of history, etc. The possibles are thus both unlimited and defined by these ends (finality and meaning). The working class and its action, far from driving towards quantification (endless growth of the present elements of society, increase in size of the constitutive 'moments'), advances on the path of the qualitative. It rejects the past to create and produce new qualities: relationships that are ever 'richer'. The various ends are only (qualitative) leaps along this path. Analysis of the 'real', by differentiating the quantitative and the qualitative, does not hesitate to attribute quality to the (total) revolution. This total revolution, though divided into distinct phases and movements, has as its starting point proletarian revolution and its active development, both free and determined. Not because freedom consists in cognition of a pre-existing determination, but because it develops the determinations while diversifying (differentiating) them. Openings onto the future, milestones along the way, correspond to determinations and tendencies, not to determinisms.

Nietzsche? Like Marx, the poet Nietzsche revealed and denounced some monstrous metamorphoses, starting with that which made circumstantial results of history into metaphysical truths, and made the body into images and ideas. History is disqualified. Meaning comes neither from the past nor from the future. Where is it sought? Where does it reveal itself? In the present. 'Value' is applied to the present, giving this meaning by valuing it. Even the 'values' of faith and theology, belief and morality. Even the 'values' of history! Now, these values and meanings are dead, all of them. From where then can value and meaning arise today? From sticking to the *vécu*, lived experience, not to accept it but, on the contrary, to metamorphose it by the force of adhesion, to transfigure the *vécu* into *vivre* [living]. Grasping the present reveals its depth, no longer bound up with origin and end, with theological and philosophical questions. The body turns out to have been unknown and misunderstood. With the exception of Spinoza, philosophers since Socrates had ignored the body and its riches, its organs as bearers of meanings and values. Only Spinoza grasped the identity of the conceived, the perceived, the lived: the body contained far more than a space filled with a material; it contained the infinite, the eternal. Other philosophers, in their metaphorizing, had ignored the body on their way towards abstraction, the pure 'legible-visible'.

What then is the superhuman? To define it as a projection or a project, a hope or a desire in the usual sense of the word, is a philosophical error, which metaphorizes the superhuman, aesthetically or ethically. When Hegel, contradicting himself, proposed that the creative consciousness should 'entrust itself to absolute difference', grasped in its 'being there' (cf. *Phenomenology*), he presaged Nietzsche's contention. The superhuman is nothing more than adhesion to the present, with the result that the body gives a glimpse of what it contains: chances and determinisms, repetitions and differences, rhythms and reasons (Dionysus and Apollo). Suffering has as much meaning as joy and pleasure. Night has as much meaning and more depth than day, death – that return – more than life. As poets have understood better than philosophers, and differently

from theologians. Adhesion, the 'yes', creates the maximal difference –
the superhuman – while having the air of denoting a minimum difference, acceptance, *'amor fati'* in the Stoic sense. The meaning of the 'yes'
and the start of the superhuman is 'everything and right away', which
implies the terrible test of return: the all, the present grasped as all, can
return. The Gay Science does not falter against this vision: it tests and
'verifies' itself in it.

2) *But do we really have to choose?* On closer examination, very close, of
each element, the reasons for choice disappear and collapse.

Hegel?
Hegel is the state, nothing but the state, only state. And the state 'fastened
to its prey'![1] Real, or at least realized since Hegel. But does the state as
modern reality coincide with the Hegelian state? This has the grand
appearance of a castle; the modern state looks more like a large bourgeois
house, the main buildings flanked by a number of dependencies, shops,
workshops, rubbish tips. The grand style has gone; nothing remains of the
fine rational construction except the lack of horizon, the stifling. Since
Hegel's time, the bureaucracy has revealed its essence, its tyrannical and
complicated performances more clearly than its competences. Bureaucratic
knowledge and brute force, those are the two faces of the state.

   For Hegel and in Hegelianism, knowledge triumphs. Knowledge and
power harmonize to the point of being identified with reason, in an
initial and final trinity. In the modern society and state, on the other
hand, what do statesmen need? Information more than cognition. For
what aim? The manipulation of 'men', crowds and individuals. Which
relieves the state of the humanist pretext that it still had for Hegel.
Science, or rather, the sciences? These find their place in the apparatuses
of production and control. Knowledge as such? It is relegated into a
ghetto, the university. For information, statesmen have their services,
their teams. In relation to them, knowledge functions as a 'databank'.
Cognition, then, is frozen into institutional knowledge, and relegated to
a margin instead of occupying the centre, as for Hegel. This does not
prevent it from a double use: in materiality (production) and in ideality

---

   1 ['*C'est Vénus toute entière à sa proie attachée*', Racine's line in *Phèdre* about 'Venus
fastened to her prey' is an ever-popular quotation. – Translator.]

(politics). It serves and does not reign. In short, the state, ever more a brute force, makes use of knowledge.

To accept the Hegelian conception means agreeing to place oneself at the service of the state, in other words, of the leaders of the state, selected (the wrong way round) by their own apparatuses. Those competent in this or that, those with 'knowledge', form councils and become counsellors of princes. Those competent in nothing, but who show particular skill in manipulating people and using skills, become political leaders: modern princes, with the risks and perils attached.

Marx?
His postulate of the possible is hard to verify. It rests on a fragile basis: the analogy between nature and society. As in nature, there is a maturation of social beings, critical points of growth, then decline and death. Death may be heralded in advance, predicted, by analysing indications and symptoms (contradictions). This postulate, generalized to classes (rising, declining), nations, societies, to the state and to states, to modes of production, is not consolidated as truth (as acquired knowledge) on the so-called 'epistemological' level. As for seeking where and how Marx contributed to theory (to cognition), this is not to be sought in this naturalist philosophy of history, but rather in Marx's economics (surplus value) or his history in the strict narrow sense (the genesis of social formations, including capitalism and the bourgeoisie).

For Marx, a new rationality, qualitatively superior to philosophical rationality, is born from social practice at a given point in time: from industry and labour. Now, this presupposition, not very explicit, is no more verified than is the naturalist postulate that aligns social life with natural life. Is it correct that Marx received from the 'rising' bourgeoisie, by the mediation of the English economists and Hegel, the notion of labour as 'value'? Yes and no. Yes, in the sense that he recognized, as Smith and Hegel had done, the importance of production. No, in the sense that he held that an original *reason* (a rationality) arose from labour, not yet spelled out by the English economists and Hegel – but more strongly and with broader perspective by the great Frenchmen: Fourier and Saint-Simon.

That said, the division of labour, until now not surmounted even if not insurmountable, has shattered this optimistic theory. The superseding of labour is not being brought about by a 'polytechnicism', a multi-functionality of the worker, but by automation. Something that Marx had sensed without perceiving the inevitable shattering of the 'values' and 'meaning' of labour that has resulted from it today.

But this is nothing alongside the political paradox inherent to Marxist thought: struggle on the political level to put an end to politics (to lead the state to wither away). A specific but surprising dialectic is that the working class, for Marx, asserts itself by negating itself. It supersedes itself by superseding capitalism. Does this dialectical assertion not contain a risk: the loss of momentum and identity, the withering away of the working class itself?

Nietzsche?

What risks! If the superhuman begins here and now, in jubilant adhesion to the act (to the body) and the present, where does it lead (me)? Where does someone end up if they do not enter the realm of the will to power, and yet grasp the depth of this will, with its diversities, masks, travesties? In a wandering with no assigned direction? Towards heterology, without managing to escape the question of the language or support to adopt (or not) for this 'reality'? Avoiding conventional metaphors that have entered the language, what is the risk of returning to a poetic naturalism, in which sun and night, thunder and lightning, sea, lakes and winds, lead a great prophetic dance?

The greatest risk is that of constructing an 'elite' that sees itself as a new aristocracy, masters without slaves, etc. Egotism, egocentrism – these criticisms of Nietzschean living are without foundation. The 'subject' rebuilt on new bases has nothing in common with the old 'ego'. The accusation of elitism, on the other hand, does have an impact. This elite would cultivate its art of living within the existing society, using its resources without seeking subversion and destruction otherwise than on the level of writing (literature). Separate in appearance, subversive in illusion, this elite would have no hold on the real, save by way of discourse and writing. Such a caste, unable to become a class, remains marginal in relation to people who act and have wealth and power, or both. In short, Nietzscheanism runs the risk of reaffirming what Nietzsche hated: the intellect, the intelligentsia. Ghettoes, turnstiles, verbal negativism have not put an end to nihilism, and do not seem designed to do so.

Something about Nietzsche's poetry recalls the quest for the Grail, in the version of Wolfram von Eschenbach (where the Grail is not a sacred vessel, a holy cup, but a magic object, a talisman, a precious stone, conferring superhuman powers on its possessor).[2]

We might reply by refuting the parodies and caricatures of Nietzscheanism. Today, the Nietzschean would practice both discretion and prudence. He would abstain from speaking too much, and above all from writing. He would seek to live and express himself in actions full of meaning. But what criterion enables us to distinguish poetic practice as recommended by Nietzsche from its parody, in an age when mimesis plays a dominant role?

3) Which saint to devote oneself to? And if there is no saint, no luminous figure, if there are no stars above the shadow, shall we go and look elsewhere, in the company of the guides of shadow, the gurus, the *griots*, in other words the psychoanalysts, the 'modern' neo-philosophers, the inspired?

Excluding this second crass hypothesis, what remains of the confrontation? This: rather than choosing, the three 'moments' should each be kept in mind. To choose, in the customary fashion, would mean adopting the one and dismissing the others. Why?

Simultaneously:

a) Hegel, Hegelianism? With the reality it represents this is a given of action, the obstacle and enemy that can only be combatted with its own weapons. If something has been shown, it is indeed the fascinating and adverse character of Hegelian doctrine, not so much as doctrine, but as the truth of an intolerable reality that blocks the way. An unavoidable double action, on the theoretical and the practical level, aims, on the one hand, at Hegelian doctrine and, on the other hand, at what this expresses: the state that has set itself up and imposed itself, indefinitely persevering in its being if it is allowed (if we accept, with Hegel and the Hegelians, that 'being' in the philosophical sense finds its code and its deciphering, its elucidation and its accomplishment, in the state).

---

2 Cf. Pierre Gallais, *Perceval et l'initiation*, Paris, Éditions du Sirac, 1972, pp. 23–39, who shows a correspondence between this Western symbolism and that of Iran (ancient Persia, that of Zoroaster).

b) Marx indicated the objective possibility of a breakthrough: a social and political possibility, which only a revolutionary class could carry out (the working class, if it asserts itself as political 'subject', and to the extent that it does so). If it is true that this assertion has never been accomplished massively and decisively, something is always happening somewhere or other that maintains this meaning, in other words, the production of new relations and objective differences.

c) Nietzsche indicated the subjective possibility of a breakthrough by displaying what is contained in the 'pure' act, initial and final: adhesion to the present, in a human body; a 'yes' to life. This leads to a poetic practice, creator of subjective differences.[3]

4) By way of an afterword to this confrontation, here are a few deliberately subjective aspects. Why insert them here? To show the importance of Nietzsche as *revealer* (in terms closer to knowledge: as the person who expressed meanings and values, thus the universal decoder and thereby destroyer of codes, requiring either the invention of a different code, or the superseding of coding-decoding!).

The present writer read Nietzsche as the result of pure accident, at the age of about fifteen, during a Christian education: everything that was then translated, plus some texts in German.

Zarathustra: the book you believe you have already read on first reading, but believe you are always reading it for the first time, the book that redeems.

Yes, but it is a symptom of the era: then comes the effort to return to the norm (work, practice, history, action), given the extreme difficulty experienced by an adolescent in creating his own life – and contradictorily, the effort to join a revolutionary or subversive movement, capable of effective action.

At twenty-five years old, therefore, despite the Nietzschean dazzle: a shadow among shadows, and even the very embodiment of shadow. Struggling with not just one shadow. Hence the encounter first of all with Hegel (again by purest chance: on the desk of André Breton), then with Marx. Hence also misunderstanding: adhesion to Marxism because

---

3 By way of example: objective breakthrough, Lip, 1973 [see note 10 on page 16 above]; subjective breakthrough, Solzhenitsyn, 1973–4.

of a capital theory, that of the withering away of the state. Hence joining the French Communist Party (PCF), a movement that was inevitably frozen in Stalinism and fetishism of the state. Hence a number of diversions.[4]

In the course of these diversions, and while slowly finding my way to the light, the idea of a *double breakthrough* never disappeared: by way of politics and the critique of politics, to supersede this as such by way of poetry, eros, symbol and imaginary, by the refusal of distortion and alienation, and by grasping the present.

5) The objective (socio-economic) breakthrough and the subjective (poetic) breakthrough meet up together in space. It is in space that differences are inscribed and still more are 'realized', from the least to the most extreme. Unevenly illuminated, unevenly accessible, bristling with obstacles, and itself an obstacle in the face of initiatives, shaped by these, space becomes the site and milieu of differences. The test of conflicts and the test of space tend to coincide, for everything that asserts itself and seeks a breakthrough, objective or subjective.

Is this project of space, the task on a planetary scale of a double productive and creative activity (aesthetic and material), the empirical substitute for the superhuman, a replacement product? No. It implies a superseding (Überwinden) on the scale of the world, casting the dead results of historical time into abolition. It contains a concrete test, bound up with practice and the totality of the possible, according to Marx's most radical thought, bound up too with the entire restitution of the palpable and the body, according to Nietzsche's poetry.

This project rejects into the nothingness of dead results the Hegelian space, the work of the state, where this establishes and displays itself. As the work and product of the human species, space emerges from the shadow, like a planet emerging from an eclipse.

----

4 Cf. Henri Lefebvre, *La Somme et le Reste*, Paris: Bélibaste, 1973 [1959] (an incomplete reissue). [A full re-edition was made in 1989 with Meridiens Klincksieck and again in 2008 with Anthropos.]

Index